Superstud

ALSO BY PAUL FEIG

Kick Me

Superstud

Or How I Became a 24-Year-Old Virgin

Paul Feig

THREE RIVERS PRESS
NEW YORK

Copyright © 2005 by FEIGCO, Inc.

Published in the United States by Three Rivers Press, an imprint of the Crown
Publishing Group, a division of Random House, Inc., New York.
www.crownpublishing.com

THREE RIVERS PRESS and the Tugboat design are registered trademarks of
Random House, Inc.

Library of Congress Cataloging-in-Publication Data
Feig, Paul.
  Superstud, or how I became a 24-year-old virgin / Paul Feig.—1st ed.
  1. Teenage boys—United States—Sexual behavior.   2. Feig, Paul.   3. Sexual
  ethics for youth.   4. Man-woman relationships.   I. Title
HQ27.3.F38   2005
306.7'0835'1—dc22   2004029239
ISBN 1-4000-5175-4

Printed in the United States of America

Design by Ruth Lee-Mui

10   9   8   7   6   5   4   3   2   1

First Edition

I was going to dedicate this book to my wife, Laurie.
But she didn't want me to.

I thought about dedicating it to my mom and dad,
but they've both passed away
and there's enough embarrassing stuff in here that
I'm pretty sure they wouldn't want me to anyway.

Since my wife didn't want the dedication,
then I can't really dedicate it to my in-laws.
And I can't imagine that any of the relatives on my side
of the family would want their names in here.

It's just way too weird to dedicate this to any of my friends,
especially when you see what some of the subject matter is.

I'd dedicate it to the famous people who've inspired me in my career,
but their estates would probably sue me.

And so I would like to dedicate this to Heather MacArthur,
whose name I picked at random out of the phone book.
I don't know who you are but you sound like an interesting person.

Please contact the legal department at Three Rivers Press
if you have a problem with your appearance in this dedication.

Happy reading!

Contents

Book Three: Life After High School

Book Four: The Ballad of the Homesick Virgin

Book Five: Close Encounters of the Nerd Kind

The Hapless Romantic

I've always been a hopeless romantic.

If I had a dime for every time in the past that I have walked on the beach at night by myself, humming the theme from *Against All Odds* or that Chicago song "After All That We've Been Through" (or whatever it's called) or that Barry Manilow song "Come into My Arms" (or whatever *that* song's called) as I fantasized I was actually walking hand in hand with one of the myriad of girls I happened to be in love with at that moment, I'd have at least enough dimes to get myself a good-sized sandwich, drink, and dessert. I've driven more miles in my car at night with the radio blasting the love-gone-wrong songs of Elvis Costello or Bob Dylan or the Tangerine Dream soundtrack from *Risky Business* than most cross-country truckers log in during any given year. And I've gotten misty in more Woody Allen relationship films (*Annie Hall, Manhattan,* and *Hannah and Her Sisters,* specifically) than, well, probably anybody.

There's just always been something about trying to find those perfect moments in life, the ones where you feel loved and needed and fulfilled, that has driven me to do so many embarrassing things over the years. They never seemed embarrassing at the time but, once looked back upon, they cause me to cringe in the same way I cringe when I think about the time I wore a powder blue disco jumpsuit to high school with the mistaken impression that it would actually make me look cool.

It didn't.

But despite my lifetime membership as a semi-mature, card-carrying geek, and despite the misconception some people have of the nerds of this world being asexual creatures who care more about Japanese anime drawings of women than real living, breathing females, I've actually spent a lot of time and energy looking for romance. And I've misguidedly spent a lot of money trying to buy it, in the form of expensive dinners, impressive gifts, and good tickets to pricey events, all meant to kick-start the blossoming of *Love* from an otherwise unwilling prospective girlfriend. And because of all this, I can definitely confirm that the old saying *is* true—"You can't buy love."

Well, unless you're a millionaire. Then you probably can. Just not quality love.

You have to be a billionaire to buy that.

But I digress.

I'll never forget the moment when I realized how desperately I wanted true romance in my life. It happened on a Saturday night. I was about twelve and was in Kalamazoo, Michigan, for a guitar competition. My mother and I drove up and spent the weekend in the hotel where the judging was taking place, and I was having a great time. Even though I wasn't much of a guitarist, for some reason I had picked just the right piece to play on my classical guitar for that day's competition, and the planets had aligned so that when I got up to perform in front of the judges, I was actually good, scoring an amazing 100 out of 100 points. I went from ranking as one of my guitar teacher's biggest embarrassments to being his star pupil within a matter of minutes and was feeling no pain as I went into the evening's celebrations. The music association that ran the competition was putting on a dance for all the participants, and the whole thing seemed magical to me as soon as I walked in the door with my mother. The large hall was packed with young musicians of all ages, and the band performing was amazing, made up of professional players who were using the event to really show off what they could do on their instruments. I was standing and watching as they performed the Dan Fogelberg/Tim Weisberg song "Tell Me to My Face," which was one of my favorites at the time, and the lead guitarist, who was also an older friend of mine from music school, was performing a truly amazing guitar solo.

There was something about the all-encompassing power and volume of the music and otherworldliness of the flashing lights and being surrounded by people who were talented and creative and not the kind of people who were mean to you or wanted to beat you up that all combined to make one of those magical moments that sometimes occur in life—where you feel transported out of your body, away from all your earthly cares; in which you see the world in a different light, as a collection of people and energy, and you suddenly love it all and want to experience it all. As I stood there watching and listening, my twelve-year-old brain taking in so many new emotions and stimuli and suddenly feeling so happy to be alive, I noticed a girl standing in front of me, with her back to me. She seemed to be about my age, maybe a year or two older, and was a few inches shorter than I was. I had the feeling that she was very pretty, but I couldn't tell since I was looking at the back of her head. But I remember staring at her hair. It was long and dark and hung down straight and simple as it magically reflected the lights from the stage. I stared at the perfectly straight center part in her hair, and then followed the silken-looking tresses as they spilled onto her shoulders and hung down her back. She was thin and delicate and was wearing a simple shirt and jeans. And because she was swaying lightly to the music, the ends of her hair were floating back and forth gently, brushing against her shirt as if they were ghostly fingers caressing her softly. I was close enough where I thought I could smell the powdery aroma of her perfume and the sweet scent of her shampoo, although it's hard to say if it was coming from her or one of the many other girls crowded around us. But I was suddenly overwhelmed by it all as I continued to stare at the top of her head. To this day I don't know why I was so affected by the part in her hair, but I couldn't stop looking at it, at her. It somehow made her seem so human, so real and attainable, and I was overtaken with the strangest feeling—a realization that if you could get a girl to fall in love with you and to become your girlfriend and marry you, you would possess that person, just like she would possess you. Not in a desperate way or in a way that meant she was something you owned, but in the sense that she was yours, that she was a fellow human who had dedicated her life to being with you, just as you had dedicated your life to being with her. You could be hers, and you would belong to each other. If I were to become her boyfriend, I thought, then I could see that part in her hair every day. I could reach out and touch it if I wanted to. I could kiss the top of her head and she would love me. And if I married her I would actually have a person in this world to whom I belonged. The thought so overwhelmed me that I literally felt everything else around the two of us melt away, as if she and I were the only people in the room. She obviously had no idea this was happening behind her and simply continued watching the band, swaying contentedly to the music. But I felt lighter than air as we stood there, and I didn't want the moment to end within my lifetime.

It was then that I felt a poke in my back and one of my friends from the music school said hi and introduced me to his mother and then my mother said hi and we all started talking and by the time I was able to look back at the girl, she was gone. I spent the rest of the night trying to figure out who she was and get a glimpse of what she looked like but I never did. There were too many people and too many thin girls with long straight hair, wearing simple shirts and jeans. And the truth is I don't really think I wanted to find her. I didn't want to know what she looked like or if she was nice or not, because, in my mind, I'd had a perfect moment with a perfect girl, a girl who looked exactly the way I wanted her to look and who looked at me the way I always wanted a girl to look at me, and who would have fallen in love with me if only she had turned around and seen how much I cared for her. I had experienced my first moment of true love and emotion and it would never be ruined for me by reality. I had discovered what I wanted out of life and now I would simply have to find the real thing. And just like that, I had a new goal.

I wanted to be in love.

Little did I know how badly I had set myself up. Because when you decide to go looking for perfect moments, you're asking for a whole lot out of life. It doesn't mean that you won't find those perfect moments. It just means that you're going to have to look pretty hard.

But hey, what the hell? I was born an optimist.

And I think that's where all my troubles began.

BOOK ONE

The Rope Feeling Chronicles

I. Bliss Interrupted

Let's face it. Masturbation has never been a proud activity. It's very seldom that people will brag about the fact that they have masturbated. You don't often hear the response to the question "What did you do today?" being, "Oh, ran a few errands, paid my bills, masturbated, made dinner." It's just not an activity you really want to brag about. Or speak about. Or even admit to yourself that you do. When your body decides that it yet again wants to engage in a little round of onanism and your brain gives in like a beleaguered mother acquiescing to her child's incessant demands for candy, your brain still won't really let itself admit what's about to happen. The walk to whatever place has been decided upon as the conjugal site is usually filled less with thoughts of "Man, it's really great that I'm going to do this" than "This isn't right" and "I wonder if I have a problem?"

Or at least it has been for me.

The "problem" started when I was a kid. I was raised as a Christian Scientist, which is the religion that is mostly known as the one that tells its followers not to go to doctors when they get sick. The whole faith is based on not giving power to the physical world, the idea being that you can avoid sickness and bad things happening to you by basically keeping your thoughts and desires above the realm of the body and earthly entanglements. And so this means that you're really not supposed to think about things like sex and bodily pleasures. And this is all well and good if you can turn your libido on and off like a light switch. But if you're a normal, healthy human being who has the genetic code of the *Homo sapiens* in his or her DNA, then it's a little hard to deny your body what it wants, especially when you're going through the ravages of puberty.

Fortunately or unfortunately for me, I discovered masturbation at a very early age. After climbing the ropes in gym class during the second grade, I had unwittingly experienced my first orgasm. This then led to me figuring out how to re-create this experience in the privacy of my own bedroom and in the bathroom I shared with my parents (but not while they were in there, obviously). This intensely pleasurable act, which I referred to back then as "the rope feeling," was something I wasn't really even sure was sexual at the time. I knew that it felt great and made me very happy, but so did the act of eating a box of day-old Peeps. And so I merrily engaged in this self-pleasing act for several years, happily unaware that what I was doing might be considered wrong by some segments of the community. No, except for the occasional rubbed-raw spots that resulted from periodic overuse, my early years spent with the rope feeling were painless, carefree, and blissful.

The salad days of self-love, if you will.

It wasn't until I was on a vacation with my parents at a budget hotel in the Caribbean when I was twelve years old that my orgasmic little world was shattered permanently. We were in our room after a fun-filled day at the pool, and my dad was listening to the radio. A local call-in show was on, and it had a very religious bent to it. The heavily accented

Jamaican deejay was taking phone calls on the topic of morality and behavior. As I sat on the bed playing a game of solitaire, a woman caller phoned in and started talking about masturbation, saying she had recently caught her son in the act and was wondering what she should do to keep him from doing it again. This sent the deejay into a long tirade about how God doesn't approve of masturbation and what a major sin it was in His eyes. Feeling a hot flash run up the back of my neck, I tried desperately not to look up at the radio, for fear that my father and mother, who were lounging in chairs by the window, might see my reaction and realize that I too had been indulging in this forbidden act. As I listened on in horror, eyes fixed solidly on the cards in front of me, the deejay uttered the following sentence:

"Besides, everyone knows that each time you masturbate, God takes one day off of your life."

All the blood rushed out of my head and I felt like I was going to faint. *Everyone knew this?* Nobody told *me* about it. I remember my father throwing a look at my mother and making a concerned face, but I couldn't tell what the face meant. In retrospect, I'm pretty sure it was a mixture of "Turn that garbage off" and "I don't think it's good for Paul to be hearing superstitious nonsense like this." But, of course, I at the time interpreted it as, "See, I TOLD you that a boy loses a day off of his life every time he masturbates."

The wheels in my brain started spinning like a game of Battling Tops. How many times had I done what I now knew the Lord was willing to kill me to stop doing? How many days had I lopped off my life so far? I was in an absolute silent panic, like a person who'd just discovered he'd eaten poisoned food. But it was too late for me to throw the poison back up, because what was done was done. Those days were lost. And now I knew only one thing:

I had to stop doing it immediately.

To save my life.

I was suddenly filled with anger. How could the rope feeling have done this to me? What just a few minutes earlier had been my closest friend and comforter was now revealed to have been the serpent in the Garden of Eden. The rope feeling had unwittingly gotten me to eat its apple and was now mocking me for each day of my life that I had sacrificed to it. Why didn't you keep a record of how many times you did it?! I yelled at myself. People always say life's too short. Well, now you've made it even shorter.

I immediately refrained from subtracting any more days off my life for the rest of our vacation and, once I returned home, vowed to keep myself distracted by other activities. The rope feeling wasn't going to knock me off before I had lived what was now left of my life. Besides, I had plenty of other things with which to distract myself—all my hobbies, like my guitar, my magic tricks, the TV, spending time with my next-door neighbors, sending my G.I. Joes into imaginary battles, mastering the recipes in my *Betty Crocker's Cookbook for Boys and Girls*. Why, an enterprising young man like myself would have plenty to keep his mind busy and off thoughts of anything that God didn't want him to do. I was going to get myself off of His hit list for good. Things were going to be A-OK.

One particular day a few weeks later, I decided that a little quality snooping-around-the-house time would be the perfect way to keep my mind off my ex-lover. Walking to my bedroom, I realized that the top shelf of our hall closet had never been properly explored. I opened the door and looked up. All that appeared to be up there was the punch bowl set my mother pulled down once a year when she would begrudgingly host Thanksgiving for our relatives. I went and got a stepladder out of the kitchen and climbed up to see what else was residing up there. I found a bunch of old party favors behind the punch bowl box, things like shiny toot horns and noisemakers and plastic leis, all the kind of stuff that I used to see revelers wearing and making noise with when my parents and I would watch the Guy Lombardo New Year's Eve specials. All my friends' parents would watch *Dick Clark's New Year's Rockin' Eve,* but at my house, with parents who married at thirty-seven, conceived me when they were thirty-nine, and had both lived through World War II, Guy Lombardo was about as "rockin'" as our New Year's Eves would ever get. I put on the bright green lei, and then I made the noisemakers make their noises. But every sound they produced was loud and irritating, sounding more like Psychological Operations devices an army would use to drive a dictator out of his stronghold than something that was supposed to make a party sound fun. So I took off the lei and started to put the party favors back. It was then that I saw a shiny hat behind everything else. I pulled it out. It was a molded plastic bowler derby that was made more festive by a layer of green cellophane wrap covering it. I took down the hat and put it on my head. It was too big and fell over my eyes. Plus, it smelled a lot like mothballs. I removed the hat and was about to toss it back into the closet when I noticed something.

Something shocking.

On the top of the hat, glued beneath the clear green cellophane, was a picture of a topless woman. She was photographed from the waist up and had her hands over her head, laughing as she held the exact same hat as the one she was on, keeping it aloft over her hairdo.

And because her arms were up, her breasts were completely exposed, front and center.

I couldn't believe it. I suddenly experienced the strangest mix of surprise, excitement, and fear. The surprise and excitement were easy to explain, but the fear was there because it scared me that my dad had a picture of a naked woman in our house. Did he know it was up there in the top of the closet behind the punch bowl we drank out of on the holidays? He must, I thought. How can you have a hat with a naked woman on it in the house and *not* be aware of it? And even if for some reason he'd forgotten about it, it weirded me out to think that my dad had actually at one time looked at a picture of a naked woman. The thought of my parents doing or enjoying anything even remotely stimulating sexually was colossally upsetting to me. So, adding pornography to the mix was devastating, to say the least. And what about my mom? Did she know the naked lady hat was up there? I couldn't imagine my mother condoning it being in our house, knowing how religious she was. I mean, she used to get upset when Goldie Hawn would dance around in a bikini on *Rowan & Martin's Laugh-In,* but at least Goldie was dressed and covered with writing. The woman on the hat was completely nude.

My mind started to spin.

What if my mom *did* know about the hat with the picture on it? What if she thought it was okay? What if she *bought* it for my dad? Did she and my father have some strange other life filled with pictures of naked ladies and erotic party hats and sex dinners with other adults in our neighborhood? I was starting to feel angry at the hat for ever having come into our lives and tearing our happy home asunder when suddenly I got very nervous.

What would God have to say about all of this?

True, my parents were married, but I couldn't imagine that a picture of another woman without her clothes on could be viewed as anything but wrong in His eyes. I mean, the

Guy knocked a day off your life just for masturbating. Imagine what He'd think about a dirty picture.

I stared at the lady on the hat, wondering if my unearthing of her had alerted God to her presence in our house. Did I just get my parents in trouble with the Almighty? I mean, I knew He could see everywhere, but maybe even *He* hadn't bothered to check behind our punch bowl.

I suddenly began to feel strange. But not strange because I was afraid of what God was thinking.

It was more of a "rope feeling" strange.

I had always loved looking at pretty girls in school and at beautiful women on TV but had never seen any of them naked, save for the time I accidentally opened the door when my aunt Emma was getting out of the bathtub. But that had not been a pleasant experience by any means. In fact, it had caused me several weeks of nightmares in which my naked aunt would lock me in her bedroom and try to make me sleep with her. But now, as I stared at the naked breasts of the woman on the hat, I started to feel something else; something I had felt many times before but never in this context . . .

An overwhelming urge to visit with the rope feeling.

I was immediately thrown into crisis. Was it worth it to give away another day of my life just to succumb to the siren song of a party hat? And if God got mad when I indulged by myself, then how much madder would He be if He found out I was doing it with someone else, even though that someone was only a picture? My brain may have been telling me not to indulge, but my twelve-year-old libido simply had a louder voice.

I closed the closet door and snuck the hat into the bathroom.

The lady on the hat and I dated intensely for about a week. However, after this initial flurry, she very quickly began to lose her appeal. I think the problem was the slightly surrealistic quality of the picture itself, which had been tinted and airbrushed so that the woman had an almost cartoon-like appearance. On top of that, she simply wasn't my type. In her day, I knew she must have been the Belle of the Ball, but that was an era of lipstick and powder, of heavy makeup and excessive body weight. While her breasts were voluptuous, so was the rest of her body. Her arms were puffy like my friend Mike's mother's, and her shoulders and waist looked pretty doughy. She also seemed to have her gut sucked in, the way Captain Kirk used to do whenever he'd wind up in a fight with his shirt off. And on top of all this, her hair was in a bee-hive, a look that always made me think of the playground ladies at my school. It was the overweight women at our local bowling alley and the older ladies from our church who still found the stacked-up, impenetrable giant pinecone of hair to be attractive—not anyone under fifty, and certainly not the kid who thought Maryanne from *Gilligan's Island* was the sexiest woman on TV. No, the hat lady's naked breasts were the only allure she held for her twelve-year-old admirer, and those had both unfortunately lost their appeal.

And so I retired the party hat to its place behind the punch bowl, bid farewell to the days I had eliminated from my life, and apologized to God for my egregious lack of self-control.

But the whole experience had cracked the determined resolve I had found after hearing the terrifying words of the Jamaican deejay. And now that my libido had discovered the joys of visual stimulation, my willpower was at an all-time low. And thus my mind started to play a dangerous gambit.

I began to tell myself that since I was young, and since both of my grandmothers were in their eighties and still in good health, that I had longevity genes and wouldn't really need the ninety-third year of my life anyway. I could indulge occasionally and still only lose a small period at the end of my days when I'd probably just be sitting around in a wheelchair staring at the TV anyway. If anything, the rope feeling would be a form of altruistic preemptive euthanasia, my way of not being a drain on the payroll taxes of a future generation by shortening the time the government would have to pay my Medicare bills. It seemed like the perfect plan. I just knew I had to dole the sacrificed days out very slowly.

I was up for the challenge.

Little did I know that my own mother was conspiring against me.

II. The Day the Earth Didn't Stand Still

The very next day, I walked into the bathroom and discovered one of my mom's fashion magazines, a full-sized color newspaper called *W*, sitting on the clothes hamper that served as an ersatz coffee table across from our toilet. My mother had always been an amateur follower of fashion and in the last few years had begun buying occasional issues of women's clothing magazines. She generally never left them around the house, since she'd read them at the beauty parlor and then give them to her hairdresser. But on the few times she'd bring them home, I would try to flip through them whenever no one was around. I enjoyed looking at all the pictures of the fashion-show models, even though there was always something about them I found slightly creepy. They always looked like they were mean, and their bodies were usually so tall and thin and their makeup and hair so strange and severe that they looked more like villains from a sci-fi movie than women who were supposed to be desirable. That said, there was definitely something alluring about them. It was probably the fact that as they were walking down the runway, they were wearing shirts and dresses that were wide open all the way down to their navels, the sheer material barely covering their breasts. I would always wonder, as I still do today when I see a fashion show, where on earth a person could actually wear those styles without being arrested or accosted. I could only speculate back then that Paris must be one mighty liberal town.

Since I had never really gotten to spend any extended quality time with one of these fashion magazines, I quickly locked the bathroom door, got comfortable on the toilet, and started flipping through the pages of *W*.

As usual, it was the standard collage of small pictures of models walking down runways, this time dressed in very unrevealing fall fashions. I could tell that this issue was going to be a bust and started turning the pages with waning interest.

And it was right then that I turned the page and felt like I was suddenly punched in the face. My entire brain jolted. My eyes blinked. I couldn't breathe.

For there, on a full page, full frontal, about one and a half feet tall, was a head-to-waist photo of a sweetly smiling, completely naked young woman standing in a field. She looked to be about twenty-one years old, was thin with long blond hair, a pretty face, and two very exposed breasts. It was an ad for some kind of body cream, so I guess the purpose of the photo was to show the women who read *W* magazine how soft and perfect this product would make every inch of their skin. And while *W*'s female readership may have been able to look at this picture and very impassively judge the effectiveness of the product, for a twelve-year-old boy who had just spent the past week trying to become aroused by a woman from the 1950s who was built like one of the chorus girls in a Marx Brothers movie, this was the mother lode.

If the party hat lady had pulled up the corner of the lid on the Tupperware container that held my libido, then the naked girl in the magazine had torn the lid off and flung its contents all over the kitchen. I stared at the picture of the woman I was holding in my trembling hands, as affected as if I had been handed the Holy Grail, and knew one thing for absolute certain: I was about to happily kiss several days of my life good-bye before I unlocked that bathroom door.

The next day, I literally sprinted home from the bus stop, having spent the entire day at school dreaming of my return to my blond-haired, printing-pressed concubine. I came in the door and my luck got even better. My mom wasn't home. Now I wouldn't have to slink into the bathroom and stress over trying not to let the paper make any noise as I opened it. If *W* made a crinkling sound today, that was just fine. My mother would have no idea what I was up to. I was free to concentrate solely on my time together with the girl who was now everything to me.

I walked into the bathroom and all the color drained out of my face.

She was gone.

I ran through the house, searching in a panic for my beloved *W,* but it was nowhere to be found. So desperate was I to find my new girlfriend that I immediately called my mother, who was working in the office at my dad's store.

"Mother . . . uh . . . where's that *W* magazine that was in the bathroom?" I asked, sounding panicked. I immediately tried to cover, suddenly aware of how badly I was outing myself. "I've . . . uh . . . I'm doing a project in one of my classes on fashion and need to bring in some pictures."

"What class are you doing a project about women's fashion for?" she asked in a tone that said she was suddenly concerned about the unorthodox curriculum in our school district.

"It's for social studies," I fired back, realizing the hole I was digging myself into if my mother decided to take it upon herself to call my social studies teacher to complain. But at this moment I didn't care. I was looking for my lost love and would take any action necessary to get her back.

"Your father threw it out. He said he doesn't want me spending any more money on clothes. Besides, that magazine was old anyway." She barely had these sentences out of her mouth when I said a lightning-fast "Okay, good-bye" and hung up the phone.

I bolted out of the house and into the garage. I ran over to where the garbage cans normally sat but they weren't there. My brain flashed white and a cold chill ran down my spine. Because I had just remembered it was Wednesday.

Garbage day.

I walked slowly down the driveway toward the street like a man walking toward a room that contained the body of his murdered wife. As I came around the tall hedge that separated our front yard from the street, I saw our garbage cans lying on their sides, haphazardly thrown into the dirt by our ham-handed garbage men.

The cans were empty.

It was all over. My new girlfriend was on her way to the dump. She was in the back of a garbage truck, the truck that had the big metal compacting claw I used to love watching as a little kid. She was now smashed inside the back of the truck with all the old orange peels and apple cores and rotten food and wet grass clippings and dirty diapers that people throw away. She was irretrievable, even if I were to follow the garbage truck out to the landfill to rescue her. The perfect picture on the perfect piece of paper I had fallen in love with the previous day was now soaked, smashed, and dead.

I had loved and lost. And as I quickly found out, it was *not* better than never to have loved at all.

III. Lookin' for a Love

I found myself caught in a netherworld for the next several days. Without my *W* girlfriend, the rope feeling just wasn't the same. I needed her back or I needed someone new. But there was nowhere else to turn. In a pathetic act of rebound, I even tried returning to the party hat lady but, alas, she now held even less appeal than she did when I first broke up with her. I tried to tell myself this was all a good thing, that being forced into self-control was saving days at the end of my life that might actually be made more productive by future medical breakthroughs. But again the threat of a shortened life was starting to take a backseat to the surging hormones of adolescence. I had tasted the forbidden fruit and was now completely under its spell. I had to find another girlfriend and I had to find her fast.

I just had no idea where to look.

It's here that I must take a moment to address any younger members of the public who might be reading this. At the risk of sounding like somebody's grandfather, as hard as it is to believe, there was a time when people actually had to leave their houses and go out into the world in order to procure pictures of naked people. In those days, computers were things as big as Coke machines, with large reels of spinning tape that made them look like colossal minimalist versions of SpongeBob SquarePants. The idea that in the privacy of your own home you could simply type a few words into a Web browser and access any kind of picture your heart desired was as foreign as the notion of being able to get into an airplane and fly across an ocean would have been to medieval peasants. No, back then if you wanted to see pictures of naked people, you either had to go out to a store, approach a sales clerk, and buy them, or you had to hope that another one would turn up in your bathroom or in the closet behind your mother's punch bowl. Short of that, the only way to satisfy a craving for pictures of naked women was to try to find pictures of women who were *almost* naked.

My search began and quickly grew intense, as I scoured every magazine, catalog, newspaper, and book in our house for anything that showed the slightest hint of the female form. I had some luck with my father's *Life* magazine *Year in Review,* a thick, oversized coffee table book that contained a couple of small, arty photos of scantily clad fashion models. One was even wearing a sheer top I could see the hint of a nipple through. She and I had a brief fling for a couple of days, but she ultimately proved too obscure and mysterious for a long-term relationship, not to mention nearly impossible to sneak into the bathroom without being detected since she resided in a book the size of a tombstone. The ladies' underwear section of the various department store catalogs in our house offered the occasional thrill, but the underwear the women were wearing in the pictures was usually of the giant underpants variety, with bras so big they looked like two white hubcaps with shoulder straps. Plus, the female models all sort of looked like the moms in our neighborhood. Pretty moms, granted, but moms nonetheless, and definite mood killers. No, things were not going well on my quest for low-rent erotica, and they only got worse. My lowest point came when I tried to use the written directions that I had discovered inside a box of my mother's tampons under the sink. The piece of paper featured a line drawing of a woman with her clothes off, a picture with about as much sexual detail as the figure on a Do Not Walk sign. When I emerged from the bathroom after that barely successful encounter, like an alcoholic who ends up drinking rubbing alcohol out of desperation, I realized that I had finally hit rock bottom.

God must be having a good laugh at my expense as He ticks the days off my life, I thought. Maybe it's time to give it all up and start reading the Bible.

Does it have any pictures in it? I wondered.

IV. Paradise Found

The next day, I went to the mall with my mom. While she was off buying yet another color-coordinated purse-and-shoes combo, I went over to the bookstore to buy the latest issue of *Mad* magazine. As I was looking at the magazine rack, I pushed aside a copy of the substandard *Cracked* and accidentally uncovered an issue of *Modern Photographer* magazine. My heart skipped a beat. There on the cover was a naked woman who was sitting hugging her knees to her chest. This covered any of the body parts that would make her actually naked but the effect was still earthshaking. Looking around cautiously, my heart pounding, I picked up the magazine and quickly flipped through it.

I couldn't believe my eyes. It had pages and pages of naked women in it. Most of the pictures were black and white and were all rather obscured by arty lighting and filters, but there was no denying that this was a magazine full of nude ladies. Just then, I heard a couple of old women walking down the aisle toward me. I immediately stuffed the magazine back behind an issue of *Ranger Rick* and dashed off into the science fiction aisle. Pretending to be interested in an H. G. Wells anthology, I waited impatiently for the women to leave. Unfortunately, they got engrossed in a knitting magazine. Then two other women walked up and started having a discussion about how unattractive the picture of Richard Nixon on the cover of *Time* magazine was. Frustrated, I headed for the door to find my mom as my mind tried to process my new discovery. Did every issue of *Modern Photographer* have nude pictures in it? And how could a twelve-year-old buy an issue if it had a naked woman on the cover?

Before I could fully grapple with these thoughts, I looked over to my right and saw something that stopped me in my tracks. Over one of the bookshelves, where it was normally labeled "Literature" or "Biography" or "Cookbooks," was a sign that read . . .

"Photography."

I realized I'd seen the sign over that section many times before and had always thought what a mundane topic it was. But now the section took on a whole new meaning to me. I wanted to go over to it but was sure everybody would know what I was up to. But then I realized that anybody seeing me over at this section would merely think I was just some nerdy kid who was into taking pictures. It was the perfect cover.

I walked up to the wall of books. There were hundreds. A lot had titles that told you they were filled with unexciting diagrams of shutters and electric lights and scientific facts about darkroom chemicals. However, there were others that seemed like they might hold some promise. I pulled down one that was titled *How to Take Pictures of People*. There were shots of pretty girls on the cover, as well as a few pictures of couples and old people. I flipped through the book and hit a chapter titled "How to Work with Models." And, sure enough, there were indeed pictures of naked women. Once again, they were arty, black-and-white images with strange lighting and a grainy texture that obscured a lot of the details, but you could still tell what everything was. I wasn't sure if these pictures would do the job I had in mind or not, until I realized that they were already working. I quickly glanced down and was horrified at the distended shape of the front of my pants. I looked around in a panic and noticed that there were people flipping through books on both sides of me, only a few shelves away. Before they could notice my midsectional shame, I quickly crouched down to obscure it, acting as if I was looking at the books on the bottom shelf, and waited for the indelicate moment to pass.

But it simply wouldn't. It couldn't. Because every book on the lower shelf had a title that told me it was filled with pictures of naked women.

> *Modern Nude Photography*
> *How to Photograph Nudes*
> *The Female Form: A Study in Nudes*
> *The History of Nude Photography*
> *Yes, You CAN Shoot Nudes!*

The titles spun and jumped out at me like newspaper headlines about the "Japs" and the Nazis in old black-and-white movies about World War II. The photography section had suddenly turned into a red-light district. I couldn't catch my breath and began to feel faint as whatever blood was left in my head rushed out of it and made a beeline for my crotch. Suddenly, just the word *nude* was enough to send me into premasturbatory delirium, as if the world had just become one giant flesh pit calling my awakening young libido hither. I tried desperately to think of things that would let me regain control over my lower region but nothing worked. An upcoming math test, kissing Grandma, a dead squirrel I had seen earlier that day—nothing could get the word *nude* and all the associated imagery that comes with it out of my head. My legs were starting to cramp from being crouched down in a baseball catcher's position for so long, and I realized that I was going to have to stand up and get away from the burlesque show in front of me if I had any hope of returning my overexcited condition back to normal. And so I took a deep breath, stood up as best I could, and headed quickly for the exit at the front of the store, walking like Groucho Marx rushing out of the "college widow's" room in *Horse Feathers*.

"Excuse me, young man!"

My nightmare. I stopped and turned to see an angry-looking middle-aged female clerk staring at me suspiciously. I was fortunately able to place a low display table between my below-the-belt region and her line of vision.

"What's in your pants?"

A hot flush ran up the back of my neck. What kind of question was *that*? Was that how adults talked in the real world? Did they persecute people for being outwardly aroused? Was getting a boner in a public place, even though you were fully dressed, against the law? At that moment, I could only assume it was. I stared at her, terrified.

"What do you have in your pocket?" she said as she walked out from behind the counter and started toward me. The fear of the moment did what the images of kissing my grandmother could not. The blood rushed back out of my middle region and returned to my frightened brain. The nudes were gone.

"Just my Cub Scout knife," I said, sounding like I was about to cry. I wish I could say my emotion was merely a ruse to get sympathy from the woman. However, I truly was about to weep from the fear and humiliation of it all. I pulled out my pocketknife and showed it to her. She looked me over for a second and then nodded.

"The way you were rushing out of here, I thought you stole something," she said in a tone that showed she had no intention of apologizing to me. "A lot of you kids have been shoplifting from me lately. But you're not going to get away with it, you hear me? None a ya."

Despite my indignation at having just been lumped in with all the mean shoplifting kids who used to beat me up in school, I nodded at the woman and hightailed it over to Winkleman's to find my mother.

And as I ran through the mall past girls and women who I knew were all naked under their clothes, one thing was now crystal clear to me:

I had to get one of those photography books back to my house, mean cashier or not.

V. Mission: Sorta-Possible

A few days after my amazing discovery, I got on my bike and rode farther than I'd ever ridden, in order to return to the mall bookstore. Lakeside Shopping Center was miles from my house, and I had to cross many dangerous intersections to get there. But I would have ridden naked through a room full of laughing bullies and cheerleaders just to accomplish my goal. I knew I couldn't ask my mom to drive me, because then she'd see the books I was buying and want to look through them, which would then lead to her figuring out what a sexual deviant her son had become. No, this was a trip I had to make alone; it was like an Indian manhood ritual, and part of me felt like it would be a test of how far I would be able to push God. If He really was mad about my masturbatory obsessions and needed to prove to me that He was not to be messed with, then He could simply run me over with a truck on my way to the mall and put both of us out of our misery. But if He let me get to Lakeside and back with my books of artistically photographed naked women, then He was at least telling me that Free Will existed and I was more than welcome to cook my own goose. Whatever the outcome, I couldn't help feeling like God was all over me like the proverbial cheap suit. You see, that was sort of the problem with being a Christian Scientist. As my father would say to me when he was trying to make me feel good about life, "God is always with you, closer than the air you breathe." Which meant that I had no chance of ever getting away from the Lord in order to get some faux pornography without Him knowing about it. And this seemed more like the annoying work of a nosy neighbor than a deity that was supposed to be protecting me. Who knew that God was the Gladys Kravitz of the universe?

I got to the mall, sweaty and tired but full of nervous energy. The task before me felt monumental, as if I were on my way to steal the Pink Panther diamond equipped with only a Swiss Army knife and a garden hose. There were many obstacles and pitfalls that I knew I'd have to navigate. First, I had to go through all the books in the photography section in order to find one with a title and cover that wouldn't give me away to the store clerk and yet which contained the maximum amount of exposed female flesh. Doing this ran the risk of drawing attention to myself, since the clerk was already sensitive to the specter of loitering preteens and would probably be watching my every move. I would have to be swift, yet discerning. Second, I had to have a good alibi in case I encountered any of my schoolmates while I was looking through the books or, more dangerous, if I was stopped after having already made my out-of-character purchase. I knew from experience that a shopping bag never went uninspected by one's peers at a mall, and the privacy-invading question of "What'd you buy?" and consequent unceremonious grabbing away from me of the bag would have to have a convincing response in order for the possession of photography books by a nervous kid who didn't even own a camera not to raise suspicions. And third, and most important, I had to figure out how I was going to have all this interaction with nude photography books in a public place without getting a raging hard-on in the process.

Having anticipated all of these variables, I felt fairly certain I had each of the obstacles covered. Behold:

For Obstacle One, I would approach the sales clerk, say hello in my nicest and most "I'm a good kid who because of my moral upbringing would never in a thousand years consider stealing anything from your store" tone of voice. Then, I would tell the woman that I was doing a school project on photography and was wondering if they sold any books on the topic. Then, while searching through the books for naked pictures, I would furrow my brow in a very thoughtful way that would say to her or anybody else who happened to see me in my search that I was both engaged in a sober quest for the driest of technical information and that I would rather be outside playing than having to slog through a wall of boring old photography books on a sunny Saturday afternoon.

For Obstacle Two, I would inform any of my classmates who might inquire about my purchase that my parents had told me they were buying me a camera for my upcoming birthday, and so I had taken it upon myself to do some reading up on the subject. I might even throw in that I was thinking of joining the yearbook staff and wanted to make sure my photographic skills were at a high enough level that I wouldn't miss one memorable moment from our current school year once I was in possession of said birthday camera.

And for the terrifying Obstacle Three, I had what I thought was a foolproof plan. On a previous trip to the bookstore with my friend Mike, we had discovered a book in the true crime section on the topic of forensic science. In this book were pictures of dead bodies cut open on lab tables and bloody crime scene photos. I had been so horrified and sickened by the book when we first looked in it that I couldn't eat lunch that day. And so I figured that just the prospect of telling myself I would look in that book (conveniently located next to the photography section) would be enough to negate any stirrings that might occur downstairs. And if not, then the doomsday plan of actually looking in the stomach-turning book would certainly do the trick. No erection can withstand the power of a really gross picture, I figured. I had also taken out a further bit of insurance by wearing my newest and least broken-in pair of Toughskins jeans, which were stiff and unbending enough to conceal whatever uncontrolled activity might happen within them. These precautions, along with the fact that I knew I would already be nervous because of the guaranteed scrutiny of the suspicious sales clerk, made me feel very certain that I could avoid having my overexcited hormones give me away during this very high-stakes mission.

And with all this running through my brain, I approached and entered the bookstore.

As expected, the kid-hating clerk was sitting behind the register. Unexpected, however, was that she was reading the Bible. The shock of this almost made me abort my plan, but the thought of having to ride my bike back to the mall on yet another day was enough to keep me moving forward. As I approached the counter, the woman looked up and gave me a disapproving look. I went into my con, putting on the widest-eyed, most sincere Sunday school smile I could muster.

"Hi, can I ask you a question?" I said, using a tone that sounded a lot like the one I would use when I was trying to get my mother to buy me something.

"You're that kid from the other day, aren't you?" she

asked. It was hard to tell if she thought this was a good or bad thing.

"Uh . . . yeah," I replied, trying to sound breezy and not at all nervous, which is exactly what I was. Just say "I'm doing a report on photography and wondered if you had any books on the subject," I told myself.

"I'm doing a report on women's fashion and wondered if you had any books on the subject."

The minute it was out of my mouth, I realized the meaning of the maxim "Oh, what a tangled web we weave . . ."

She made a face like she'd just smelled dog shit and said, "What the heck kind of school makes a kid your age do a report on *women's fashion*?"

"Uh . . . oh . . . uh," I stammered eloquently as flop sweat broke out on my forehead. "I mean it's a report about cameras. You know, the kind they take pictures of fashion models with."

"Why don't you go to the library?" she asked, studying me as if she were trying to see inside my soul.

"They don't have the books I need there."

"Well, this ain't a library, you know. If you want to use a book for your report, you're gonna have to buy it. We ain't runnin' a bookmobile here."

"I *know*," I said defensively, starting to feel indignant. "I've got money. I was going to buy them." I wanted to add a snippy "I'm not poor, you know" but decided that confrontation was not in my best interest.

"Well, the photography section is over there, but if I see you just readin' all the books, I'm gonna throw you outta here."

The local Dairy Queen by our house for years had a dirty and ripped old poster on the wall behind the cash register that showed a photo of a lion yawning in the middle of a field that read "The Customer Is King." Obviously this woman had never seen it. Desperate to get away from her, I nodded and headed over to ground zero.

I looked up at the photography section and Obstacle Three quickly became my main adversary. For some reason, just being in front of the section I knew contained all the potential pictures I had been dreaming about was enough to cause an immediate reaction. My Toughskins now proved to be as effective at containing things as a sheet of Kleenex would be at plugging a hole in Hoover Dam. Panicking because I knew the woman was staring right at me, I immediately leaned way in to the bookshelves, pretending to look up at the top shelf.

"You're gonna need a stepladder if you want to get up to that top shelf," she called over, begrudgingly trying to be helpful.

"No, that's okay. I'm fine." I wanted nothing more than for another customer to come in and distract her for a few seconds so that I could step over to the true crime section and hit myself in the libido with the autopsy book. Alas, things only got worse.

The woman walked over and stood right next to me. "Show me what book you want to see and I'll get it down for you. I can't let you climb the ladder yourself, in case you fall off and break your neck. And quit leaning against those books, you're gonna bend 'em."

Desperately trying to keep my wits about me, I immediately squatted down to hide my condition from her. "I don't really need anything from up there," I squeaked as my eyes came face-to-face with the nude section.

"Well, you can't look at any of those books down there," she said disapprovingly. "They're all filled with naked people."

It was at this moment that I started to curse the apparent hair trigger I'd inherited from some long-dead ancestor.

Because even though the nightmare I was currently involved in should have caused complete and total reversal of my arousal, the presence of the word *nude* in front of my eyes, coupled with the saleslady's utterance of the word *naked*, were all combining into an irreversible boner that it seemed might take days to subside. I now knew I only had one course of action.

I had to get out of there, book or no book.

As I stared up helplessly at the woman, not daring to stand while she was so focused on me, I said, "I've gotta go meet my mom for lunch. I'll have to come back later."

Just my luck, the woman took that moment to soften up, suddenly discovering she had a conscience as she stared down at the pathetic twelve-year-old crouching on the floor in front of her. "Look, darlin', you don't have to rush out of here because of me. I'm just trying to help you." And with that, she pulled out a book and handed it down to me. "What about this one? I've seen people buy it before. I hear it's good."

The book, entitled *Happy Snappin': A Child's Guide to Photography,* was literally the last book on earth I wanted. I reached up and took it from her.

"Thanks, I'll buy it," I said.

Using the book as cover, I quickly stood up, then held the book down in front of my groin with both hands, the same way I'd seen Daisy Duck hold her purse as she stared at Donald with love in her eyes. It was a fairly graceless move but it provided me the smokescreen I needed.

"Aren't you even gonna look at it?" For a woman who appeared to hate kids, she sure seemed like she couldn't get enough of talking to them.

"No, a friend of mine has it. It's really good."

"If your friend has it already, then why don't you just borrow his?"

For the second time that week, I felt like I was about to start crying. I could feel the shovel strikes hitting around my feet as I dug my grave deeper and deeper. *Just get out of here* were the only words going through my mind. "He lost his," I lamely retorted.

"Well, if that's the book you want, then I'll ring you up." And with this, she turned and started back to the register. Surprised and suddenly energized by my momentary freedom, I quickly scanned the bookshelf for a familiar title. And there, like an old friend, was the book I had looked at a few days earlier: *How to Take Pictures of People*. A cry of "Naked models, ahoy!" went through my brain as my future suddenly looked brighter.

I snatched the book down from the shelf and put it behind the copy of *Happy Snappin'* I was holding. Then I quickly rushed over to the checkout counter, where I knew I could hide my perpetual arousal from the saleslady. As she started to ring up the two books, I suddenly launched into a nonsensical rant about my mythical school project, trying anything to distract her from focusing on the second book in my pile. My heart was pounding like a John Bonham drum solo as I chattered away about how hard seventh grade was, terrified that she was going to decide to flip through the new book and stumble across the nudity-laced "How to Work with Models" chapter. But she didn't. Fortunately, it seemed my time spent with her in the previous five minutes had somehow warmed her up to my prepubescent charms. Looking guiltily at her Bible sitting next to the register, though, I knew that hers was not the judgment about which I needed to worry most.

VI. Arrested and Jailed Development

Fortunately, even God couldn't kill the excitement that was swelling inside me as I rocketed my bike back home from the mall that day. I now had a new naked lady—nay, *several* naked ladies—and this time they weren't going to get away from me.

I had beaten the system.

My acquisition of the model-filled photography book proved to be a roaring success for the rope feeling and me, as I began cutting days off my life like blades of grass under a riding lawnmower. Over the course of the next several years, the photography section at the mall bookstore became my home away from home, a never-ending stag party that I could drop in on anytime to survey the female landscape, like Hugh Hefner coming down the stairs at one of his parties at the Playboy Mansion. In addition to this, I had started culling images from other sources as well, having developed a sneaky system of going through my mother's fashion magazines after they had been relegated to the garbage can and cutting out any pictures that showed the slightest inch of forbidden female flesh. I kept this ever-growing pile of titillating clippings stashed in the bottom drawer of my dresser, cleverly hidden inside the box that held the old Corgi miniature crane my uncle had bought me when I was five. The further I progressed into my teenage years, the more my room became an advent calendar of adolescent sexual angst—whatever drawer you pulled, whatever door you opened, whatever lid you lifted had a semi-erotic surprise hidden inside. I had created my own personal City of Women and found that I was quite content overseeing it.

It was around this time I started to hear that a lot of the guys in my school were looking at *Playboy* magazine. I had always dreamed of getting my hands on a copy and yet knew I couldn't buy one because of my age, not to mention that handing one to a cashier felt like it was the same as walking up and saying, "Hello, I'm a chronic masturbator." Most of my *Playboy*-reading peers seemed to have older brothers they would borrow their magazines from, and I even heard a few guys say that their fathers had subscriptions. The idea that a kid's father would have *Playboy* in the house was truly terrifying to me. Knowing that my father had a "naughty" party hat in our closet was bad enough, but the idea that my dad would have the mailman hand-deliver a monthly magazine filled with pictures of naked women who were half his age was on a par with hearing that my father was out killing guys "just to watch them die." I had visions of these kids' sex-crazed dads as drooling, lascivious monsters who had to be locked in cages in their basements next to the furnace and thrown raw meat along with their pornography just to keep their families and neighborhoods safe from their voracious sexual appetites.

But the more I thought about kids my age getting to peruse heart-stopping pictures of naked Playmates and Girls of the Big Ten, the more annoyed I became. What was most galling about it was that while they were getting to look at

Playboy, I was having to dig through garbage cans for fashion magazines and creep around mall bookstores spending all the money I earned working at my dad's store on expensive books containing "artistic" pictures of women draped in gauze standing in dimly lit fountains or dressed as topless matadors covered with blue body makeup. I was spending tons of time and energy amassing my collection of G-rated erotica while they were just being handed prepackaged and far more effective collections of masturbation-inducing pictures. It was like finding that after years of hard work and loyal service you had been passed over for promotion by the boss's idiot son.

And yet, for some reason, I felt almost superior to my *Playboy*-reading peers. I guess it was because of the ingenuity I had displayed in the face of necessity. Any moron could just grab a *Playboy* and pleasure himself, but it took a real connoisseur of the female form to hand-select his own personal lusty Louvre. And while my fellow males were training themselves to one day unsophisticatedly fall in love with large-breasted strippers and the Snap-on Tools bikini-clad calendar girls, I was honing my skills as an aficionado of beautiful women, one who could look upon a roomful of fashion models and pick out the one who was most exquisite. No, my peers were developing the erotic tastes of truckers and hillbillies while I was becoming a junior David Niven, appreciator of fine female perfection. Let them have their *Playboy* magazines, I thought. I've got the true onanistic pioneer spirit.

Unfortunately, as I was lauding myself for my self-pleasing superiority, what I didn't realize was that the peers I had outdistanced in the realm of self-gratification had advanced into a whole new world that the experts like to call Human Sexual Relations.

My realization of all this occurred one innocent day when I was walking down the hall in my high school. I was a sophomore and was feeling the freedom of no longer being a freshman, of knowing that even though I was on the third tier of seniority in the blackboard jungle of Chippewa Valley High, at least I wasn't on the bottom. As I walked along feeling somehow mature and wise beyond my years, two freshmen guys came out of a classroom. As one headed off down the hall, the other stopped in the doorway and yelled very loudly after him, "Hey, if she doesn't want to kiss, then she's not gonna fuck!" He then looked over at me and gave me a laughing look that said, "Can you believe what an idiot my friend is?"

I was completely shocked. Partly at the crude nature of the whole event—the fact that someone would yell the f-word down a crowded hallway, especially a freshman who was supposed to be terrified of the older students and hence lying low to avoid drawing attention to himself—but more at the idea that anybody in our school, and a *freshman,* no less, was actually comfortable and familiar with the real act of sex.

Actual sex.

With other people.

Not cutouts from magazines and photography books.

What shattered my world so much was the level of knowingness on his face as he shared his look with me. It was the face of someone who'd either already had sex or at the very least had experienced everything leading up to it. And like the logic that says for every cockroach you see in your apartment there are hundreds of others lurking unseen in the woodwork, I was suddenly forced to realize that there was a lot of sexual maturation going on around me. No longer could I look at the couples making out in the hallways and assume they were simply content with stopping at first base. I had been living in a dream world, I realized, and I didn't know how to feel about myself. Clearly, kids my age were not supposed to be having sex. Our church had taught us that you were supposed to be chaste until your wedding night. So if God got mad when you masturbated after He told you not to, I could only imagine how pissed He must get at you for basically telling Him to "go jump in the lake" by going all the way with someone you didn't even plan on marrying.

The one good thing I took away from this unsettling revelation was the reassurance that if God had all this sacrilegious sex to disapprove of and people to punish for it, then maybe He was at a point in His life where He was willing to cut me some slack in the masturbation department. Maybe He'd even let me slide on the whole lose-one-day-each-time thing, since I was obeying the premarital chastity rule. I mean, once He saw how out of control my fellow students were, He might even give me back the days I'd given away. It only seemed fair. Besides, it'd been so long since I'd heard the deejay utter the warning that maybe it was no longer in effect. Heck, maybe it only applied to Jamaican kids.

And so, using my amateur Socratic logic, I tried to release myself from all the residual guilt and angst I had been experiencing over the past few years, tried to forget about the sacrificed days, forget about the Curse, the Divine Disapproval, and just continue my inoffensive relationship with my ink-and-paper ladies. How could God possibly still get mad at me about that?

I've now lived long enough to know that something bad generally happens when you start asking questions like that.

And so it did.

God started talking to me.

VII. Hello, God, It's Me.
The Dorky Kid.

At the risk of sounding like I had suddenly turned into Emily Watson in *Breaking the Waves,* I had in essence turned into Emily Watson in *Breaking the Waves,* minus the bus trip hand job to the old Danish farmer.

Because of a new concept that had been introduced recently in one of my Sunday school classes, which said I could always find guidance in life by listening to "God's still, small voice" inside me, I had started having discussions with Him.

And He was neither still nor small.

At first it was simply little moments of advice and guidance that I told myself were coming from God. (I was an only child and was always talking to myself anyway.) After a while, however, I started hearing these moments as a conversation, in which my own personal inner voice would start being lectured to by what I believed to be the voice of God. The dialogues started off fairly innocuous and didn't involve any sexual judgments. They generally went something like this:

Me: "Gee, I wonder if I should do my homework or watch a *Lost in Space* rerun on Channel 50?"

God: "Well, do you think that you'll be able to do your

homework after you watch the show? Or are you then going to procrastinate again and watch the back-to-back *Brady Bunch* reruns that are on afterward?"

Me: "Well, my plan is to do my homework afterward but there's always a chance that I'll end up watching *The Brady Bunch* if I see it's one of my favorite episodes."

God: "Then you'd probably better just do your homework now and skip watching TV until tonight."

Me: "But I want to watch *Lost in Space*."

God: "But you don't even like that show."

Me: "I like the old ones that are in black and white. Those are really good. It's just the ones that are in color where they meet up with space bikers and giant talking carrots and stupid stuff like that that I hate. Especially the ones with Bloop, the weird monkey with a big black dome on his head that I think is supposed to make you think he's got a huge brain or something. Those are really dumb."

God: "So, if one of those episodes is on, then you should turn off the TV and do your homework."

Me: "Okay, that sounds like a plan."

And then I'd go and watch *Lost in Space,* even though it was a really stupid one where the Robinsons meet up with a space circus, and then I'd watch *The Brady Bunch* and put off my homework until late at night. And all during the time I was watching TV and goofing off, I'd hear:

God: "You shouldn't be doing this. You should be doing your homework. You told Me you would."

Me: "Yeah, yeah, I know. I will."

And God would simply shake His head and give me the same look my father would when I'd admit that I'd forgotten to take out the garbage.

This kind of inner dialogue started taking place more

and more frequently until one day God decided to confront me as I eyed the photography books on my shelf and considered a rendezvous in the bathroom.

God: "You shouldn't do that, you know."

Me: "I know. I haven't said I was gonna. I was just thinking about it."

God: "Well, *stop* thinking about it. You know my rule. You do it, you lose a day off your life."

Me: "Is that for real? I mean, it sounds kinda weird. Isn't it just something that Jamaican deejay guy made up?"

God: "You think I'd have let him say it if it wasn't true? You think I would have let you hear it? Don't you think I did that on purpose, that I had your dad turn on the radio just then so that you'd hear My warning and realize that you were supposed to stop doing that terrible thing you keep doing? Why do you think I had you go to Jamaica in the first place? I never would have gotten that on the radio in this country."

Me: "But why is the rope feeling such a terrible thing? I mean, it's not hurting anybody."

God: "Well, let's see here. Spilling your seed. Giving power to the material. Looking at women as sex objects. Disobeying the Word of God. You want me to keep going?"

Me: "But how do I know You're really God? I sort of feel like I'm just talking to myself and telling myself stuff in Your voice because I'm trying to stop myself from doing something that I don't know if I should be doing or not. You might just be me."

God: "I'm not *your* voice. It's really Me."

Me: "See, I feel like I just said that to myself. It even *sounded* like my voice."

God: "Because that's how I talk to you. I talk to you in your voice but it's a little different in attitude so that you'll know it's Me. But, hey, if you don't believe Me, then go ahead and disobey Me. It's no skin off My teeth."

Me: "No, no, I believe it's You. And I promise I won't do the rope feeling anymore."

God: "You're going to do it right now, aren't you?"

Me: "Uh . . . I don't know. Can't we talk about something else?"

And then, of course, I'd head to the bathroom, photography book in hand, and feel guilty until I got swept up in the moment, and then once the moment was over, the guilt would wash over me like a tsunami and I'd look at the book and want to throw it away and would vow never to spill my seed again and then I'd try to avoid God for the rest of the day. But He'd always take a shot at me afterward.

God: "Way to go, man. Thanks for lying to Me. Say good-bye to one more day. It's the day your grandchildren were going to throw you a party."

God started hitting me hard and heavy in the months after that. By the time I turned fifteen, God was living full-time inside my head, chattering away like a hyperactive teenage girl after four double espressos. There wasn't a move I could make or a thought I could think without God giving me advice and passing judgment on me. But it was the act of masturbation that seemed to obsess Him the most.

And then one day, He suddenly had a new tactic. Sensing that I had grown slightly immune to the lose-a-day-each-time law (because when you're a teenager, the end of your life seems so far away that you can't imagine yourself being old anyway), He came up with a much more immediate deterrent:

He would ruin my day.

It started as more of a vague threat.

God: "You're gonna go and masturbate again, aren't you?"

Me: "Probably. Actually, yes. Definitely. What's it to You?"

God: "Well, you should know that if you do, then I can't protect you for the rest of the day. If something bad's gonna happen, then there's nothing I can do about it."

Me: "What kind of bad thing could happen?"

God: "Hey, anything. Car accident, broken leg, tornado, heart attack, cancer. A million things can go wrong during a day. Get My drift?"

Me: "Is something bad gonna happen? Do You know about something You're not telling me?"

God: "I'm just sayin' . . ."

And so, after I would once again ignore His warning and indulge, I would spend the rest of the day walking around on eggshells, waiting for tragedy at every turn. Most days, nothing bad would happen. But on the days when something *did* go wrong, if I'd get in trouble with my parents or flunk a test or get pummeled by bullies in the locker room, I knew it was all due to my forbidden dalliance with the rope feeling. But since I was able to reason with myself that God's interpretation of a bad day didn't include me actually getting killed, then I figured I could put up with any ruined twenty-four-hour period if it meant getting to enjoy a few daily moments of tension-releasing bliss.

And that's when something really bad happened.

VIII. The Whip Comes Down

One week after I turned sixteen and had gotten my driver's license, I threw caution to the wind on a morning when I believed I had heard a particularly strong warning from God in my head. I tried to abstain but found myself to be too weak in the face of my latest photography book, which featured pictures of a naked model posing amidst poems by Elton John's lyricist, Bernie Taupin. I took my latest lover into the bathroom and the trap was set.

At lunchtime, I offered to take my mom's Dodge Coronet to the car wash, in order to pull off a quick joyride with my friend John. When I picked him up, we cranked WRIF on the radio and had a great time driving down Gratiot Avenue, singing along to Foreigner and Led Zeppelin. John would always crack up when I played the short drum break from Boston's "Rock and Roll Band" on my dashboard in perfect sync with the song, and when the track came on as we crossed into Roseville, I got my biggest laugh from him to date. It was truly one of those "it's great to be young and alive" moments of teenage bliss that makes those years twixt thirteen and eighteen bearable. However, seeing that we had been out longer than a car wash would normally take, I turned the car around and started to head back. John was trying to talk me into stopping at the house of a friend of his so that we could look at a go-kart the guy had built out of a stolen shopping cart. I, however, didn't want to get in trouble with my mom. I always avoided getting in the slightest bit of trouble with my parents the way most kids avoided looking like they cared if their parents got mad at them. As John made good-natured fun of me and we started singing merrily along to Aerosmith's "Big Ten Inch," John suddenly thrust his arm out in front of my face as we approached an intersection, pointed out my side window, and yelled, "Turn here! Now! He lives down here!" He said it so quickly and emphatically that I spun the wheel and immediately pulled an illegal left turn. Within a fraction of a second that seemed to morph into slow motion, John started laughing uproariously and I, feeling the thrill of having broken the law so easily, started laughing too, or at least until I looked over and saw a tan Dodge Aspen station wagon with fake wood paneling that contained a large family heading toward me as my car veered over the line into its lane. Before I could react, my car caught the side of the station wagon and smashed into its back half, sending their car spinning. As the impact occurred, I could see the faces of a bunch of shocked eight- and ten-year-olds in the backseat as the impact threw them out of their seats and up into the ceiling. The sound was awful, a huge dull thud that didn't sound anything like car crashes did in the movies, and incongruously ringing out above it all was the sound of John laughing like a hyena and Aerosmith playing away merrily. As I heard the spinning Aspen's tires screech and then crash into the curb, my mother's car threw up a cloud of noisy steam from under the now folded and twisted hood as we rolled to a stop. The feeling of absolute fear, panic, dread, and remorse that shot up the back of my neck and overtook my brain like an explosion of fire was enough to make me wish I was dead. Neither John nor I was hurt, but we exchanged a look that can only be translated as a very inarticulate "Oh, shit." I switched off the radio, mocking me as it was with its blithe indifference to what had just happened. I was too terrified to look at the station wagon. Did I just kill people? Was there a dead or dying family strewn about inside a car that was going to explode into a huge fireball, the way cars always did in movies after they got in accidents? I slowly got out of the Coronet, willing to give up everything in my life if I could just somehow be transported away from there.

Fortunately, I saw the Brady Bunch–sized family clambering out of the car, looking shaky but uninjured. I walked weak-kneed over to them as the kids immediately started looking at the station wagon that was now completely caved in on one side and very obviously totaled. The mother, who had been driving, looked at the side of her car and started crying uncontrollably, saying, "My car, my beautiful car!" over and over again. (I'll leave the cynical jokes about anyone saying a sentence like that in reference to a Dodge Aspen station wagon to the more heartless among us.)

Everything became a dreadful blur after that, as police cars and ambulances arrived. I remember, at one point, as the woman was crying and having what seemed like a nervous breakdown while she recounted the accident to a police officer, I weepily came up and asked if I could give her and her family a ride home. She looked at me like I was a serial killer and started backing away, saying, "Stay away from me," in the same tone of voice she would have used if I was stalking toward her with a butcher knife. The whole accident was one of those terrible experiences where everything is awful and surreal despite the fact that the sun is shining and cars are driving past you filled with staring people who haven't been in a terrible car wreck and so are going happily about their day, not knowing that you're living through the worst moment of your life to date.

As my father drove John home and lectured us both about how irresponsible we were and how lucky we were that we hadn't killed anybody, I sat in a dungeon of guilt and condemnation and thought about the one thing I knew for certain at that moment:

God had fired a warning shot over my bow.

He'd told me that something bad would happen if I didn't listen to Him and I didn't listen and something bad had happened. I had pushed the Big Man too far.

His voice was speaking quietly in my head, calm as an Old West sheriff who now knows he has your complete and undivided attention.

God: "I let you off easy this time. But the next time you don't heed My word, things are gonna turn out a lot worse. Trust Me."

Me: ". . . yes, Sir."

That night, I vowed to never masturbate again. I threw out all my magazine clippings, packed away all my photography books, and did everything I could to deny myself my "attentions."

And I did this for thirty-eight days.

I went through every mental state during this period of abstention. At times I thought I was going to go insane, and the clock seemed to move at a geological rate. At other times, I marveled at how strong my will was. There were even some moments when I felt complete and utter superiority over the people of the earth. I was doing what this voice in my head that was calling itself God wanted me to do and I wasn't wavering. He had spoken and I had listened. My conscience was clear. God and I were like old pals now. He'd give me the thumbs-up whenever I'd walk past the bookstore at the mall and not go in. He'd high-five me when I'd let one of my mother's fashion magazines sit unopened on the hamper as I sat on the toilet and used the bathroom for the only things it had been built for—to dispose of bodily waste in, and to take a shower in, and to brush my teeth in, and to *not* masturbate in. And except for the fact that I felt like I was going to have a heart attack and that my testicles were going to explode, I was one hundred percent committed.

I had won.

IX. The Calm Before the Storm

On the thirty-seventh day of The Accomplishment, my parents and I took a weekend trip to Chicago. As we checked into our hotel, I stopped in the gift shop and picked up a few magazines. I bought a *Mad,* a *Scientific American,* a *People* that had a picture of Luke Skywalker on the cover, and a *National Lampoon*. I had never read *National Lampoon* before but my next-door neighbor Craig had always told me it was really funny. When I took the magazines up to the register, the cashier gave me a disapproving look as she rang up the *National Lampoon*. I figured that it probably had to do with her judgment of the humor in the magazine. I'd had plenty of adults tell me that *Mad* was stupid and juvenile and so figured that she was passing the same judgment on this new humor magazine. Shaking her head to herself, she put the magazines in a bag and handed the bag to me with a scowl. Figuring she was simply a snob, I headed up to my parents' hotel room and didn't give the episode a second thought.

That evening, with my parents asleep in the bed next to me, I sat up in the dark with my penlight reading *Mad* and *People*. After about an hour, though, I encountered a very revealing picture of *Charlie's Angels* co-star Kate Jackson in a bikini and felt the stirrings of my old exorcised demon. Committed to my cause, I quickly closed the magazine, turned off my penlight, and tried to fall asleep.

God: "Good work. Kate Jackson's too old for you anyway."

Me: "Not a problem. Besides, I'm tired."

God: "Attaboy."

X. The Storm

On the thirty-eighth day, after a fun-filled afternoon of sight-seeing and shopping, my parents and I headed up to our hotel room to get ready for dinner. As my parents got dressed and I waited, I flipped through my copy of *Scientific American* and decided that, once again, it was far too obtuse and scholarly for me to read. I always bought it both to impress whoever was working the register and because I was ever hopeful that there'd be an article about UFOs or aliens or other things that fell firmly into the fiction side of the science world. I was about to pull the *National Lampoon* out of the bag when my mother emerged from the bathroom and said, "Ready!"

"Finally!" said my father, and I put the *Lampoon* back in the bag.

That night, after we had watched *The Tonight Show* and had laughed all the way through both Johnny Carson's mono-logue and a panel appearance by Rodney Dangerfield, my dad turned off the light, and he and my mom fell asleep. As my dad snored loud enough to shake the television off the dresser, I turned on my penlight and pulled out the *National Lampoon.*

I started flipping through the magazine and was surprised at how adult it was. It had swear words all over the place, as well as very frank, irreverent talk about sex. But it was a scary irreverence for a sixteen-year-old who was afraid of the idea of intimate physical contact with another person, this idea of a world of people who had casual sex and then made jokes about it. However, wanting to feel mature, I tried to convince myself the magazine was funny and forced myself not to be shocked.

In the middle of the issue there was a story about the kinds of girls you can sleep with in college, and it featured photos of unattractive women in "sexy" poses. Nerdy librarian types, angry feminists, uptight theology students—they each had a black-and-white picture of a different coed dressed unappealingly. I read it and thought the article was rather funny, even though I was thrown by the notion that college students seemed to have sex all the time.

And it was then that I turned the page.

There in front of me was a picture of a nude woman that was labeled "Anthropology Major." The gag was that she was a girl who didn't shave any part of her body. And so here was a black-and-white picture of a very hairy woman who wasn't in the least bit attractive.

Except for the fact that she was completely naked.

And except for the fact that I been abstaining for thirty-eight days.

My eyes went wide.

Enter God.

God: "Oh no, c'mon! You've made it *thirty-eight* days. And that woman is horrible. You can't possibly be considering doing this."

Me: "I'm not. It's just . . . I mean . . . are You really saying that I can *never* do this again?"

God: "Well, yeah, sorta. Or you've got to go for *at least* a year."

Me: "You've gotta be kidding me. I was sort of amazed that I made it this long."

God: "But look how good you feel about yourself. And if you do this, it nullifies everything you've done so far. You stop, you go back to zero."

Me: "That's not fair. I have to get *some* credit for trying so hard."

God: "What credit should you get? This is something you shouldn't have been doing in the first place."

Me: "And so You're telling me that nobody else in the world does it? That I'm the only one?"

God: "Whoever does it isn't a good person. If you want to be a bad person, then go ahead and be my guest. Just remember that if you're not concerned about losing days off the end of your life, what if you're not *supposed* to live to be ninety-three years old? What if I decided when I made you that you were only going to live until you were twenty? If that's the case, if you head into that bathroom and do what you're thinking about doing, how do you know that you haven't used up all the remaining days you had in reserve? This could be the one that makes you drop dead."

Me: ". . . is that true?"

God: "Maybe. Hey, it's not My job to let you know that stuff. You should have been keeping track. What, I'm not busy enough running the world, now I have to keep count of how many days you're masturbating off your life?"

Me: "I don't know. You sure seem to have enough time to sit in my head and give me a hard time about it constantly. Don't You have a famine to solve or something?"

God: "Fine, do whatever you want. But just think how terrible you're going to feel about yourself afterward."

I sat there and stared at the unattractive picture of the very unattractive hairy nude woman. I looked over at the bathroom door and shined my penlight at it. I stared, I tried to talk myself out of it, and then I sighed and got out of bed.

God: "Where are you going?"

Me: "I just have to go to the bathroom, that's all."

God: "Then why are you taking the magazine with you?"

Me: "Because I want something to read in there. Gimme a break, would Ya? My stomach's all goofed up. I might have to sit there awhile."

God: "You'd better not masturbate."

Me: "I won't."

I lied.

The minute I was finished, I was filled with absolute disgust at myself, at my weakness, and at the picture of the hairy naked woman. I had let myself down and I had thrown away my gargantuan effort of the past thirty-eight days. I felt terrible, worse than if I had actually dropped dead. And I knew that there was nothing God could do to punish me that would be worse than how much I was already punishing myself.

And right at that moment, my father knocked on the door.

"What are you doing in there?" he said impatiently. "I've gotta go to the bathroom."

In my panic at the unexpected interruption, I pulled my pajamas back up and threw open the door . . . and promptly forgot that the magazine was sitting on the floor next to the toilet. My father pushed past me and shut the door. My heart was beating out of my chest. He was going to see the picture. Maybe he'd just think I was reading a funny magazine and innocently happened to have dropped it open to that particular page. I wanted to knock and explain my innocence but then I just might make it worse. Maybe he didn't care. Maybe he'd laugh at it and then we'd have a fun talk about his college years. I got back in bed and waited, terrified. God knew how bad I felt about what I had just done. There was no way He would rub my face in it like that. Right?

My father finally opened the door. He had the magazine open to the exact page with the naked hairy woman on it. He stared at me, and then he shook his head in total and absolute disgust, with a look that said he knew exactly what I had just been doing and that he didn't approve in the least.

"You'd better not let your mother see this garbage" was all he said as he shoved the magazine back at me, in a tone that indicated he had lost all respect for his only son. And then he climbed back in bed and sighed as if to show that I had disappointed him greatly, and went back to sleep.

Oh, man, I thought as I crawled back into bed. God completely ratted me out.

What an Asshole.

After this, God seemed more like a bratty little sister than the Ruler of All Space and Time to me. And so His warnings in my head started feeling more annoying than anything else. I started going against His will just to spite Him for being such a little friggin' tattletale. I started telling God to shut up. I started telling Him to go and end a war or something. And after a while, I figured, He just decided to give up, because His voice started to get weaker and weaker every day. And while it never fully disappeared, it at least seemed more manageable from that point on.

Not that I was freed from the guilt that had been programmed into me. It just transferred over to another ethereal being. Because when my grandmother died a year later, I started to torture myself with the thought that since she was now probably able to look in on her loved ones from the afterlife, maybe the only times she decided to look in on me just happened to be the very moments when I was doing the thing in the bathroom that would horrify her the most.

But, after stressing about this for a few weeks, I just figured that she was a grown woman and could deal with it. And, if she couldn't, I wouldn't have to find out how terrible she thought I was until I died.

And I figured I could deal with that.

Well, as long as I hadn't masturbated away too many years of my life, that is. I wasn't ready to deal with her *that* soon.

BOOK TWO

Hellooooooooooooooooooooo, Ladies!

Clueless in Mt. Clemens

When I was in seventh grade, Mr. Ramos, our science teacher, came into class one day and had all the girls leave. Once they were gone, Mr. Kemp, our school's other science teacher, brought in all the boys from his class and had them sit in the missing girls' seats. As we exchanged looks and wondered if we were in trouble, Mr. Ramos and Mr. Kemp started a tag team lecture about sex. It was all very clinical and nothing that I hadn't heard from my next-door neighbors:

A man and a woman got into bed together, things went into certain places, a bunch of technical stuff happened inside the woman, and then nine months later a baby was born.

As the teachers talked and showed diagrams of a woman's uterus and a man's testicles, there was a lot of tittering from my fellow students, especially when there was any reference to the "penis" or "vagina," and Mr. Ramos kept telling everyone to "grow up."

After about fifteen minutes of lecturing, the teachers told us to write down any questions we might have about sex on a piece of loose-leaf paper and then hand it up to the front. "There's no such thing as a dumb question in this classroom," said Mr. Kemp reassuringly. "Anything you're confused about or unsure of is legitimate, and Mr. Ramos and I are here to answer anything you ask, man to man." He told us not to put our names on the paper, so that our questions would be anonymous and therefore free us from any concerns we had about being embarrassed in front of our peers.

When all the folded papers were handed up to the front, Mr. Ramos opened the first one, read it to himself, and shook his head with a world-weary sigh. He then read the question out loud.

"It says, 'Hey, Ramos, why don't you let the whole class come in your mouth?'"

The entire room erupted into uproarious laughter, with some kids shaking their heads in disbelief at the sheer audacity of the question, and I could tell from his smirk that one of the tough kids on the other side of the room had written it. And as everybody was laughing knowingly at this question, I was thinking the following: "What's so funny about letting everybody in the room walk inside the teacher's mouth? It's not even possible. That's the weirdest joke I've ever heard."

I use this story to illustrate something that I'm sure is already one hundred percent apparent to all of you—I knew nothing about the real-life world of sex when everyone else around me apparently did. I knew *what* sex was, and I knew *how* it was supposed to work, but I didn't know how any of it translated into the real world outside of what I could do by myself in the bathroom. To me, sex with another person was something that happened on a distant planet. The people I saw in the world around me every day clearly couldn't be stripping off their clothes in private and co-mingling their bodies with those of other human beings. The most sexual thing I could conceive of anyone actually doing was hugging and kissing. Even when somebody was described as having been involved in "wild sex," my image was of a spirited session of groping and rolling around on the living room floor while fully clothed. It just didn't seem possible anything more advanced than that could be occurring between the people I saw every day in school and at the mall and at the grocery store and in my neighborhood and on TV.

In my mind back then, sex was something dirty, an activity taken part in by people who were unmarried and out of control. And even if they were married, in my mind sex had to be something that was inherently wrong, an urge you gave in to in a moment of weakness. Looking back, it seems that I had taken a bit too seriously the part of my religion that said we were supposed to look away from our physical bodies and dwell on more spiritual matters. I simply couldn't see a time when sex was justified, other than when you had to make a baby.

And even *then* I couldn't get my head around it.

When I'd see a prim and pretty young woman at the drug store who was pregnant, I would be unable to fathom the idea that she had actually had sex with her husband. I could only imagine that if they did, it was in the most formal of ways; that they had both faced it as something that had to be done in order to carry on the family name, and so it was performed mechanically and impersonally, allowing all involved to retain their dignity and make sure the woman would not be sullied by what I knew had to be a messy and inherently degrading act. How else could she now be walking around dressed conservatively in a neatly ironed blouse, with flowered barrettes in her perfectly combed hair, while letting the world see that she was with child? How could she say hello to the older cashier who smiled sweetly and asked when she was "due" if she wasn't ashamed of the fact that her round belly was informing all who saw her that she had engaged in sexual intercourse? How could she head into the crowded parking lot and show her fellow shoppers that she had given in to what I knew had to be the basest of animalistic instincts unless she and everyone around her knew that she had done it in the most innocent way possible? And how could I even begin to grapple with the idea that everyone I'd ever met in my life who had children—my parents, my friends' parents, the people at church, my teachers, the den mothers in my Cub Scouts chapter, even our school's playground ladies— had at one time or another had sex, and that more than likely they all had sex on a regular basis? The answers I tried to sell myself never seemed quite believable and so, like you do when you're brought a steak at a restaurant, instead of thinking about how the cow it came from was slaughtered, gutted, skinned, and chopped up into pieces, I chose to believe that somehow pregnancies just happened and that nothing unsettling ever occurred to bring them into existence.

And it's because of this that, to me, the sentence "Hey, Ramos, why don't you let the whole class come in your mouth?" was simply a statement that contained words from a foreign language.

And, unfortunately, I've always been a slow learner when it comes to foreign languages.

Hell on Wheels

I've always had a lot of enthusiasm.

I can get enthusiastic about almost anything if it holds any appeal to me. And once I'm enthusiastic about something, I'll embrace it with an obsession found only in drug addicts and people who collect Pez dispensers.

I've been enthusiastic about many things in my life: stand-up comedy, magic, guitar, drums, banjo, juggling, science fiction, *Mad* magazine, Charlie Brown books, UFOs, astronomy, Hot Wheels, G.I. Joe, *Monty Python's Flying Circus,* fashionable clothing, Steve Martin, George Carlin, Lenny Bruce, Groucho Marx, *Saturday Night Live, The Brady Bunch,* building model cars, trying to be a stuntman, and, of course, whatever girl I happened to have a crush on at the time. And among all these was one obsession I was even more enthusiastic about than normal:

Roller skating.

It all started when I was ten and one of the kids in my Cub Scout troop had a birthday party at our local roller rink, the Skate-o-Rama. I had never been roller-skating before, having only attempted ice-skating, at which I was hopeless. This was in the days before hockey skates were easily attainable, and so I had been sent out by my father onto the frozen ice at the bottom of our sloping backyard to skate in a secondhand pair of men's figure skates procured from his army surplus store. My ankles proved to be as weak as those of a spindly ninety-year-old woman, and I spent the entire afternoon watching them bend inward painfully, making the bottoms of my legs look more like I had just suffered a horrible shattered-bone injury than that I was a kid having fun in a winter wonderland. And because of this, as I headed into the roller rink for the first time, fully bedecked in my Cub Scout uniform, I was filled with my usual sense of dread toward all things I'm certain I will fail at.

However, to my surprise, the moment I walked into the rink, I was hooked. The music was loud and rocking. The lights were colorful and made the place feel like a dimly lit carnival. The rink was packed with people having fun, and the sight of so many skaters flying around the oval track at top speed made me feel like Holden Caulfield at the end of *The Catcher in the Rye* as he watched his sister Pheobe going round and round on the carousel: something just seemed right about the world when I was inside this place.

Things got even better when I put on my rented skates and found that I actually had a natural aptitude for roller-skating. Whereas ice-skating was all about trying to balance on a thin blade of metal, roller-skating gave you four wheels laid out in a rectangle, which meant that as long as you could get used to the fact that you were standing on something that moved, you were pretty much as stable as you would be on a pair of platform shoes. The freedom and the lightness I felt as I zoomed around the painted concrete floor on my eight rented wheels was euphoric. Whenever I was on my bike I was constantly slowed down by the potholes and cracks in the streets of my neighborhood, things that kept me from ever being able to soar with the velocity I always imagined I could attain if only I could find the perfect kinetic medium. And now I had found one that seemed almost organic. To have your vehicles strapped onto your feet so that they were simply an extension of your body was both brilliant and life changing. By the time the party had ended, I was able to skate as fast as anybody in the rink, even the mustached teenage guys who were trying to see which one could go the fastest without falling down. I was all power and speed as I weaved through the mass of unsteady skaters in my Cub Scout uniform while Led Zeppelin blared over the sound system and the floor flew past underneath my feet. I felt the roller rink air rushing against my face, an air that smelled like the soft pretzels and hot dogs and Cherry Icees at the snack bar, and the whole thing was like a religious experience.

And if every religion needs a messiah, mine was a group of alluring females referred to in the skating world as the Roller Rink Girls.

The Roller Rink Girls were a subgroup of feminine species that I had no idea existed until I set foot inside the Skate-o-Rama. They were extremely pretty girls in their early to mid-teens who were just on the verge of becoming burnouts and freak chicks. They had a uniform that they all wore, consisting of hip-hugger blue jeans and tight-fitting powder blue T-shirts that featured an iron-on image of a skating cartoon rabbit. The rabbit was staring impassively out from the T-shirt and was filled in with the colors of the American flag, complete with stars and stripes (laid out in the vertical fashion of Peter Fonda's helmet in *Easy Rider,* a movie I hadn't seen but knew because of a poster in the record store at the mall). I had never seen a cartoon character with an expression as cool and detached as that on the Roller Rink Girl rabbit, and there was something about it that just seemed to scream, "Only beautiful women dare wear me." What added an intriguing and, for a ten-year-old boy, hypnotic element to this was the fact that on most of the girls, the rabbit's head was stretched and distended by the burgeoning breasts growing beneath the T-shirts upon which the rabbit lived. I watched the Roller Rink Girls stare at teenage boys about whom they would whisper and laugh and then glide hand in hand with during the Couples Skate. I thought they were the most mature, exquisite creatures I had ever laid my eyes on during my ten years on earth. And I vowed that one day I would couples-skate with one of them.

I spent the next three years going to the All-Ages Skate every Saturday from ten in the morning until two in the afternoon. During those years, I had bought my own pair of roller skates, which was a definite status symbol among the roller rink crowd. I also scandalized my nondrinking, Christian Scientist family by talking my mother into buying me a Budweiser roller skate carrying case, which was an oversized briefcase tiled with red and white Budweiser beer labels. As much as I always tried to avoid the vociferous, anti-alcohol hand-wringing of my father and grandmother, I was more interested in impressing the Roller Rink Girls, who I was sure would see my boozy skate container and wonder if there was more to me than my geeky exterior suggested. I taught myself how to skate backward in the hopes that one day I could do a Couples Skate the way the coolest guys at the rink did—by skating backward while the girl skated forward, facing the guy as he put his hands on her waist and she put her hands on his shoulders. This to me seemed like the absolute pinnacle of romance, a rolling demonstration of your attraction to each other, and while I would occasionally muster up the courage to ask a girl from my school to do a Couples Skate with me in the standard hand-in-hand/both-skating-forward formation, I dreamed of the day that I could convince a Roller Rink Girl to go face-to-face with me as we skated slowly to Barry Manilow's "Mandy." I knew that if I could just get one of them to stare into my eyes as we went round and round while Barry sang about the girl who came and gave without taking, I'd be that much closer to getting one of them to kiss me in front of all the people who thought I was just another dorky kid who spent his Saturday mornings skating around in circles.

I then tried to increase my odds of catching the Roller Rink Girls' mascaraed eyes by taking freestyle skating lessons at eight o'clock every Saturday morning before the All-Ages Skate began. Convinced that if I became a showier skater I could make them notice and admire me, I began to learn how to do jumps and spins as if I were preparing to join the nonexistent Olympic roller-skating team. My goal was to be allowed to skate in the forbidden section, the empty eye-of-the-storm center of the rink that forms when a mass of teenagers skate around an oval-shaped floor. This was the place where the rink referees would congregate and talk. They were all older members of the freestyle team and would use the middle section to practice and exchange pointers on whatever moves they happened to be working on at the time. And, to me, these rolling authority figures always looked like the coolest people on earth. I was sure that by joining their ranks, I too would be allowed to skate and spin and thus be cool in this highly visible bit of real estate in the center of the rink. I even had a song that I had appropriated as my own—the very overwrought and rabbinical "The *Exodus* Song." One particularly embarrassing memory is of Violet, the cute but dowdy eighteen-year-old referee who played the records for the rink, putting on "The *Exodus* Song" and then, as if she had just remembered upon seeing me look up at her that *Exodus* was "my" theme, saying rather halfheartedly, ". . . go, Paul." Upon which I skated enthusiastically out to the center of the rink and, with the eyes of the entire population of the All-Ages Skate upon me, immediately found myself in way over my head. I wasn't that good a freestyle skater and didn't have the nerve to attempt any difficult spins or jumps for fear of falling, and so simply skated as fast as I could and launched repeatedly into wobbly arabesques, looking very much like the world's nerdiest airplane gliding back and forth over the center of the rink. During this, I saw the initial looks of anticipation from the crowd that I might be someone who was going to impress them with flips and twirls slowly fade from their faces. By the time I was sailing across no-man's-land for the fourth time with arms outstretched and one leg extended behind me as if I were Peggy Fleming's talentless little brother, I had lost them for good. I slowly blended back in with the other skaters and waited for what felt like an eternity for the stupid "*Exodus* Song" to end.

It wasn't until I turned thirteen that good luck finally befell me at the Skate-o-Rama, in the heart-stopping form of a girl named Sherry. She was one of the more senior Roller Rink Girls and had decided to sit in on a freestyle class one Saturday morning. As if the Fates finally decided that *something* good should happen to me after two years of faithfully attending my Saturday-morning class, I was assigned by Violet to fill Sherry in on the basics of skating backward (about the only freestyle move I was good at).

Sherry was sixteen years old and absolutely beautiful. She was taller than I was, and I was only about four inches away from the six-foot mark. She had a very sculpted face and looked a lot like a teenage version of Jacqueline Bisset in *The Deep,* with the body to match. To me, she was so physically mature that it was almost off-putting. But I quickly got past that and fell head over wheels in love with her. And whether it was because she found me amusing or harmless, she and I actually became friends. She would never hang around with me when she was with the other Roller Rink Girls, but I didn't care. She was about as much as my geeky psyche could take even from afar. And I immediately began to dream of turning our friendship into an epic romance.

As the weeks went by, Sherry occasionally allowed me to skate a Couples Skate with her. And, to my delight and secret arousal (kept secret only by the fact that the rink would dim the lights to almost nonexistent during the period of the Couples Skate's two romantic songs), she let us skate in the me-backward/her-forward configuration. My heart would pound like a loan shark beating down a deadbeat's door whenever I'd put my hands on her waist and she her hands on my shoulders and the two of us would glide around the rink face-to-face as the few friends I had at the All-Ages Skate would watch and think I was cool for the first time in my life. Sherry and I would talk and laugh as I made jokes and acted platonic while inside my head I was watching us at our wedding ceremony, fantasizing about kissing passionately on our honeymoon in Hawaii. There were times when I even got the distinct impression that if I were to lean forward and kiss her, Sherry might possibly let me. But, alas, I had nowhere near the nerve ever to attempt such a forward move and so settled for believing that Sherry was my secret Saturday-morning girlfriend.

We even began talking on the phone during the week, although our discussions were of the most innocuous kind. And while at first I fancied these conversations to be possible stepping-stones to a real relationship, I slowly began to realize that to her I was simply someone to pass the time talking to, a diversion to keep her from having to do her homework. But I didn't mind.

Because, despite whatever delusions I might have had of a drop-dead gorgeous girlfriend who was three years older than me, my relationship with Sherry did wonders for my fragile self-esteem. I was now walking into the Skate-o-Rama with a swagger in my step, convinced that all who saw me knew I was the thirteen-year-old former nerd with the beautiful and mature sixteen-year-old girlfriend; that I was the freestyle skater who had transformed himself from an ugly duckling into a graceful, studly swan. I started attiring myself better, wearing dress pants and fancy tuck-in shirts and the occasional V-neck sweater that made me look like I had just stepped off the set of *American Bandstand*. I even started wearing a turquoise ring I had bought when visiting my aunt Doris the previous summer in Albuquerque. And as I skated around the rink, saying hello to the referees and my fellow freestylists, I was sure that the eyes of every girl in the place were upon me, that I was now the Saturday-morning regular whom they secretly hoped would ask them for a face-to-face Couples Skate. Yet they all knew that my heart and soul belonged to Sherry, the woman who had been wise enough to see through my once-dorky veneer and recognize the Prince Charming that lay within. And so I was certain they had all vowed to steal me away from her, if only they could get the chance.

And then one day, their chance came.

Every month, the Skate-o-Rama would do a "snowball," which was where all the patrons would stand around the edges of the rink as one couple skated to a slow song, and then, when the referee blew a whistle, the couple would break apart and each would ask someone else to skate. Then, after these two couples skated for a little while, the whistle would blow again and then the two couples would split apart and then each person would ask another person to skate, making it four couples on the rink. And then the whistle would blow yet again and four couples would become eight. And then, as the old shampoo commercial used to say, "and so on, and so on." The idea was that after a lot of whistle blows and several songs, the entire population of the Skate-o-Rama would be out on the floor gliding hand in hand, having gotten to skate with people they would never normally have met.

A rolling mixer, if you will.

I had watched a number of snowballs over the years but had seldom participated. As in gym class, I was terrified of being picked last or not being picked at all. And so I had always avoided the snowball by strategically buying a hot dog and Icee right before it began, so that I could safely watch and dream about the day when I'd be brave enough to join in on the fun.

But as I would sit and chew on the brains and spinal cords those gray boiled skating rink hot dogs were made out of, I would stare dreamily at whichever opening couple started off the snowball. There was something so magical about seeing them bathed in colored lights as the mirror ball spun overhead and they weaved gracefully around the floor, always skating in the face-to-face fashion, staring into each other's eyes as all the waiting snowballers around the edges of the rink watched and secretly wished they were one of them. To me, it seemed like being the opening couple was the way to go. Because you would be the one who would then be doing the asking, and those whom you asked would be in awe of you. If I could just be part of that opening couple, I thought to myself, I would have everything.

And then one Saturday, it happened.

I had mentioned my secret snowball desire to Sherry the previous week and so she had asked Violet if she and I could start it this Saturday. I couldn't believe it. Sherry looked so pleased when she told me that I was sure it was a prelude to her informing me that she'd realized I was the one she had decided to spend the rest of her life with. There was no other explanation I could think of for her setting this up. Being the opening couple was always reserved for the coolest older skaters who were actually boyfriend and girlfriend. To be the opening couple was a way of telling the world that you were one, that you had committed yourself to each other.

Or at least you had for the length of the snowball.

But commitment was commitment in my book, and an opening was an opening. And Sherry had just opened a huge door that I was about to jump through with the entire population of the Skate-o-Rama bearing witness.

As the time counted down to the snowball, I was both giddy and nervous. Should I kiss Sherry as we skated? If I did, would it be one of those moments from the end of a bad romantic comedy where, when our lips meet, everyone in the rink watching us bursts into applause and cheers? Or would it be too forward of me? Would she be insulted and slap me? I wasn't sure what to expect and so used my cool new self-confidence to tell myself that I would simply have to play it by ear.

The moment would tell *me* what to do.

And then the moment arrived. Violet went through her usual explanation of the snowball over the sound system and had everybody line up along the railing that surrounded the rink. Then she dimmed the lights, turned on the mirror ball, and hit the colored spots that illuminated it. Sherry skated up next to me as I waited to skate onto the rink and took my hand. I looked at her and my heart lifted gently out of my chest and started to soar through the air over the rink, doing graceful circles around the mirror ball that sent off a thousand beams of reflected light that moved like weightless sparkling diamonds across the floor and walls and ceiling. Dave Loggins's "Please Come to Boston," which was Sherry's favorite song, began to play over the sound system, and the music encircled us like a velvet sheet as we rolled weightlessly out onto the rink. I turned and started skating backward, then held out my arms to Sherry. She skated up to me, and we took hold of each other. I stared with my thirteen-year-old eyes at her beautiful sixteen-year-old face and felt like I had been in love with her for several lifetimes. And so, emboldened by all the human energy around us, I decided to take a shot.

"Sherry," I said just loud enough for her to hear me over the song I have never forgotten my entire life, "I really, really like you."

She smiled sweetly and said, "I know you do. And I like you too. But just not in that way, you know?"

Even though her words weren't what I wanted to hear, for some reason they didn't hurt me at that moment. Because I was holding her and we were skating and she was looking into my eyes and smiling the most beautiful smile I had ever seen aimed at me.

"Really?" was all I could muster.

"I'm sorry," she said with what I thought was an almost sad look. "It's just that . . . well . . . you're too young for me and I sort of have a boyfriend already. Plus, I think we're just really good friends. You know?"

It was everything that I had always known, whether or not I'd let myself believe it since we met. Sherry wasn't going to be my girlfriend. Ever.

And yet I didn't feel sad. Because she was still in my arms.

"That's why I wanted to do this," she said, glancing around at all the people staring at us. "I wanted everyone to see what a great guy you are. And I wanted you to show these girls just what they're missing."

I was surprised by this, and, despite myself, I smiled. She suddenly seemed like my big sister at that moment, and I realized that she was right. When you're a teenager, a three-year age difference *is* a big deal. But now she had given me a newfound confidence, and it was up to me to use it and improve my life.

The whistle blew and Sherry gave me a supportive wink as she let go of my shoulders and I let go of her waist and the distance between us grew. I stayed skating backwards for as long as possible as I watched her turn and head over to some older guys to ask a lucky one of them to skate with her. And then I turned, knowing that things between her and me would never be the same again.

It was then that I saw a pretty girl my age whom I had also been watching for months, a girl I had always wanted to skate with. And so I skated over to her.

Sherry was right, I thought. I'm a good guy, and it's time to prove it to the rest of the girls here as much as it's time to prove it to myself.

I stopped in front of the girl, gave her a benevolent smile, and held out my hand to her.

"Would you skate with me?" I asked sweetly.

And.

She.

Shook.

Her.

Head.

No.

But it wasn't merely a "no, thank you but I'm too shy to go out on the floor with a nice and together guy like you in front of all these people" shake of the head. It was a shake of the head and a face that looked like I had just asked her to fish one of my turds out of the toilet; a shake and face that said, "Eeuw, for*get* it!"

Completely thrown, I looked at her friend standing next to her and held out my hand. She too made an "as *if*" face and shook her head, and then the two girls looked at each other and stifled laughs.

I went to the next girl I could find but she also said no. Having been turned down publicly by one girl, I found that every other girl followed suit for fear of being the one to pick the rotten fruit. As I turned to find a friendly female face to skate with, the spinning mirror ball and its minutes-earlier magical sparkles of light now swirled dizzyingly around me, the way stars spin around the head of a cartoon character who has just been hit with a sledgehammer. But all I saw was one hundred girls' heads look down in unison to avoid my eyes. In utter desperation, I looked over and saw Violet. She saw what trouble I was in and immediately came to my aid. It felt very much like having my mother come out to skate with me. And as Violet took my hand and we skated around the floor far behind Sherry and her new partner, I suddenly wished I could be transported out of the Skate-o-Rama and into a bomb shelter somewhere far from the world of delusion I had created for myself in this rundown skating rink two miles from the house in which I grew up. When the next whistle blew and we split apart, yet another of the female referees was waiting to be my partner. And after the number of couples on the floor grew big enough to camouflage me, I quickly skated off the rink and disappeared into the bathroom, where I stayed standing in a stall, staring at the obscene graffiti for ten minutes, hoping that by the time I came out, the world would be transformed into a place where nice things would occasionally happen to people when they were supposed to.

Sherry and I never really hung out much after that, and it was only a few weeks later when I decided that my time on Saturdays would be spent more productively working at my dad's store, so that I could earn enough money to buy a stereo for my bedroom. And several months later when I arrived for my freshman year of high school, I saw some of the Roller Rink Girls, who had now gotten rid of their blue T-shirts with the impassive skating rabbit on them and replaced them with halter-tops and real rabbit fur jackets.

I guess none of us, not even a cartoon rabbit, made it out of the Skate-o-Rama alive.

My Trophy Date

Every school has one. You can tell when she's around. Guys suddenly go quiet as she walks past; smiles and nods are aimed at her; teenage boys elbow each other and snicker between themselves when she passes, secretly wishing that she would say hello to them. She is both an obsession and a distraction. She is both desirous and disturbing.

In short, she's the girl with the biggest boobs in school.

In our school, that girl was Jill Holsteader. I had been a classmate of hers since the fifth grade. Even back then, it was obvious that she was developing faster than any other girl in our school system. She had a cute face and long blond hair, but she also had sort of a bad leg. It wasn't a full-fledged handicap. You would just simply notice, if you watched her close enough when she walked, that her right knee didn't seem to work as well as her left, that it seemed to bend in a bit when she put weight on it. But she was a nice, friendly girl whose tight striped sweaters probably awoke the dormant sexuality of more fifth-grade boys that year at Clinton Valley Elementary School than Marcia Brady's short skirts ever could hope to.

I have to admit, however, that I was scared of Jill back in

my grade school days. There was something so unsettling to me about a girl my age whose body was doing very adult things. There was an older woman in our church when I was that age who also had enormous breasts but they were always hidden beneath an oversized floral-print blouse. So, instead of defining her bosom, the blouse made it appear as if she had a pony keg hidden under her shirt. I've heard a fat woman's behind when it's hidden under a too tight dress described as looking like "two dogs fighting under a blanket" when she walks. But when this woman from our church walked, the effect was more like someone had strapped a fat, struggling elf to her chest. I'd had several nightmares over the years about that woman, usually involving her stripping off her shirt and chasing me around the church topless, trying to crush my head between her breasts like a filbert in a nutcracker.

It wasn't until I got to high school that I started to become enamored with Jill. By that time, not only had her breasts doubled in size but she had fallen in with what we called the "freak chick" crowd, the pretty but scary girls who were into smoking and drinking and drugs and who you knew were having sex or at least stopping to touch all the bases short of home plate on a daily basis. They were the rock 'n' roll groupies in the long leather coats who were experimenting erotically with the cool, older freak guys in our school who had mustaches, tight pants, and their own cars. I couldn't tell if Jill was one of the sexually advanced crowd or not but, judging from the company she kept and the way she was dressing, I figured the chances were pretty good that her two most prominent features had made their way into the hands of at least a few advanced guys in my school.

Okay, I have to admit something right here. Sure, I could tell you that the reason I was suddenly attracted to Jill was because of my raging adolescent hormones, that I had suddenly decided I wanted to become sexually active and that the sight of Jill's prematurely large breasts sent me into head-spinning, pubescent delirium.

But I'd be lying.

I simply wanted a girlfriend.

I was desperate to be able to walk around the school hand in hand with a girl, to kiss her good-bye at the door to our next class, and then be able to walk her home with my arm around her waist. And I knew that if I was going to have a girlfriend, I wanted her to be somebody the rest of the people in my school would be impressed with, someone they'd shake their heads in amazement at as she and I walked past, gazing lovingly into each other's eyes. I wanted a young woman who would make them say, "Wow, that guy really must be something. Look at the girl he's with."

In short, I was looking for a trophy girlfriend. Apparently, I was having some sort of teenage midlife crisis. And instead of buying an expensive new bike or a wardrobe of designer school clothes, I chose to go the eye candy route.

And there was no greater eye candy walking around our school than Jill Holsteader.

There was only one problem: How would I get her to agree to go out with a geek like me? Especially when I had never been out on a real date in my life?

The answer seemed clear. I'd have to ask her to go somewhere so amazing that she'd be unable to say no, a place no rock 'n' roll–obsessed freak chick could resist.

Fortunately, an idea presented itself pretty quickly. I had been a huge REO Speedwagon fan for the past couple of years and heard on the radio that they were going to be in concert at Cobo Hall in downtown Detroit. Just so you know, this was REO Speedwagon before *High Infidelity* came out, the album that took them to commercial success but lost them most of their original fans because it was, as the freaks in my school would say, "wimpy." No, the REO Speedwagon I wanted to see was the *You Can Tune a Piano But You Can't Tuna Fish* version, the ones who played "Keep On Rollin'," and who put out a live album with the song "157 Riverside Avenue" on it, a rocking fast blues jam that used to cause me nightly to grab my Fender Stratocaster, turn *off* my amplifier, turn *up* my stereo, and dance around air-guitaring Gary Richrath's solos until my mother tapped on my bedroom door, nervously asking me to turn the stereo down as if I were Billy Mumy in that *Twilight Zone* episode where he could turn adults into jack-in-the-boxes and wish them into the cornfield. In those days, I thought that REO were rock gods, and the idea that I could bribe Jill Holsteader into going out with me to see one of my favorite bands was so powerful that I felt like God Himself had intervened in my favor, as if He actually wanted to see what I would look like with Jill Holsteader as my girlfriend as I rocked out like a cool guy at a major arena concert. I really believed that I was at a turning point in my life.

All I needed was a couple of tickets.

Early the next morning, I drove with my friend Mike, who could draw Grog and the other *B.C.* comic strip characters as well as the guy who really drew them for a living, down to the Cobo Hall ticket office to wait in line for tickets. Mike was in a bad mood because he had wanted us to camp out overnight in line, which was what you did if you were cool and living the rock 'n' roll lifestyle. He had even gotten his mom to agree to let him do it. To me, however, the thought of spending all night on a sidewalk in downtown Detroit surrounded by a bunch of burnouts had about as much appeal as sleeping in the Dumpster behind my dad's army surplus store. Fortunately, I had gotten my mother to save the day by telling me in front of Mike that I couldn't camp out overnight and that if I wanted tickets I would simply have to go down in the morning and see what was left. I had set up this elaborate plan with her in advance so that she could take the blame for being overprotective and I could save face in front of Mike, whose mother seemed to have no problem whatsoever with her own son spending the night sleeping on a sidewalk in what was then the murder capital of the United States. As Mike and I drove along and I complained to him about what a square my mother was, I secretly sighed in relief at the fact that I had spent the previous evening watching TV and sleeping in my toasty bed with the electric blanket on (the blanket I wasn't allowed to use as a little kid, for fear that I might pee my pants in the middle of the night and electrocute myself). I mean, hey, I liked REO and all, but they sure as hell weren't worth dying for.

We got downtown at about 8 A.M., only to find that the line was wrapped all the way around the parking lot. It quickly became clear to me that the only method for getting good seats was indeed to have slept there overnight. Mike looked at me with contempt and said, "Great. I hope your mom's happy. Let's try to find the back of the line." He stalked away and I guiltily slouched off after him as a cold rain started to fall.

Hours later, completely soaked and freezing, we finally made it up to the ticket window. I had visions of the guy slamming the window closed just as we arrived, like I used to see in old movies about gamblers trying to place last-minute bets at the horse racetrack, but fortunately Cobo Hall was proving to be vast enough to provide all the REO Speedwagon fans in that parking lot with a ticket so far. As I walked up to the window, feeling as nervous as I would be if I were about to meet the queen, the man inside, a skinny guy in his fifties with a bristly mustache and glasses that made him look like Wally Cox from *The Hollywood Squares,* looked at me and said, "How many?"

"Two," I said proudly, as if he would know that one of the tickets would be used by me to squire a fairly attractive girl with enormous breasts from my school to the concert. "What seats are available?" I asked, hoping to be given a choice of location by the ticketmonger as he consulted with me about the subtleties of which seats had the best acoustics and view. I felt very grown up, like my dad when he'd take me to the box office of the Fisher Theater to pick out tickets for the Detroit Symphony Orchestra. However, no seating plan of the concert hall was brought out. Instead, the guy just looked at me like I'd asked him to blow me and said, "How the hell should I know? Look, kid, do you want your tickets or not?"

I informed him that I indeed did want my tickets and so he shoved two of them at me, grabbed the forty dollars I held out to him, and signaled for Mike to step forward while jerking his head to the side as a way of telling me to move, with a look that said if I was still standing in front of him in the next two seconds he'd summon one of the huge security guards standing on either side of the ticket window and have them give me a bum's rush into a mud puddle. I moved quickly away and looked at my tickets. The section, row, and seat numbers meant nothing to me, having never been to a concert before. But I knew one thing and one thing alone—those tickets said REO Speedwagon on them and I had them in my hand. My date with Jill was only one proposition away.

Even though I was normally a huge chicken when it came to talking to girls, and would on any other occasion have had a heart attack simply at the thought of asking Jill out on a date, the power that came from holding two tickets to a rock concert swept all other worries and doubts from my mind. Those two oblong pieces of printed card stock in my possession were a suit of armor, a love potion, and a hypnosis disk all at the same time. Jill would be rendered powerless in their presence, of this I was sure. A pound of pot and a free rabbit fur jacket couldn't have been a more powerful siren song. And it was with this confidence that I approached Jill as she entered our French class, looking especially good in a tight sweater with big black stripes that were stretched and distorted by the upper body they were covering.

"Hi, Jill," I said with a definite swagger in my voice, "how's it going?" I could practically feel the tickets glowing white hot in my back pocket, tucked behind the enormous blue Goody comb I used to keep back there.

"Oh, hey, Paul," she said. We had joked around and said hello just enough over the years for my interaction with her to not seem like anything out of the ordinary. With supreme confidence, I dove in.

"Hey, Jill, I went down to Cobo Hall this weekend and got a couple of tickets to see REO next week. You wanna go?"

I was masterful. It was a whole new me. I sounded cool, not desperate. I was casual, yet pointed. My attitude said that I could have asked any girl in the school and yet had selected her to be my lucky date. My face showed her that if she said no, it wouldn't mean a thing to me either way, and that she'd have to assume that I would simply move on to the next pretty girl in her group. It was a supreme performance, and for once in my adolescent life, it actually worked.

"Sure, Paul," she said, sounding surprised and flattered. "That'd be great. I love REO." Yes, if you were cool, you called them "REO." The "Speedwagon" part was for losers. I called them "REO," and Jill called them "REO." We should just get married right now, I thought.

"Great," I said, my heart in my mouth, "it'll be a lot of fun." I suddenly worried that I had strayed into geek territory with that last sentence, since I'd heard the phrase "It'll be a lot of fun" mostly out of the mouths of the elderly gentlemen at our church, used when they'd ask my mom and dad if they were coming to a taffy pull at their retirement home. But the tickets in my pocket were protecting me that day, because the next thing I knew, Jill gave me a very sweet look, a look that seemed to say she had never thought about me in a romantic way but now was considering it.

"I think we're going to have a *great* time."

I felt a hot flash run up the back of my neck as I tried not to faint. The results were in, and they were official. I was going out on a date with Jill Holsteader, the girl with the biggest boobs in our school.

Take *that*, cool guys!

I spent the next week impressing all my friends and enjoying the moments when I'd get to say hi to Jill in the hallway. It was like my impending date with her had given me the key to a whole new city. The freaks now acknowledged my existence. When Jill would say hi to me while she was standing in the hall with Cheryl Hodges and Kari Krinski, two of the most "mature" freak chicks in our school, Cheryl and Kari actually wouldn't be mean to me. True, it wasn't as if they'd called me over and asked me to hang out with them, but since they had both called me a "retard," a "faggot," and "Poindexter" on several occasions over the past four years, I took their nonabuse as a sign of acceptance. I would occasionally glance back after I passed, only to see them whispering to each other as they watched me walk away. I let myself imagine that a discussion regarding what they were now finding attractive about me was taking place. Even if this were somehow true, I'm sure that my attractiveness ended at the point where the REO tickets met my hand. But, hey, if you can't buy admiration, what in this world *can* you buy?

The night of the concert finally arrived and I was both excited and nervous. Not only did I have my first date with Jill and all the angst that would come with that, but this was also going to be my first solo driving trip into downtown Detroit. I had gotten my driver's license that summer and had been given the exclusive use of my grandmother's old Plymouth Fury III, a car so big and boxy that if you were to hollow it out, you could hold a square dance inside it. My father had given me all kinds of terrifying advice to prepare me for my long-distance trip into the wilds of the nation's murder capital, helpful tips like "Don't sit at stoplights for any length of time" and "If you think someone is following you, drive directly to the nearest police station." My obsession with how I was going to time my trip to avoid stoplights and figure out where all the police stations were in downtown Detroit helped to take my mind off my natural inclination to become terrified at the prospect of an evening with an experienced freak chick. Whenever the panic would start to creep up on me, I'd go into my bedroom, fire up my Marantz stereo, and put on REO's "Roll with the Changes." Yes, that was my anthem for the night. I, Paul Feig, former geek and burgeoning cool guy, was indeed going to roll with the changes as I dated the busty Jill Holsteader, rocked out to one of my favorite bands live, and tried to avoid getting killed at traffic lights in downtown Detroit.

I picked up Jill in front of her house. I had sort of hoped

I'd get to say hello to her parents, in order to cement my legitimacy as a potential boyfriend. Parents usually liked me, and if Jill decided for some reason I wasn't right for her after our date, I was hoping to have the added insurance of her mom and dad to talk her into reconsidering, since I was "such a nice young man, not like those other bums you go out with." But I quickly found out that wasn't the way the freak world worked. No, if you were dating in the land of sex, drugs, and rock 'n' roll, then you picked up your date at the curb in front of her house.

As we drove downtown, I was struck by how little Jill and I really had to say to each other. We talked about school and the classes we were both in, but beyond that it didn't feel like we had much in common. It was like going out to dinner with someone you work with—once you've caught up on all the office gossip and talked about what a jerk your boss is, you suddenly find yourself staring at your food and killing conversation time with erudite phrases like "Mmm, good bread" and "Wow, this place is crowded." But Jill was very nice as we rode down the I-94 freeway while we tried to talk, and I was surprised that she wasn't at all intimidating. In fact, because she was wearing an oversized jean jacket that hid her breasts, she started to seem like just any other girl from my school. We chatted about our French teacher, Mr. Zaloff, an extremely strange man who talked like a monster. His teeth didn't appear to have the ability to separate when he spoke, as if someone had wired his jaw shut long ago, and his voice rasped and sputtered like a ten-pack-a-day smoker talking through a kazoo. When he would say "bonjour" to us every day, it sounded less like the romantic greeting that Maurice Chevalier might say as he walked down a Parisian street and more like somebody belt-sanding a metal garbage can. I had perfected an imitation of Mr. Zaloff in the two and a half years I had been in his class and so was able to get big laughs from Jill as we drove. Things are going okay, I thought to myself. Just keep moving forward like the boys in REO. *"You got-ta, got-ta, got-ta, got-ta keep on rollin' . . ."*

We got to Cobo Hall and I found myself in the first traffic jam of my life. Or at least the first traffic jam I couldn't get someone else to bail me out of. The previous summer, when I still had my learner's permit, my father had let me drive the second half of our yearly trip to Chicago. As we approached the city, we suddenly found ourselves in a massive traffic jam where two freeways intersected. As car horns blared and people tried to cut in front of me, I panicked like a first-time skydiver who refuses to jump out of a plane and basically stopped the car in the middle of the highway so that I could do a Chinese fire drill with my father and escape to the back-seat. But here in the shadow of Cobo Arena, as hundreds of cars filled with long-haired concertgoers tried to inch their way into the single-lane opening of the arena's parking garage, I tried everything in my power to appear cool and unaffected as I secretly shat my pants. While I slowly and nervously maneuvered my grandmother's aircraft carrier of a car through the sea of souped-up Cameros, TransAms, El Caminos, and Dusters, I looked at the occupants of the other vehicles. It was at that moment I suddenly realized this was the first real rock concert I had ever attended. I'd managed to fool myself into thinking the Saturday-afternoon Beach Boys concert my friend Craig had taken me to the past summer at the pastoral Pine Knob outdoor concert theater had made me a veteran of live rock shows. But seeing the rough-looking mustached and bearded burnouts of all ages crammed into their muscle cars, swilling down cans of beer and bottles of Jack Daniel's, passing around joints and screaming "FUCKIN' A!" at the top of their lungs as their car stereos blared out

Ted Nugent and Led Zeppelin songs, I realized that I was completely out of my element. This crowd seemed like pure, mind-altered aggression. Chances were slim that if one of these guys decided he wanted to beat me up, I could win him over by doing my impression of Dan Ackroyd doing his impression of Jimmy Carter or by making a quarter disappear by doing the French Drop sleight-of-hand move I had learned in my Bill Tarr's *Now You See It, Now You Don't* coin magic book. The most I could hope for was that the sight of Jill and her enormous bosoms walking next to me would get me the same respect that I seemed to be getting in the halls of my high school.

Make sure Jill takes her coat off when we get inside, I mentally noted to myself.

After forty-five minutes of nerve-wracking gridlock, we were finally routed into an auxiliary parking lot next to the Detroit River. The parking lot guy yelled at me to pull my car into a narrow space and then proceeded to have other cars park tightly behind me, hopelessly trapping my Fury in the middle of a giant automotive jigsaw puzzle. I could see that if there was an emergency that required us to get quickly out of Detroit, it would be quicker to simply run the twenty miles home than try to extract my car from that sea of metal. Jill and I got out and started the long walk to the concert hall. She looked cute in her jeans and Earth Shoes, with a wispy see-through scarf tied around her neck. I wasn't sure if the scarf was supposed to keep her warm, since it only covered a one-inch strip around her throat, but the effect was slightly European and strangely appealing. As we walked and talked, I started to look at her closer than I ever had before. She was odd looking, when you got right down to it, and not at all what you'd call pretty, at least not in a traditional sense. She had a nose that looked a little like a cleft chin, sort of like Karl

Malden's nose in *The Streets of San Francisco*. It wasn't totally unattractive on her, but at the same time, it wasn't something you'd ever seen on the face of a girl whom you considered to be good looking. She also had a slightly odd mouth, with teeth that looked more like a row of little tombstones than something you'd chew food with. Her hair was very straight and clung to her head, as if she'd just taken off a static-filled knit cap, and her eyes had small bags under them that made her look perpetually tired. Watching her walk with her hands in her jacket pockets, her breasts hidden beneath a layer of denim, her flat hair blowing slightly in the breeze as she talked about the vacation she and her family had taken that summer to Benton Harbor, her imperfect knee causing her to have a slightly uneven gait, I couldn't tell if I liked her more as a potential girlfriend or a little sister. True, we were both the same age, but there was something very vulnerable about her at that moment, a quality I had never before picked up from her. She seemed almost innocent, and it made me feel more protective toward her than romantic.

All those feelings were immediately revised, however, when we got inside the arena and she took off her jacket, revealing a very tight flowered T-shirt that erased any and all questions about what she might look like topless. The bottom line was that Jill Holsteader knew exactly what made her special, and she didn't try to hide it. And as I saw the eyes of every guy in Cobo Hall lock onto Jill's boobs like heat-seeking missiles, she was no longer innocent and no longer a potential little sister to me.

She was once again my trophy date.

We walked into one of the small tunnels that led to the arena. When we came out the other end and stepped into the massive concert hall, I was immediately overwhelmed. I'd never seen anything like it. There were thousands of people inside this enormous place, and they were all yelling and laughing and shouting and smoking and preparing to go wild. It was both thrilling and completely terrifying, a Hobbesian rock 'n' roll nightmare. Trying not to panic, I looked at our tickets and attempted to figure out how to decipher where our seats were. Pot smoke enveloped me like fog on a London bridge, and my first thought was about how I'd ever get the smell of weed out of my clothes so that my parents wouldn't think I had spent the evening getting all "doped up," as my dad used to say. But I quickly realized that this was a lost cause, since everywhere I looked I saw people smoking joints, rolling joints, selling joints, or passing lit joints to the people next to them. It was like being an extra in the world's biggest Cheech and Chong movie, and I resigned myself to the fact that I would have to get myself out of trouble by making an emotional speech to my parents when I got home about how upset I was to be surrounded by so many drug addicts whose fiendish smoking of the demon weed had carelessly ruined my clothes. Right then Jill took a deep whiff and smiled wistfully, saying, "Man, I love the smell of concerts." Trying to pass my first freak attitude test, I also took a deep breath and said, "Yeah, so do I." Unfortunately, I did this just as somebody walked past smoking a clove cigarette. I burst out into an involuntary fit of coughing, complete with red, watering eyes. Jill laughed, thinking that I was trying to be funny, and so I laughed too, as I desperately tried to suppress the second round of hacking that would have given me away. Trying to hide my watering eyes from her, I looked down at our tickets again. I really wanted to come off like an experienced concertgoer to Jill, but I simply had no idea how the section and row numbers on our tickets translated into where our seats might be. Fortunately for me, a big guy in an official yellow security windbreaker came up to me and said, "Hey, kid, you know where you're going?"

I wasn't sure how to handle this, because to say what I wanted to say—which was "No, I sure don't, sir, thank God you're here to help me"—didn't seem like something that would play as anything other than dorky and non-freak-like. So I became a teenaged Laurence Olivier and decided to act like I couldn't hear him. By doing so, I was able to lean in to indicate he needed to speak up, whereupon I casually held my tickets out so that he could see them. He grabbed the tickets out of my hand, shined his flashlight on them, then gave a little derisive chuckle and said, "You're up there in the nosebleed seats." And with that, he pointed toward what I first thought was the roof, but which turned out to be the uppermost corner of the arena.

Jill and I started our upward trek, a journey so prolonged and so steep that we should have brought a Sherpa along with us, as well as ropes and oxygen. I was far too embarrassed about our crappy seats to actually look Jill in the eye as we climbed, and so I threw the occasional backward glance toward her, giving a sheepish smile and shrug that I hoped would indicate I was as surprised as she was at how bad our seats were and that the next day I would definitely be giving the con artist who had duped me with these tickets a firm talking-to. We continued to climb. Since both smoke and heat are known by science to rise, the higher we got, the higher and hotter we got, processing what must have been several cubic tons of secondhand pot smoke through our lungs. I wasn't sure if it was the high altitude, the heat, or the first time intake of airborne PCBs that was causing me to become so lightheaded. Just keep climbing, I told myself. If you can get to the seats, you'll be fine. Just don't faint in front of your big-breasted girlfriend.

We eventually arrived at the row and seat numbers that matched the ones on our tickets. We worked our way into the center of the row and finally found the seats that belonged to us. I sat down heavily and tried not to look completely winded. It's here that I have to make a fairly unappetizing admission. I've always had a problem with the way I sweat. For some reason, while most people on the face of the earth seem to sweat from their armpits, I for some strange genetic reason sweat exclusively from my scalp. I can keep a shirt going for days without a trip to the laundry, even in the hottest weather, but get me in a situation where my body temperature rises a fraction of a degree above normal and suddenly my head looks like a red bowling ball covered with wet spaghetti. As I sat trying to act cool and not show how hot and winded I was, the sweat began to pour from my head as if my body had turned into a fountain in front of an Italian catering hall. I spent the next several minutes pointing out interesting things to Jill just so I could keep her eyes off me as I used the arm of my long-sleeved T-shirt to try to mop off my brow the best I could. As I finally began to cool off and see the light at the end of my sweat-filled tunnel, a loud "WOOOO HOOOOOOO!" pierced the air. Both Jill and I jumped and looked over. We saw three guys in their early twenties approaching in the row behind us. One of the guys, who was very clearly in a chemically and/or alcoholically altered state of mind, threw his arms in the air and screamed, "WOOOO HOOOOOOO!" again at the top of his lungs. To this day, few sounds fill me with more fear than the sound of a drunken guy WOOOO HOOOOOOO-ing in enthusiasm, because this sound is often a prelude to either a minority person, a foreign person, a gay person, or a geeky person getting his or her head caved in. The drunk guy's two friends laughed and shook their heads in that "our friend is so crazy" way that signals to those around them that there's very little chance they're going to try to control their obnoxious cohort. The three guys worked their way down the row and then took their seats, which were directly behind us. As the drunk guy plopped down heavily in his seat, he inhaled like a pearl diver who had just come up from a three-minute underwater journey.

"God *DAMN*, Spenser," the drunk guy said loudly. "Whose seats are these? God's?"

Jill laughed at this, then turned around to look at the guys. I immediately smelled trouble. When you're a geek out on a date with an attractive burnout and she finds the funny older drunk guys behind you amusing, chances are that your date is going to end up interacting with those guys for the rest of the evening. And at that point, you have no choice but to go along for the ride. Who knows? I thought. Maybe they won't notice her or they'll think she's too young. I wasn't sure if I should also turn to look at them, since you never know what it will take to make drunken guys decide they want to kick your ass. I'd seen enough westerns to know that sometimes an innocent sidelong glance could result in hearing the words "What are *you* lookin' at?," which is followed by the drawing of guns or a saloon brawl that always ends up with someone flying through the air and breaking all the bottles and the mirror on the wall behind the bar. However, wanting to seem like I was interested in everything Jill was, I too turned and looked at the guys.

They were all around twenty-one years old and two of them were pretty good looking. They had long hair and mustaches and both looked like versions of the lead singer from Three Dog Night. Their drunken friend was much scarier looking, with a hint of insanity about him. He had bulging eyes and bad skin, and the minute Jill turned around, he noticed her.

"Hey, there, pretty lady," he said, pulling off a line that I had only heard guys like Dean Martin and Frank Sinatra use on TV variety shows. His two friends looked down at Jill, and I saw all three of them zero in on her breasts.

I was definitely in trouble.

"Hey, what's goin' on?" one of the handsome guys said to Jill, his attitude both cool and on the prowl as he leaned down toward her from his row.

"Hi," Jill answered with a smile. I had seen her give this smile to many people when they said hello to her, myself included on occasion, but was now concerned that its unconsciously flirty nature was going to give the wrong signal to these guys who were much more mature than I was. And I was right.

The next ten minutes turned into some sort of burnout cocktail party, which saw the two handsome guys chatting up Jill, Jill laughing and listening to their banter doe-eyed, the drunk guy tossing out uninhibited off-color comments for comic relief, and myself relegated to the role of the unnoticed waiter who stands off to the side waiting for a break in the conversation so that he can inform the diners of the dinner specials. At first I tried to convince myself that they thought I was her boyfriend and so were ignoring me as a way of dealing with their jealousy and frustration, admitting to themselves that they could never get her away from a catch like me. But this delusion quickly passed. I realized that these guys were hitting on Jill big-time and I was a nonexistent presence, a featured extra in a scene they had titled "Let's Hit on the Lonely Chick with the Huge Cans." It was time to take action, I decided.

"Hey, you guys come to concerts here often?" I interjected. It was possibly the lamest thing I could have said. I didn't even know where it came from, other than it was literally the only thing I could think of to ask them.

The guys all stared at me and it felt like the whole arena went silent, as if we were in an Old West saloon and the piano player had suddenly stopped playing. The two handsome guys exchanged a look that said, "Who's the fag?" The drunk guy then smirked at me and said, "Why? You need a date?"

One of the handsome guys laughed as the drunk guy turned to him and held up his hand for a high five. However, Jill gave the other handsome guy a playful but disapproving look. Being experienced in the ways of trying to look like a nice guy so that he could get laid, the handsome guy punched his handsome friend in the arm and said, "Hey, man, that's not cool. You shouldn't make fun of her little brother."

Jill stifled a laugh at this as I opened my mouth to respond. As if on cue, the lights in the arena went down and the crowd roared and the announcer came on and said, "All right, Detroit, are you ready to rock?" The crowd roared louder and the drunk guy WOOOO *HOOOOOOO*ed and I abandoned any and all hope that I would be able to let them know I wasn't Jill's little brother and was in fact her date for the evening. REO Speedwagon came out onstage and a wall of sound blasted out of the speakers and amplifiers. The concert was under way.

Having only been to a mellow outdoor Beach Boys concert before, I was surprised at how loud the sound was. What was more of a surprise was that up in the farthest reaches of the arena where we were sitting, the sound was terrible. It was loud, and it echoed and bounced all over the place and sounded as if we were listening to the band play inside a public toilet. I was also completely thrown by the fact that the drummer's arm hitting the snare drum was not synching up at all with what I was hearing. It dawned on me that we were so far from the stage that the speed of sound wasn't fast enough to reach our ears in a timely fashion. But, despite its defective aural qualities, the music was really blasting and everyone around us started going wild. The handsome guys started yelling "FUCKIN' A!" and the drunk guy started WOOOO *HOOOOOOO*ing so loudly mere inches from my head that my eardrum started crackling. It would have been intolerable except that REO was still my favorite band at that moment and so I tried to use my excitement of seeing them to get my mind off my discomfort. I clapped and cheered and looked at the people around me and noticed that they were dancing and jumping around to the music. I looked over at Jill. She was swaying and nodding her head to the beat, keeping her dignity while those around her lost their minds. She looked over at me and gave me a smile that said she was happy I had asked her to come. Maybe this was going to turn out all right, I thought. At least when it's this loud, there's no way she can talk to the guys behind us.

It was right then that I saw a hand tap Jill on her shoulder. We both turned to see that one of the handsome guys was leaning over to talk to her. He yelled something that I couldn't hear. Jill shook her head to say she didn't hear him either. He leaned down, cupped his hands over his mouth, and put them over Jill's ear. He said something and then smiled, and Jill looked at him and nodded. Then he leaned in again, cupped his hands back over her ear, and told her something that seemed to go on for minutes. Jill's face had that look you get when somebody you think is funny is telling you a joke and you're anxiously waiting for the punch line. I was getting very aggravated, since I had no idea what he was saying and because he had his stupid mouth so close to Jill's ear. What is so important that he has to distract her from the first few minutes of the concert I paid twenty bucks for her to see? I wondered angrily.

After what seemed like an eternity, the guy finally finished his oral dissertation. Jill laughed and nodded, and the handsome guy stood back up and gave her a smile and she smiled back and then she went back to watching the band. I looked back at the guys and saw that the one who had distracted Jill was now yelling something into his friend's ear. Who knew handsome guys were so goddamned chatty? The guys then laughed and high-fived as their drunken friend continued to WOOOO *HOOOOOOO,* lost in his own altered state.

I leaned over to Jill and said, "What did that guy want?"

She just shrugged and rolled her eyes, chuckling warmly, and said, "Oh, nothing. It was just stupid." And then she went back to watching the concert. I wasn't sure but I had a feeling I was starting to see her freak chick side in all its glory.

A little while later, REO announced they were going to "slow things down a bit" and began to play their power ballad, "Time for Me to Fly." Jill and I sat down, as did most of the people in the audience, seeking a breather from all their rock 'n' rolling.

"Oh, I love this song," she said.

"Yeah, so do—" was all I could get out before the handsome guy's head appeared between Jill and me.

"They fuckin' rock, huh?" said the handsome guy. Or at least that's what it sounded like he said, since he was turned toward Jill, leaving me with the back of his head in my face. I was about to become indignant with Jill for talking to the guy again when she did something that surprised me. She shut him down.

"Yeah," she said, "Hey, I really wanna listen to this song, okay?"

I couldn't believe it. Maybe she was getting as irritated as I was at this guy who was incessantly inserting himself into our evening together. She didn't say it to him angrily, but it had the kind of firmness that only pretty girls seem to be able to get away with, a tone that says, "Hey, you're kinda bugging me, could you back off?" Maybe this date was going better than I thought.

The handsome guy nodded, slightly thrown, and said, "Yeah, that's cool." He then sat back up in his seat behind us and watched the band.

I looked over at Jill, who was now leaning forward, elbows on her knees, watching the band intently. She would occasionally close her eyes and sway her head lightly to the music. She looked very pretty with the different-colored lights from the stage reflecting off her skin. I felt very attracted to her at that moment and started wondering what the end of our evening would be like. I definitely knew I wanted to try to kiss her when I dropped her back off at home, but I also wondered how I would react if she wanted to do more than just exchange a good-night kiss. What if she wanted to make out? What if she wanted to park somewhere and go further? Was I prepared to do this? Of course not. Just the thought of it made my stomach fill with butterflies swinging pickaxes. But I liked entertaining the idea that I might have to make a decision about it. I wondered if my planned admonition that she and I should wait until we'd been going out longer before we started to get more intimate would be met with derision or admiration. Would I be "the first nice guy" she'd ever been with, one who cared more about love and romance and getting to really know her than simply about trying to get my hand down her shirt? Would she suddenly feel self-conscious about her promiscuous freak chick status and turn over a new leaf to start dating me? Was this the beginning of one of those relationships that finds itself fifty years later at a golden wedding anniversary party, with me making a palsied toast of "To my high school sweetheart: May the next half century be as wonderful for us as the last half century has been"? I wasn't sure, but sitting there staring at Jill in the softly lit Cobo Arena as my favorite band filled the air with a moving rock 'n' roll ballad, I knew that anything seemed possible.

And then it happened.

The drunk guy, who was sitting in the seat directly behind Jill, suddenly leaned forward and vomited down the back of Jill's seat. It was one of those real stomach emptiers too, as if the guy had just won a hot dog–eating contest an hour before. A huge, thick streak of barf ran all down the back of Jill's chair and started to pool up at the base, just inches from the back of her pants. Because she was sitting forward listening to the band, she didn't realize what had happened. However, both the smell and the fact that I quickly put my hand on her back to keep her from sitting back made her turn around. She gasped as she saw the puke and quickly stood up. The two handsome guys then also noticed what had happened, as they looked over and saw their friend leaning over the back of Jill's chair, holding his head.

"Aw, Spenser, you dumb fuck!" yelled the chatty guy. And with that, he hauled off and hit the drunk guy as hard as he could in the shoulder. The drunk guy fell sideways onto a skinny freak kid next to him, who then quickly pushed the drunk guy back, so that he now slumped onto the other handsome guy's shoulder. That handsome guy then punched the drunk guy in the chest, making him once again slump forward with his head on the back of Jill's chair, thus rendering the last few seconds of repositioning Spenser completely useless.

Jill was staring at her barf-soaked seat incredulously, as someone a few rows behind us yelled, "Sit the fuck down!" The handsome guy turned and yelled, "Shut the fuck up!," then looked at Jill and reached out to grab her arm. "Come up here," he said to her, almost fatherly, "you're sitting in this asshole's seat." Holding her forearm, he motioned for her to use the armrest as a step to come back to his row. As Jill did this and the handsome guy helped steady her, he grabbed the back of the drunk guy's shirt with his other hand and lifted him out of his seat. "And, Spenser," he said angrily, "you're sittin' in your own puke, you fuckin' dipshit." And with that, he somehow forced the drunk guy to stagger up and over the back of Jill's seat, then grabbed his shoulder and shoved him down into her vomit-covered chair with a wet splat that even REO Speedwagon couldn't drown out.

It had all happened so fast and authoritatively that I was completely stunned. One second I was staring at Jill with love in my heart, and the next Jill was sitting behind me between two handsome guys and I was next to a semi-conscious, drunken idiot whose entire back was covered with his own vomit. It was one of those moments where I knew I was probably supposed to take a stand and get in a fight with the handsome guys, demanding that one of them trade seats with me so that I could sit next to Jill, or at least insist that they take their friend out to their car and then find a janitor to clean up the seat so that Jill and I could go back to enjoying the concert. But, alas, I didn't. I just sat there as Spenser the vomiting drunk passed out with his head on my shoulder while I tried to breathe through my mouth. I guess I knew that even though I'd have any jury completely in my favor if the facts of my case were heard, an arena rock concert was not the place where logic had any chance of winning. Plus I was struck with the fact that, in many ways, the handsome guy had done the most chivalrous thing possible in a moment that had simply stunned me into inaction. A woman was in trouble and he had immediately risen to the occasion. How could I then get upset without looking like some whiny guy who was only thinking about how to resume sitting next to his date? Wasn't I being just as chivalrous as the handsome guy by stoically staying put and keeping an eye on the ne'er-do-well who sullied m'lady's throne, thus freeing her up to watch the concert in peace? This will have to score me more points with Jill, I thought to myself as Spenser doubled over again and threw up next to my shoes.

As the evening wore on, it slowly became clear that I was scoring absolutely no points with Jill. Apparently the phrase "Out of sight, out of mind" applies even when the out-of-sight one is only two feet away. The problem was that once the handsome guy had Jill next to him, he went into pickup overdrive. Every time I turned around to look at Jill, she had the handsome guy's mouth right next to her ear as he chatted away merrily, gesticulating and laughing and apparently regaling her with stories about something she found interesting. It's weird for me now to think that Jill was only about sixteen years old when this happened, and yet she was being majorly hit on by a guy in his early twenties. I guess he had already formulated his defense for when the police came to pick him up for statutory rape—"But, Officer, I had no idea she was underage. I mean, look at the size of her breasts!"—and so decided to stay the course. Unfortunately, Jill looked like she was having a great time, and the few instances when she'd notice me looking, she'd give me a shrug and a platonic smile that felt more like something your sister would give you when you'd find her stuck in a conversation with Grandma than any kind of apologetic look that said, "I know that I'm trapped with this guy right now, but after the show, I'm going to really make it up to you." And so as REO went from one of my favorite songs to another, I found myself caring more and more about what was happening onstage and less and less about Jill.

When the concert ended, the lights came up and the handsome guys came and collected Spenser, who had managed to sleep through the entire concert. As he was heading off down the aisle, he suddenly woke up again and screamed, "WOOOO *HOOOOOOO!* REO *SUCKS!!!*" As the guys all headed down toward the exit, Jill walked up behind me, looking excited.

"Hey, guess what?" she asked in a tone that said she had news she was sure would make me happy. "Those guys asked me to come to a party at their house. They said you could come too. You wanna go?"

And it was at that exact moment that I realized something.

Jill had never really considered this a date.

Maybe when I was so casual in asking her to go with me that day in French class, an attitude I thought had made me seem cool and studly, I was actually casual to the point where my proposition had come out like that of a friend who was simply asking another friend to help take a ticket off his hands. Maybe I was supposed to have been clearer in stating my intentions. Maybe when you ask a girl out on a date, you're supposed to start it by saying, "Hey, you know, I really like you a lot and was thinking that maybe you and I should go out . . . you know . . . on a date." But wasn't it the automatic assumption that if a member of one sex asks a member of the opposite sex to go somewhere after sundown that the asker has romantic feelings toward the askee? Do we really have to be so unsubtle in this world?

"They told me there's gonna be a lot of girls there too," she said helpfully. "Maybe you'll meet someone."

Yes, Virginia, we really *do* have to be that unsubtle.

I told Jill that I had to get going, that I had promised my dad I'd come home early so he wouldn't worry about me. I would never have admitted such a nerdy thing to her earlier in the evening, but what was the point of trying to be cool now? Better to take off my mental girdle and let my geek hang out. She laughed and said she was going to drive over to the party with the guys and that she'd see me in school on Monday. I told her to have a good time and then watched as she sprinted off after them, looking very much at home among the other freaks and burnouts still hanging around in the arena. I then slowly made my way out of Cobo Hall, stopping only to buy an REO Speedwagon concert T-shirt so that I would at least have proof that I had done something that didn't revolve around science fiction or cartoons for once in my life.

When I got home, my dad was still in his den, doing his store paperwork for the day. I stopped in the doorway and he looked up at me.

"So, how'd your date go?" he asked. "You have any trouble downtown?"

"Well, a car full of murderers tried to gun us down at a stoplight but I was able to drive to a police station and have them arrested," I said.

He stared at me for a second, then said, "Since you're here to joke about it, I'll assume you followed my advice. So, how'd you and that gal get on?"

"Fine."

"You two going out again?"

"Nah, I doubt it," I said with a shrug. "I think we're better off just being friends."

My dad stared at me as if he suddenly knew everything that had gone on just by looking in my eyes. Then he gave a little chuckle and said, "Yeah, you got plenty of time before you need to get tied down with a girlfriend. I wouldn't worry about it."

"I'm not worried about it," I said, trying a bit too hard to be casual.

He nodded and gave me a fatherly smile. "Yeah, I know, but still . . . don't worry about it. Okay?"

For some reason, at that moment, I felt like hugging him. However, I simply nodded and said, "See you tomorrow."

"Hey," he called out as I started down the hall to my room. I went back to his den and saw him putting his paperwork into his desk. "You feel like playing a few games of cribbage? Haven't done it in a while."

Even though I felt like I should say no, there was nothing in the world I wanted to do more. "Yeah, okay. If you wanna."

My dad nodded and got the cribbage board and cards off his bookshelf. As I rolled the desk chair over to the TV table next to his recliner, he looked at me and said, "Go change your clothes first. You smell like dope and vomit."

I went to my bedroom and changed into my new REO T-shirt and my pajama bottoms, and then I played cards with my dad until midnight. Even though I'd recently been feeling like I might be getting too old to play cards with my dad anymore, on that night I figured I could roll with the changes some other time.

BOOK THREE

Life After High School

Big Man Off Campus

During my freshman year of college, as much as it may shock you, I was still living at home.

I had decided to attend Wayne State University in downtown Detroit, which was where my father had gotten his business degree after he came home from World War II. This allowed me to commute to an accredited state university and still sleep in the safety of my own bed. I had decided during my senior year of high school that I wasn't ready to move away yet, since I was frankly afraid of going off to live in a dorm with other students.

This was because my short history of living away from home had been rocky. Years earlier, after deluding myself into thinking I was an outdoorsman because of my successful run as a Cub Scout, I had joined the Boy Scouts long enough to go on a weekend camping trip that saw me "initiated" by my fellow scouts more times than a guy with Coke-bottle glasses and a harelip would be hazed by the meanest fraternity on campus. During the weekend in which I was forced to interact with my so-called upstanding peers at a Boy Scout Jamboree, I:

- had my shoes and socks stolen during a freezing cold early-morning hike through the woods and was forced to run the mile back to camp through the frosty forest barefoot;
- was sent on a miles-long odyssey in the pouring rain between several other campgrounds in search of a fictitious "bacon stretcher";
- was locked inside the stinkiest outhouse at the campground for an hour at one o'clock in the morning by older scouts who proceeded to pound on the outhouse walls and then tried to tip the whole thing over;
- was put into a metal oil drum and rolled down a ravine; and
- had my sleeping bag peed on by several older scouts . . . while I was sleeping in it.

On top of this, I discovered the main activity during the Jamboree that seemed to consume my fellow scouts, whose Oath stated

> *On my honor I will do my best*
> *To do my duty to God and my country and to obey*
>   *the Scout Law;*
> *To help other people at all times;*
> *To keep myself physically strong, mentally awake,*
>   *and morally straight*

was sneaking away to a nearby Girl Scout camp in order to feel up and have sex with willing members of our sister organization. This weekend of "fun" had added up to me quitting the Boy Scouts, and once college presented the prospect of living in a dorm that could be potentially filled with former Boy Scouts and bullies (I had been taken to see *Animal House* the previous year by my cousin and, even though I thought it was hilarious, the sex/booze/drugs/persecution lifestyle of college students it portrayed freaked me out), I decided that home would be the most comfortable place for me to live for at least the first two years of my higher education.

The post–high school life was proving to be a good time for me. Something about graduating from the world of mandatory education into the world of voluntary education made me begin to blossom. Being at school because I wanted to, not because I had to, made me feel freer, more in control of my destiny, more mature, and a little bolder in my everyday interactions. And this was what led me to Stacey.

I met her one night when I was out with some friends. It was one of those casual evenings in a coffee shop where the stakes are low and nobody is expecting anything more out of life at that moment than to sit around and talk about mundane things. Stacey was a friend of somebody there and at first I didn't even notice her. She was one of those girls whom you don't quite become aware of when you first meet her, but as you talk to her and listen to her and study her face, you suddenly find yourself desperate to kiss her. Stacey was a high school senior, a year younger and a foot shorter than me, with a pretty face, full lips, and a head full of thick black hair. I had always been attracted to blondes, probably for no other reason than I was blond myself, and so was surprised that by the middle of the evening I was completely infatuated with her. Part of the reason may have been that she wore glasses, a trait I had always been a sucker for ever since I developed a huge crush on the actress who portrayed Bailey on *WKRP in Cincinnati*. On top of all this, Stacey and I were definitely hitting it off, and she was doing the one thing that was always sure to get my affections—she was laughing at all my jokes. By the time we were getting up to leave, I could tell that she actually liked me, and somewhere between the cash register and the parking lot I mustered up the courage to ask her out. To my pleasure and surprise, she said, "Yes, I'd love to." And what was more, she seemed like she actually meant it.

The next weekend, I took her out to dinner and a movie, the only conceivable date for teenagers in the Midwest back then. I pulled out all the stops, taking her to Ye Olde Round Table, a fancy restaurant that was festooned with medieval tapestries, wrought-iron chandeliers, and rusty old tools from the yesteryears of farming, sort of a T.G.I. Friday's for the Dark Ages. We ate steaks and onion rings and had a nice time, always having something to talk about and seeming to agree on everything. I couldn't believe how well the evening was going and felt my confidence growing exponentially, much more than it had ever grown before around a woman. And for the first time in my life, I started to feel cocky. I'm actually good at dating, I thought to myself. And this girl actually likes me.

Now it's time to make her fall in love with me, I told myself.

We headed over to the movie theater and I bought us two tickets to see *Wholly Moses,* a comedy that I had seen a trailer for and thought looked like it'd be funny. The theater was barely half full, and wanting to impress her with my college-going intelligence, I laughed uproariously at everything in the movie, a film starring Dudley Moore and Laraine Newman that the Internet Movie Database now refers to as "the unfunniest Biblical spoof ever filmed." As the film played, I tried desperately to work up the courage to hold her hand but just couldn't come up with a move that would give me a graceful out in case she screamed and pulled her hand away. And so I simply left my hand laying palm up on my leg next to her, hoping she would see it and then, overcome by love for both my intellect and my shyness, would take hold of my hand and elevate our relationship to the next level.

I should explain that my whole MO with women when I was dating was to try to get *them* to be the aggressors. I was so fearful of being rejected or, even worse, being accused of only caring about their bodies and not their minds that I dared not try to ever "make a move." I had seen so many TV shows growing up in which men were jerks and women ended up having to defend themselves against these grabby guys who they thought were going to be their Prince Charmings that I was too nervous even to think about being forward. From Warner Bros. cartoons where a dressed-like-a-woman Bugs Bunny would accuse Elmer Fudd of being a "masher" to episodes of my mother's soap operas that always contained a scene with a woman crying while her friend said indignantly, "He made a *pass* at you?!," I had vowed to be a perfect gentleman all the time. I figured the only thing that had to be done on my part was to make myself so irresistible to whatever woman I was with that she would not be able to control her lust and would thus throw herself at me. The only problem with this strategy was that I knew I wasn't what girls considered to be irresistible. And so my goal was to try to break them down with my unpatented C.I.C. technique: winning a girl's heart through a combination of Comedy, Innocence, and Chivalry.

However, none of these resulted in handholding this night at the Cineplex. I knew I had to pull out heavier artillery.

When the movie ended, Stacey and I left the theater. I made a big show out of opening the door for her, working on the Chivalry angle of the Feig trinity. For some reason, the obligatory love story in the film had filled my heart even more with the desperation for romance. I had seen lots of movies with love stories in them, but I was usually at the theater with my mother or my friends. Knowing now that I was on an actual date with a girl made everything seem within reach. I just had to help it along. Love was going to bloom no matter what, I told myself.

When we walked out the door to the parking lot, we discovered that it was drizzling. Not a heavy rain but enough to get you fairly wet if you were out in it for long. Suddenly deciding that this was my chance to make myself look like a modern-day Lord Byron, I said to Stacey, "I love walking in the rain. C'mon!" I then proceeded to make us walk slowly through the heavy drizzle to my car, which was parked on the far end of the parking lot. As we walked along and the rain started to soak into our clothes and wet down our hair, I had a spring in my step, convinced that I could literally feel Stacey marveling at the unpredictable, impetuous me. I was the poet, the romantic, the guy who was unlike any other guy she might meet here in Michigan, and I was certain she couldn't believe her luck. I smiled over at her as her hair was getting wetter and wetter and thought I saw a look of pleased surprise and growing affection in her eyes, as if she were thinking to herself, "Gosh, I've never walked in the rain before. I had no idea what I was missing. I think I love this man who's opened up my eyes for the first time."

We finally arrived at the car. I made a big show of taking my time to unlock her door, staring up at the sky as if to say, "I wish this cleansing rain would never stop, and I wish our time together in it could go on forever." I put her in the car and then walked around to the driver's side. I stopped again by the back bumper, posing wistfully as I stared up at the sky, making sure to position myself in a place where I knew she could see me clearly in the rearview mirror and marvel at how sensitive and in tune with nature I was. I then got in the car, my hair and clothes clinging to my body.

"God, I'm *soaked*," said Stacey, sounding like she was trying to control her temper.

But surely she had to have enjoyed our walk through the rain, I thought.

"Yeah, it's great, isn't it?" I said with a knowing smile that I was sure would make her admit how happy she was.

She sighed, a bit testy, and said, "I just don't want to catch a cold, that's all."

Apparently she wasn't yet aware of how happy she was.

I quickly started the car and turned on the radio, hoping that she was just having a momentary lapse of enthusiasm. Chicago's "After All That We've Been Through" was playing. The mood was perfect for romance as I drove back to her house.

As we rode down Gratiot Boulevard, I tried to reinforce the Comedy factor of the Feig triumvirate, knowing wit could repair any damage that wet hair and wet clothes might cause in a woman's mood. I made jokes and humorous observations about all the signs we passed, getting off such zingers as referring to a coffee shop called the Acropolis as "the old crap hole" (a joke I had stolen from a friend of mine whose mother was a waitress there) and pointing out that a picture of a Detroit rock radio deejay on a billboard looked like "somebody's insane grandpa." And, as anticipated, my plan was working as Stacey loosened up and started laughing at my low-grade lounge act. By the time we pulled into her driveway, I could tell that she was mine for the taking.

It was only once we sat parked in front of her garage with the rain tapping lightly on the windshield that I realized I had no idea what to do. I wanted to kiss her—that was a fact. I had been staring at her lips all night, which were round and red. Her whole face was something to behold, since it was all in perfect proportion. Everything about Stacey's face made it look more like it had been sculpted than born, and her mouth was the center of my universe. I thought that if I stared at her long enough, perhaps she'd lean in to me and initiate things. However, she didn't. We sat talking for quite a while, and it was apparent to me that she wasn't in any hurry to get out of the car, which was a very good sign. And her laughs at my incessant nervous jokes were starting to take on a quality of coyness, as she would look down toward the floor, then shift her eyes back up at me in a come-hither manner. If I wasn't completely deluding myself, I thought, then it seemed like it might actually be safe to lean in for a kiss.

And so, as the romantic ballad "Same Auld Lang Syne" by Dan Fogelberg came on the radio and Stacey very sweetly said, "Oh, that's my favorite song," I stared at her longingly. She stared back, and it was clear that I had been granted permission to kiss her. As my heart pounded so hard against my chest that I thought it was going to shatter my ribs, I slowly leaned forward and kissed Stacey right there in my mother's Dodge Coronet.

Since the only other time I had really kissed a girl had been a disaster of fear and ineptitude, I wasn't sure now what to expect or how I would feel about it. I had an inkling that this was a moment in which I was going to be expected to French-kiss and to French-kiss well. I had a moment of panic as I wondered if my perpetual germphobia was going to get in the way of my being able to do any extended openmouthed interaction. However, a combination of late-teen hormones and my strong desire for Stacey's attentions meant that when her mouth opened during our kiss and her tongue started to move toward mine, I was suddenly able to handle the situation. I surprised myself that I was so quickly adept at the art of French kissing, even though from her perspective it was probably a pretty amateur performance. But the euphoria that overtook me, both because I was actually enjoying the infamous French kissing I had been afraid of for years and because Stacey actually seemed to enjoy doing it with me, was life changing. I kept expecting her to pull away and end it but she kept on going. And I was loving it. I had seen plenty of people making out in my years at high school but could never really fathom what it would be like. There were times that I looked at couples engaging in an extended make-out session and would wonder if they were getting bored at all. But I now realized exactly what the allure of it was.

I was in heaven.

As we kissed and the windows steamed up and Dan Fogelberg sang about drinking beer in his car with the old lover he met at the grocery store, I felt myself falling completely head over heels in love with Stacey. Visions of us making out on our wedding night flashed through my head as she and I were transported out of the car and up into the starry night sky. There was no drizzle and no cold night air as we floated above her driveway, our once-separate futures now slowly and lovingly intertwining themselves as our souls connected and enveloped each other. I couldn't tell if minutes or hours or days were passing as I marveled at how her lips felt every bit as soft as they looked, and I hoped our encounter would never end.

I knew from stories I'd heard in high school that this kind of make-out session was supposed to quickly lead to hands entering shirts and pants, and then to the removal of said clothing, and then to the ultimate act of sexual consummation. And yet this moment between Stacey and me felt like something more than that, as if even to consider turning it into something base and primal would be to sully an encounter that seemed to have been blessed by Cupid himself. No, for this to be anything other than a sweet and tender exploration of our budding love would be to ruin it. It was all too beautiful to me.

It wasn't until the bouncy Eddie Rabbitt song "Drivin' My Life Away" came on the radio that the harsh wind of reality threatened to bring us back down to earth. The perky country two-step tune started to unconsciously turn the natural movements of our passionate make-out session into a sort of jumpy wrestling match, and it became like trying to slow-dance while the "Hokey Pokey" is playing. I desperately wanted to change the station but was afraid if I disengaged from her lips for even one second to hit the radio button that she would use it as a natural cue to end the biggest extended moment of bliss I'd yet experienced at that point in my life.

Alas, even though we survived Eddie Rabbitt and made it through a couple more songs, I felt the encounter winding down. Stacey's sensuous intensity started to wane and I could feel her searching for a natural end. Soon she pulled away, stared at me for a few beats, and then said, "I have to go in."

As she opened the door, I noticed how cartoonishly the Coronet's windows had fogged up. I immediately became embarrassed, especially since I could see the light on in her living room and had to imagine that her parents must have looked out at some point and seen the steamy love car sitting in the driveway. Since Stacey didn't seem to be concerned, I began to wonder if make-out sessions in front of her garage were a common occurrence but refused to let it intrude on my now absolute love and devotion toward her. Even if she had been known to have several suitors with whom she steamed up windows, I was now sure that our passionate tango had erased all others from her mind. She *had* to be mine now. How could she not be? I knew she felt what I did.

In the purest sense of the word, we had been, and now were, one.

"'Night," she said pleasantly. "And thanks!" And with that, she headed inside.

I spent the ride home alternating between my certainty that I now had a girlfriend and my dissecting of the evening to figure out if anything had gone wrong. She seemed so breezy and unaffected when she said good night that it threw me, but I quickly convinced myself that she was simply overcome by our intimate contact and so it was all she could do to get inside the house without professing her love for me this early in our relationship. No, I told myself, there was no downside to the evening. Your paranoia is unfounded. You took Stacey out on a date, showed her a great time, and then the two of you kissed passionately for close to fifteen minutes in your car.

If that isn't the start of a torrid love affair, then I don't know what is.

And apparently I didn't.

I spent the next several weeks trying to get Stacey to go out with me again. We talked on the phone quite a bit, but whenever I'd ask her if she wanted to spend an evening together, she'd have some excuse for why she was simply too busy. What was worse, her tone with me whenever we'd talk was very pleasant and friendly—heavy emphasis on the *friendly* part. I had always imagined that once two people had been in an intimate romantic situation, things were forever changed between them. Either the relationship didn't work out and they were too embarrassed to talk to each other ever again because of the vulnerability they had revealed, or else the love between them caused everything they said to become poetry, to become sweet nothings, to become declarations of love and devotion and pet names and playful, suggestive teasing. But when I now talked to Stacey on the phone, there was none of that. We chatted the same way we did the first night I met her at the coffee shop. We'd talk and joke about school and TV shows and our friends and never mention one word about our special night together.

Or at least she wouldn't.

I would always try to drop in little romantic tidbits from our encounter, reminding her of certain flirty jokes we made to each other during dinner and of songs that were playing during our time in the foggy Coronet in her driveway. But she never took the bait. Anything I brought up was met with an "Oh, yeah, that was fun" and then the conversation would travel the short and depressing road back to the banal.

After several weeks of this, I was ready to go out of my mind. My thoughts had been all-consumed with our make-out session, and I relived it constantly, especially when I lay in bed at night. Stacey was in my dreams. I could feel her lips as if I was still in that car with her. I longed to hold her again, to have her look at me coyly and then move in for a kiss. I wanted to feel her hands on my back, pulling me close as she adjusted her head from side to side in that way you do when you're making out with someone, turning each kiss into a new experience. I needed her to let me know that she felt the same way I did, because I was certain she was in love with me, whether she realized it or not.

Because I was head over heels in love with her.

It wasn't until several nights later, as we talked platonically on the phone yet again, that Stacey officially blew my battleship out of the water. About ten minutes into our conversation about how senile her grandmother was becoming, Stacey gave a little incredulous "wait until you hear *this*" chuckle and said the following:

"God, I'm so annoyed. I had this friend of mine completely freak out on me today. I've been hanging out with him for a while and all of a sudden, out of nowhere, he goes, 'I can't believe that you're not in love with me, after all the time we've been spending together!'" She then laughed derisively and said, "I mean, like I fall in love with every guy I hang around with. Is that *stupid* or *what*?"

I fell all over myself agreeing with her about what a moron her sad little friend was and even deluded myself for a few minutes into thinking the guy was a total chump, picturing him as a whining little kid half her age who had fallen victim to an unrequited schoolyard crush. Very quickly, however, the painful truth began to dawn on me that this poor chump had probably been through the same situation with her that I had.

"Did you ever go out on a date with him?" I asked, not wanting to know the answer.

"Yeah, but only like you and I did, nothing more," she said as casually as if our date had consisted of walking around the neighborhood with a metal detector looking for buffalo nickels.

My heart dropped into my stomach and then sat there decomposing in digestive acids.

We continued our conversation but my mind was a million miles away. I felt all the life slowly draining out of me as I realized there would be no more make-out sessions with Stacey, and that she and I would not be professing our undying love to each other anytime in the near or distant future.

Stacey was not in love with me, and she never was.

I didn't even register as a blip on her radar.

I was . . . Just a Friend™.

I spent the next few weeks trying to figure out what I had done wrong. Clearly I couldn't have started out this way in her mind. I *knew* that there was an attraction between us when we met, and that it had been there during our date. What had gone wrong?

The more I thought about this, the more the question morphed into "What *hadn't* gone wrong?"

And, suddenly, everything from our evening together seemed terrible and miscalculated.

I had been too cocky.

I had been too pretentious.

I had been too ridiculous.

I had been too immature.

In short, I had been too me. Or, worse, *not* me.

My mind locked in on two key moments. One was the obviously idiotic decision to pretend I was a guy who enjoyed walking in the rain. Clearly she was completely miserable getting wet as I forced us to walk slowly through the severe precipitation and, what was worse, I was now sure she could tell I was play-acting about my love of walking in the rain, obviously and embarrassingly inspired by Rupert Holmes's "Escape (The Piña Colada Song)." But the second and worse realization was that while I thought not trying to get to any base beyond first with her in our driveway make-out session was respectful and romantic, to her this simply meant I was an immature guy who didn't have the experience and confidence to "treat her like a woman." I wasn't entirely sure if this was true or not, but then my mind started replaying something she had said when we were eating dinner, a moment that had gone past me so fast that it only registered in my unconscious brain. As we were joking and laughing and I was talking about my classes at Wayne State University, Stacey got a very euphoric look and said in a giddy tone, "Man, I can't *believe* I'm dating a college guy." She said it more to herself than to me, as if it had almost slipped out, and it had a definite undertone of "as opposed to all these immature idiots I date in my high school." I then remember that for the rest of the meal after making this declaration, she stared at me as I talked about my studies and professors as if she was completely in love.

And that was when my cockiness had started. I knew I had her. I just didn't know *why* I had her.

So, then to have taken her to a really dumb movie and to have sat there laughing when she clearly didn't find it funny, and then to have made her walk through the rain and ruin her makeup and hair and fog up her glasses as I nattered away like a junior high student who's decided he would like to write amateur poetry for the school literary magazine, and then to wait for her to give me the go-ahead to make the first move in the car, and then, after all that, to simply make out with her for so long that she simply got bored, must have made her realize that not all college guys are created equal— and that this particular college guy was created in a nerd incubator. I was so retroactively embarrassed and horrified with myself that I wanted to call her and apologize for the evening. I wanted to beg her to give me a second chance and tell her to remember that deep down I knew she still had romantic feelings for me that were simply buried under a pile of disenchantment.

And then I realized that doing this could only result in making me even more unattractive to her. And so I told myself not to.

And then, of course, I did it.

Let's just say that the lesson I learned from that ill-fated phone call, which I won't even try to re-create here for fear of making you hate me for the whiny little sniveler I've been able to turn into at certain points in my life, is that you really don't get a second chance in the dating world. Love has to sprout naturally, like a seed that takes to the soil around it.

You can't simply beg it to grow and expect anything to happen, especially if you plant it in cement. The end result of my pathetic call to her, in which I believe I started crying, was that I am now sure whatever new guy Stacey had casually made out with at that time who had convinced himself she was in love with him was now hearing the following speech about me, the college guy she had dated:

"I'm so annoyed. I had this friend of mine completely freak out on me today. I've been hanging out with him for a while and all of a sudden, out of nowhere, he goes, 'I can't believe that you're not in love with me, after all the time we've been spending together!' I mean, like I fall in love with every guy I hang around with. Is that stupid or what?"

Yeah, I guess it is pretty stupid.

Making Out Is Hard to Do

A few months after the Stacey debacle, believe it or not, I got another shot at love.

Nicole was working as an usherette at Sterling Heights High School when I was acting in a production of *Grease* that was playing in their auditorium. I was portraying the role of Vince Fontaine, the cool deejay who gets to clown around and be the master of ceremonies for the gym dance/"Hand Jive" scene. Even I have to admit that I was in top form in this role, both as an amateur musical theater actor and as a guy. A friend in the cast had lent me his father's old shark-skin suit to wear as my costume, and it fit me perfectly. Also, I was having so much fun in the role, playing an actual cool guy, I really believed when I hit the stage every night that I *became* cool. My performance always seemed to get a big response from the audience and, believe it or not, I even had a few groupies (all right, they were mostly guys and moms but, hey, fans are fans). So, in a weird way, I wasn't that surprised when a friend in the cast told me there was a girl usher who wanted to meet me. Feeling supremely confident, I went down into the empty auditorium after the show and met Nicole.

She was an interesting-looking girl. She was definitely cute, but in a way that I wasn't typically attracted to. I still had the tastes of a five-year-old when it came to women back then and was drawn to very obviously pretty girls, the way that little kids get a crush on their most Barbie doll–like teacher in grade school. Nicole was a more mature-looking girl, in that her features were sort of grown-up. She didn't look old by any means—she just looked like a young version of somebody's mother. She had very put-together hair, almost like a hairdo, and she was wearing a fair amount of makeup. She was almost as tall as I was, making her about five foot ten or eleven. But it was the way that she immediately took command over me the minute we met that drew me in. She seemed like an automatic girlfriend, as if I had been a visiting dignitary and the country I was in had arranged an escort who was going to indulge my every wish. Within five minutes of saying hello to her, she had complimented my performance, rubbed some makeup off my cheek with her thumb, told me I was cute, linked her arm through mine as we walked out of the auditorium, and asked me out on a date. She was such a whirlwind for an awkward eighteen-year-old like myself that had she suggested we go and get married immediately, I would have done it.

There's nothing like that thrill you get when you meet someone who you know is going to be your significant other. All the angst and insecurity that usually surrounds any interaction between singles of all ages seems to melt away, and you practically hear the voice of fate giving you a poke in the ribs and saying, "Well, what are you waiting for? She's yours." (Or *he's* yours if you're a straight woman or a gay man.)

With Nicole, I had a girlfriend the minute we said hello and I couldn't have been more excited about it.

We talked constantly on the phone in the week leading

up to our first date. The funny thing about long phone calls when you're in your teens is that they are ultimately so mundane and superficial that it's almost impossible to remember what you talked about once you hang up. Nicole and I would talk for hours and yet I can't really remember anything we said. There *was* lots of flirty talk from her, though. She seemed to be a very sexual person, or at least she was in my closed-off little world. She would make double entendres constantly, saying things like "I hope it's not too *hot* the night we go out" and "After we have dinner, make sure you leave some room for *dessert*." I found this to be very exciting in the safety of my bedroom, but couldn't help feeling a bit nervous about our impending date, when I would be physically present and possibly expected to indulge in whatever "dessert" she might be planning on serving up. But after the massive enjoyment of the fifteen minutes of make-out bliss I'd experienced with Stacey and what I was sure was my newfound mastery of the art of the French kiss, I was feeling more enthusiastic than nervous about my encounter with Nicole.

In other words, I couldn't wait to get back in the saddle again, if you will.

I had decided to pull out all the stops for our date and so made reservations at a very fancy restaurant in downtown Detroit at the new and impressive Renaissance Center (or "RenCen," as we Michiganian hipsters call it). My mother and I had eaten there for lunch earlier that year, and I thought it was the classiest place I had ever seen. It was a French restaurant and, in a break with midwestern restauranting tradition, had nothing medieval-themed about it. It was all red walls and wineglasses on the tables and waiters in tuxedoes and I felt like a jet-setting world traveler sitting at one of its tables. To take Nicole here would show me off to be the highest caliber of boyfriend and would allow me to enter into a romantic fantasy world with her that would help ensure I didn't lose her after one make-out session.

I just had to make sure that I didn't get too cocky this time.

I picked her up at her house and was on my best behavior, putting on no airs other than wearing a suit and tie with a tie bar that held my collar together and pushed the knot up and out in a jaunty *GQ* fashion. Nicole looked quite pretty in flattering makeup and a frilly dress that was about knee length. Unfortunately, she was wearing the kind of shoes that I've always found to be the least attractive things a woman can put on her feet, those sort of half-heel white dress sandals that, when worn in conjunction with flesh-colored "sandal-toe" stockings, make any female's feet look like they should be attached to someone's grandma. But I forced myself to overlook her geriatric footwear and felt very happy that she was going out with me.

We drove down to the RenCen and walked through the massive concrete lobby, staring up at the architectural wonder around us. As we walked, she took my hand and my heart soared. She was quite talkative and flirty and I found myself going through a slide show of emotions. I was happy and attracted and overwhelmed and nervous and worried and afraid and it all swirled around me like a swarm of gnats on a hot summer evening. But Nicole was such a whirlwind that I wasn't able to focus on any one feeling for long. By the time we were in the restaurant and acting like grown-ups as we ordered and tried to not do something that might tip off the waiter that neither one of us had ever been in a fancy eatery without our parents, we were having a great time. True, there were moments when I felt she was a bit too much, talking too fast and making sexy faces at me that I didn't know how to respond to. But the fact that all her energies were focused solely on me was enough to keep me from thinking anything negative about our evening and possible future together.

It was only when we had left the restaurant that I started to get worried.

I know it's weird that what happened next would make me start to feel uneasy about her but it did. As we were walking down a curving concrete stairway that led to the lobby, Nicole suddenly started doing chorus line kicks. She was clearly trying to be funny and goofy, but it just wasn't coming off that way. There wasn't really anybody around to see her, so I couldn't be too embarrassed about it, but there was something trying-too-hard about her antics. She started singing really loud and shaking her hands out to the side, like she was in a number from *All That Jazz,* and she looked kind of ridiculous. However, since she seemed to be having fun and I didn't want to judge her too harshly, I laughed along with her.

And then she fell down the stairs.

I don't know what happened. She was mid-kick and suddenly her knee folded under her and she tumbled head over heels down the concrete stairway. It all happened so fast and out of the blue that all I could do was stand and watch in horror as she crashed painfully down the steps. She sprawled out onto the floor when she hit the bottom and then quickly tried to stand up. But she had clearly hurt herself. The skin on her knee looked pretty raw, and I was quite frankly surprised she hadn't broken her neck. I rushed down to her. She was trying very hard to act like nothing was wrong, but she was limping and rubbing her forehead. I tried to get her to sit down on a nearby bench, but she was intent on proving to me that she wasn't injured. She went so far in the direction of pretending what just happened hadn't happened that it started to weird me out. I definitely had sympathy for some-one trying to cover for something they did that was very embarrassing, as I had been there myself on numerous occa-sions. But at the same time there was a strange desperation about the whole scene, as if she thought I was going to end our date if she admitted she had wounded herself.

Nicole marched us off through the lobby back to the parking structure to get my car. She was limping and would occasionally let out a little whimper of pain as she talked nonstop and tried to be both breezy and seductive. Her double entendre machine was switched to high as she moved her hands all over my back and waist, saying breathy things like "I don't know how I'll ever be able to *repay* you for din-ner" and "I sure hope you're still *hungry*."

As I drove home, she slid over very close to me, occa-sionally putting her hand on my thigh and rubbing it lightly with her thumb. She would stare at me with a flat-faced, seri-ous expression that I knew was supposed to be sexy but which I found slightly distracting while I tried to watch the road, since it afforded me not a second to scratch my ear or clandestinely pick my nose, which was something I simply had to do whenever I got behind the wheel of a moving car (and, sadly, still do—hey, I don't hide anything from you guys).

And during all of this, I was feeling very confused.

Part of me couldn't wait to make out with Nicole, simply because I was looking forward to an experience as profound as the one I'd had with Stacey. But the other part of me was feeling slightly put off, unsure if I was attracted to Nicole or not. The problem might have been that she was just on the border of being "my type," and she was leaning more into "not my type" territory than the other way. I'm not proud of being judgmental about anybody's appearance, but selecting romantic partners is more of a biased weeding process than picking your friends is. You simply *have* to be physically attracted to a person if you want to be in a romantic relationship with him or her. And that doesn't mean they have to be drop-dead gorgeous. It just means that they have to possess features and attributes that you find attractive. And I simply wasn't sure about Nicole.

When we turned onto Nicole's street, she told me to pull over several driveways before her house. I did and turned off the car engine. She stared at me with the same "sexy" look she'd been using during the trip home, but now that I could look her back in the eyes, she gave me the full treatment. She quivered the muscles on her face in the same way that Ginger Grant would when she'd try to seduce Gilligan in order to get him to do something for her, undulating her lips and doing the wave with her eyebrows. The effect when this was done by Nicole, however, was much like when she started doing her kick line on the stairs—it felt sort of forced. However, knowing that it signaled we were about to have a heavy make-out session, I overlooked it and leaned in to kiss her. As soon as I did, she suddenly threw her arms around my neck and pulled me to her so hard that she almost gave me whiplash.

Our make-out session was a flurry of frenzied activity. She French-kissed me so aggressively and put her tongue so far into my mouth that I thought she was trying to get food out of my stomach. She also made her tongue so straight and stiff that all I could do was circle my tongue around it, as if a maypole dance or a game of tetherball were taking place inside my mouth. She was also pushing me backward with her lips as she kissed me, making it seem like we were playing a human head version of arm-wrestling and she was the world champion. Her mouth was pressed so hard against mine that I couldn't feel her lips—I could only feel her teeth and jawbone pushing into my teeth and jawbone. It was so painful and overwhelming that I kept moving back just to try to relieve the pressure on my face. Very quickly, however, I found myself backed up against the driver's side door with the armrest pushed into my spine and the back of my head pressed against the window. She continued to grind her mouth into mine so hard that I worried she was going to push the back of my head through the window. Not knowing what to do, I pushed back into her, trying to get my head off the glass. It was a battle of such tremendous force that I was genuinely concerned we both might break our teeth. The armrest was pushing into my backbone, and I realized the make-out session I had been looking forward to was now more like trying to fend off an attacker. All the while Nicole was moaning in ecstasy, as if we were in the final throes of sexual intercourse. I wanted to stop everything and get out of the car, and yet a weird combination of thinking things had to get better and not wanting to hurt her feelings made me keep going.

The ordeal seemed to last forever. There was definitely something erotic about it, since I was making out with a girl who was very obviously attracted to me. Unfortunately, it was more unpleasant than enticing. I had no idea how much time was passing, but after a while, the encounter started to feel like a job I didn't want to be doing. It was like when my father would force me to mow the lawn on a humid summer day. I'd feel like I'd been mowing for hours and then look up and see that I still had the majority of the lawn left to cut. With Nicole, I could tell that she didn't want to stop anytime soon, and so I had to decide whether I was going to stay in for the long haul and risk long-term facial damage or try to devise a plan to get away from her.

It was then that she started grinding her pelvis against my groin as she lay on top of me. It started so subtly that at first I didn't realize it was happening. All I knew was that I was suddenly becoming physically aroused, even though I didn't want to be. And because of the thin dress pants I was wearing, there was no hiding my condition. Nicole could obviously feel this and so it made her start to grind harder. My brain went into overdrive as I was suddenly struck with the embarrassment of having so outward a reaction. In short, it made me feel like I was naked. I hadn't prepared myself for the fact that we might be doing anything more than just kissing and possibly a little groping on our first date and so had no preformed plan about how to handle any situation like the one I suddenly found myself in. And I was afraid that she was taking my aroused condition to mean I was prepared to have sex with her, which I obviously wasn't.

I knew I had to do something, and that I had to do it before my libido served up any more surprises.

I started shifting around to disengage from her pelvis but this only made her think I too was grinding and ready for action. She was moaning even louder now, and I was getting worried that the neighbors might hear this and call the cops. The thought of having a flashlight shined in my face by a chuckling sheriff who would then think I was making a move on a poor, defenseless girl was my current nightmare. Do something, I yelled at myself in my head, and do it now!

I jerked my hips quickly toward the dashboard, and we fell over onto our sides. But it didn't stop her. She pushed into my mouth passionately, making me pull back and hit my head on the bottom of the steering wheel, which thumped and then vibrated like a low note on a cello. I tried to lift my head up for air but she stayed attached to my lips like a sucker-fish and pushed into me again, attempting to put her tongue into my mouth farther than my own tongue was in there. I pulled my head back and promptly pushed it into the center of the steering wheel.

HONNNNNNNNNNNNKKKKKKKKKKKKK!!!

The blast of the car horn made us both jump and effectively drove a much-needed wedge into the dangerously amorous moment.

"Quiet!" she said suddenly, looking very nervous. "My parents are gonna hear that and look outside."

"I'm sorry," I said, disoriented. "You pushed my head into the wheel."

Nicole stared at me with an expression I couldn't read. It sort of looked like she was annoyed and wondering what she ever saw in me. But it also could have been interpreted as her trying to figure out what to do next. I stared back, not sure what to do. Even though the make-out session had been wholly unpleasant, I wondered if I had I just put off yet another girl who was going to never go out with me again.

"I've gotta go in," she said suddenly. "You'd better pull into my driveway."

Relieved, I said okay and we both sat up. I started the car and drove the thirty feet to her house as she quickly straightened her dress and then nervously checked her makeup in the sun visor mirror. When we stopped in the driveway, she threw a worried look at her house, then turned to me and said, "I'll call you tomorrow." And with that, she got out of the car and ran to her front door.

What just happened? I wondered. What did I do wrong *this* time?

I had no idea what to expect the next day. Would she call me? Should I call her? Did I *want* to call her? And what was going on in her life that she was so aggressive sexually? Was she making up for some self-esteem deficiency? Or was she just normal and *I* was the one with the problem? The idea that I might have done something that put her off and made her not want to go out with me made me start to desire her more, despite the fact that I was now terrified of making out with her again. Simply put, it was one of those "hey, you can't fire me, I was gonna quit" situations.

Dating math:

> She wants me = I don't want her.
> She doesn't want me = I want her.

It's amazing the human race has made it as long as it has.

The phone rang. It was Nicole.

"Hey, sorry I had to run in so fast last night but I got worried about getting in trouble," she said in a low voice, as if she was trying to keep from being heard. "I'm supposed to be grounded but my dad said I could go out with you if I didn't stay out late. But I had a *great* time and I can't *wait* to go out again. And don't worry. My grounding ends tomorrow." She then went into her "sexy" voice. "And we'll be able to stay out late and do *whatever we want* next time."

It was official. I was in.

I just had no idea if I wanted to be.

The setting of our next date was a much more casual affair, simply because I had blown most of the money I'd saved working at my dad's store on the previous week's gastronomical extravaganza. This week, we just went to the movies. We saw the Richard Pryor/Gene Wilder film *Stir Crazy,* which we both thought was hilarious. However, as we laughed our way through the film, Nicole kept rubbing the top of my thigh and leaning against me, snuggling in, her head on my shoulder. She would occasionally take my hand and hold it tightly, as if she was afraid I was going to try to make a break for the exit. Is this how all girls act around their boyfriends? I wondered.

It was the oddest feeling having her so near. I had spent so many years dreaming about being this close with a girl, of sitting in a theater holding hands and putting our heads against each other's and being touchy-feely and romantic. And yet now that I was doing it, I felt really uncomfortable. I was suddenly aware of everyone around me, feeling like they were all staring at Nicole and me. In the past I'd fantasized about having just this thing occur—having people see me engaged in public displays of affection. But now it just made me feel embarrassed, like I was letting the world see too much of my personal life. And on top of all this, it was making it difficult to react to the movie. When someone's got his or her head on your shoulder, you become very self-conscious about how much you shake when you laugh.

And then there was the fact that Nicole was what I like to term a "laugh-and-looker," which means that every time we'd laugh at something in the movie, she'd look at me and we'd have to do a "wasn't that funny?" smile to each other.

I've found over the years that there are a lot of laugh-and-lookers in this world. It's one of the reasons I don't really like to go to the movies with people. If you get stuck with a laugh-and-looker, you end up missing half the film because you're always having to make that goofy smile and eyebrow raise to each other anytime something the least bit amusing happens on-screen. Nicole was a laugh-and-looker of the highest order. However, she also brought with it an added element that I found completely annoying. Every time we'd laugh and look, she'd continue staring at me and try to turn our smiles to each other into a romantic moment. So, not only would I have to look away from the movie and pretend to enjoy sharing a laugh with her, but then I'd have to stay engaged in eye contact as she went into a "sexy" look that I knew was supposed to draw me into a publicly displayed make-out session. While I wasn't completely adverse to the idea of kissing her, simply put, *I wanted to see the movie.* I had been waiting for weeks to see it, and it was proving to be so funny that I didn't want to miss any of it. And so I had to either stop taking part in the laugh-and-look moments and risk getting her mad at me, or I had to exchange chuckles with her and then give her a clueless smile when she'd try to beguile me with her flat-faced romantic look just so I could get back to the film. And this was way more work than I wanted to do while I was trying to enjoy an evening at the movies.

As we were walking back to my car after the film, I asked her if she wanted to eat. She made a lascivious face and said, "Yes, but not in a restaurant." And unless that meant she wanted to cook me pasta at her house, I could only assume that this was yet another of her famous double entendres. She then put her lips right next to my ear and whispered, "Take me home."

My face must have given away the panic I suddenly felt at that moment, because she stared at me and quickly softened.

"I really like you, sweetie," she said in a very innocent tone. "I just want to be close with you, that's all." She batted her eyelids sincerely and gave me a very sweet smile, the smile of someone who truly cared about me.

And all of a sudden I was head over heels in love with her.

We drove back to her neighborhood, and she sat as close to me as she could without being on my lap. She was nuzzling her face into my neck, and I was getting waves of goose bumps so intense that it felt like I was being immersed in a pool of seltzer. Throwing all caution to the wind, I went against everything I was warned about in driver's ed and took one of my hands out of the 10-and-2 position on the steering wheel to put my arm around Nicole. It was a great feeling, both driving with my arm around a girl *and* thumbing my nose at Mr. Jenkins, my driving instructor. So many times in the past I had driven behind cars in which I could see couples silhouetted through their back windshield with their arms around each other, kissing at stoplights and stroking the back of each other's heads as they drove. And now I was one of them, as I had always wished I would be. I was living the dream.

Nicole had us park down the street from her house again, and the minute I turned off the car, she moved toward me. I was ready for her this time and so decided to go after her as passionately as she had come at me the last time we tangled. We slammed our mouths together hungrily, like two lovers in a passionate movie, and promptly smashed our teeth against each other.

"OW!" she yelled as she grabbed her mouth. "What are you trying to do?! Break my teeth?"

"I'm sorry," I said as I also held my mouth in pain. "I didn't know you were coming in so fast."

She looked like she wanted to get mad at me, then suddenly smiled coyly and moved forward. She pointed at her mouth and said, "Why don't you kiss it and make it better?"

Our lips came together tenderly, and I was overwhelmed with the romance of the moment. It truly was sweet and made it feel like we were starring in a romantic film. I like this side of Nicole, I thought. This is what I was hoping for. Maybe she was just nervous and trying too hard the other night.

Unfortunately, Nicole quickly started kissing me harder, pushing her mouth against my sore teeth. As the seconds went by, she upped the intensity to what it had been the previous weekend and soon surpassed it. Before I knew it, I found myself once again shifting back against the car door, trying to ease the pressure she was applying to the front of my skull. She started moaning loudly again and gripping my arms so tightly with her hands to pull me forward that I finally said, "Ow, you're hurting me."

She pulled away, then gave me a playful smile. "I'm sorry. Let me kiss you and make you better."

She jumped on top of me and started grinding her pelvis into my crotch again. This time, my head was wedged at a ninety-degree angle against the door's armrest, and I became convinced she was going to break my neck. But she was kissing me so hard that I couldn't speak. I began rocking in order to move our bodies down the seat a bit and get my head off the armrest. This only caused her to grind harder and for me to get another uncontrollable and unwanted erection. As soon as I did, Nicole suddenly broke her lip lock on me and rose up on her arms.

She stared at me, then said, "I want to do something to you." She said it like it was an idea that had just popped into her head.

"What?" I said in the same worried tone that you'd use if you knew your mother was about to tell you she had decided to rob a bank.

She glanced down at my crotch, then gave me a "naughty" smile, and raised and lowered her eyebrows at me like Groucho Marx. "I'll show you," she said.

And then she reached for my belt buckle.

I immediately panicked. I know I was supposed to be happy that whatever she was about to do was occurring, but

I simply wasn't. It was the last thing in the world I wanted to happen at that moment. I quickly pulled out from underneath her and sat up, making her fall backward against the passenger door.

"No, don't!" I said a bit too emphatically.

She looked at me, surprised. "What's the matter?"

"Nothing," I said, trying not to hyperventilate. "It's just . . . I mean . . . we *just* started dating."

"Yeah, so?" she said, doing the Groucho eyebrows at me again.

"I don't want to go so fast, that's all," I said, my voice cracking like a thirteen-year-old's.

"I'm not saying that I want to have sex," she said with a smile. "I just want to try something with my mouth."

My panic index jumped like the NASDAQ after an interest rate cut. And it wasn't just because I was afraid of sex. There was another more sobering reason:

I had heard a story a few years back from the oldest sister of my next-door neighbors about a girl in her school who had been asked by her boyfriend to give him oral sex. The girl did but was so inexperienced that when the guy climaxed, the girl screamed and ran gagging from the car, having had no idea what to expect. Simply put, she didn't realize that a guy's orgasm produced something more tangible than just good feelings. And now that story was front and center in my mind.

To be honest, I myself had been surprised the first time my own body produced this by-product of a satisfying moment. I had spent years doing the rope feeling in the bathroom but, since I had started so young, it was always an internal affair, a mentally pleasing event that produced no physical evidence. And so the first time something emerged when the rope feeling peaked, I was terrified, thinking I had ruptured an internal organ.

So, the thought that Nicole might not realize what she was getting herself into, coupled with the image of her running shrieking from the car as I sat in there with my pants down and no Kleenex around with which to dispose of my orgasmic evidence, made the idea of her trying something with her mouth at this moment nonentertainable.

"That's okay," I said, trying to sound as casual as if I were turning down a piece of gum. "You don't have to."

"I *know* I don't *have* to," she laughed. Then she made her seductive face. "I *want* to."

She started to reach for my fly again. I shifted away from her toward the door, my mind racing. I knew there was no way to get out of this gracefully. And while I didn't want to hurt her feelings, it was clear I could not let this happen.

"I really don't think it's a good idea," I said in a pleading voice.

She looked at me, innocently perplexed. "Why not?"

"It's just . . . I mean . . . I don't know," I stammered. "It'll be a mess."

It sounded ridiculous the minute I said it, but it was my exact fear. Yes, it would be a mess, even if it went well. The image of a satisfied Nicole smiling at me as I lay splayed out post-orgasm on the front seat with my pants down and my own bodily fluid all over my midsection was as abhorrent to me at that moment as was the image of her screaming in terror at getting an unexpected mouthful of what the gym teacher who taught my high school health class referred to as "ejaculate."

However, she was undeterred.

"I don't mind," was all she said as she once again reached

to undo my belt buckle. There was no conventional way to fight this, I realized. Either I had to give in, which the rope feeling—addicted side of me was slowly starting to realize I wanted to do, or I had to attempt another escape tactic.

And so I did.

I proceeded to make a tender and touching speech about how, by moving too fast into sex, we were risking ruining our relationship. I said that we should take it slow, that we should get to know each other first, that we should become soul mates by exploring the nonphysical side of ourselves and our attraction to each other. I waxed poetic about how young we were and how we should hold on to our innocence as long as possible, so that when we finally did consummate our relationship, it would be something beautiful and heart-felt, not just something misguided we were doing because we thought this jaded and heartless world expected us to. To wait was to take ourselves to romantic heights unknown to those in the then culture of one-night stands and free love. Our abstinence was our intimacy, and it guaranteed our place in each other's hearts.

It was an Oscar-winning performance.

Nicole stared at me for several seconds, then gave me a sweet smile and a look of love. "That's so beautiful, honey," she said, almost sounding like she was about to cry. "You're right. We'll wait." She gave me a tender kiss on the lips, then whispered, "But not too long." And with that, she smiled, got out of the car, and ran into her house.

And thus I became what I believe to be the only eighteen-year-old guy in the history of the world to turn down a free blow job from a pretty girl.

Our relationship continued on this course for the next several weeks. I kept waiting for something akin to love to overtake me but it simply wasn't happening. Nicole and I were spending more and more time together and having more and more heavy make-out sessions, many of them down on her much more comfortable and injury-reducing basement couch, but I still didn't feel like I wanted to go any further with her into the possible abyss of sex. And the main reason for this seemed to break down to one simple fact that was slowly dawning on me:

I didn't want Nicole as my girlfriend.

I really liked her and had developed a nice friendship with her eight-year-old brother, whom I found to be very funny because he was clearly on his way to fellow geek status and quite proud of it. I also got along very well with her parents, who liked me because they could tell I was a "nice, respectable young man." Nicole and I had lots of fun seeing movies and hanging out and joking around and teasing each other and watching TV together. We'd go out for drives and eat in coffee shops and go miniature golfing and attend big-band concerts at Metropolitan Beach and get along like the best of friends. Unfortunately, it was the times when we were making out that I wasn't having fun with her. True, her desperation level had decreased with each session, and the pain factor was soon less of a major side effect of our co-mingling. But there was simply no joy for me in make-out Mudville.

It started to dawn on me that I wanted to say to Nicole the same sentence I used to get so mad about when girls I was in love with would sit me down and use it to knock the wind out of my sails—six terrible words that have ruined the egos and shattered the self-confidence of countless men over the ages. I wanted to recite those six poisoned syllables to Nicole that had been dumped so many times onto me like those clouds of red chemicals that airplanes drop over large brushfires:

"I just want to be friends."

Maybe it was because the physical attraction wasn't there, maybe it was because I liked talking to her better than I liked kissing her, maybe it was the guilt I felt knowing that her parents thought I was a nice guy while I was soon to defile or be defiled by their daughter, or maybe it was simply because I was reacting badly to the massive amount of pressure she was putting on me to take our physical coupling to the next level. All I knew was that whenever she'd try to get sexy, it was having less and less of a positive effect on me.

My mind went through all kinds of fears and self-accusations.

Did I have no libido beyond the desire to masturbate?
Was I too immature to ever open up physically to a
      woman?
Was I gay, even though I was completely attracted to
      women and completely not attracted to men?
Or was I so afraid of sex that I was simply destined
      never to have it?

These questions would swirl through my head as Nicole and I would roll around on her couch and she'd give me a pleading and impatient look that asked, "*Now* can we move on to second, third, and home base?" and I would make yet another speech about the virtues of waiting, as if I were the local chaplain. I was starting to feel like Mr. Roper from *Three's Company,* whose wife would always make cracks about how he'd never have sex with her. Was this to be my sexual future?

I wasn't sure, but one thing was becoming crystal clear to me: I had to get out of this relationship.

There was only one problem.

I had never broken up with someone before.

How did one do such a thing? I wondered. I'd seen people break up on television shows quite a bit, but it always seemed to be a terrible event that ended with a woman crying and storming out of a restaurant, sometimes after dumping a glass of water or a plate of spaghetti over the heartbreaker boyfriend's head. How would Nicole take it if I told her it simply wasn't working out and that I thought we'd be better off just being pals? I couldn't imagine it would be anything other than a tearful and possibly angry moment. Would she end up yelling at me, accusing me of being impotent or homosexual or a bad kisser whom she only pretended she was attracted to in order to be nice? Would she laugh mockingly in my face like an angry Italian woman from a foreign film and spit on the ground in front of me and tell me I was a "piece of sheet" who couldn't please a "real woman" if I tried? There were too many possible scenarios flying through my brain thanks to all the TV and movies I had watched during my first eighteen years on this planet, and I wasn't sure if my fragile ego could take the possible doomsday assault a breakup could bring down upon my geeky head.

And what if I *wasn't* supposed to break up with her?

What if she was actually my soul mate? I'd never had a girl be so attracted to me before. What if Nicole was the only woman in the world who would ever feel this way about me? Was I setting myself up for a life of walking around a broken man, forever castigating myself for having thrown away my one true love? Would I spend the next fifty years watching Nicole from afar as she met another guy and got married and had children and lived out a happy life with a husband that was supposed to be me? Was I being too picky or superficial or closed-minded or immature to realize that I had been given the gift I had always wanted, the gift of true love? And was this what true love felt like? It was all so confusing that it brought me to the worst place that one can be in a failing relationship:

Stasis.

I continued the charade of being Nicole's boyfriend, and she continued the charade of acting like it was perfectly normal for your eighteen-year-old boyfriend to lecture you about the evils of sex anytime you wanted to do anything more than just kiss.

And so it went, day after day, week after week, like two gerbils on a wheel trying to get to the bowl of food in front of them. Nicole had even begun sneaking glasses of wine when I came over, saying that they relaxed her, which I realized meant I was literally driving the poor girl to drink. Something had to be done and so, in true geek fashion, I decided on the most direct and effective course of action available to me:

I would move out of the state.

All right, look. I know this was a cowardly way to end a relationship and I'm not at all proud of it. But, looking back, it was clearly what I thought was the most constructive solution to my Nicole problem. See, I had always been acting and performing throughout my school years and had known early on that I wanted to do something in the entertainment industry. But for an ambitious kid living in Detroit, that meant the most I'd be able to do would be to act in local commercials or maybe get into radio or perhaps become a TV anchorman or a writer for an advertising firm, none of which seemed glamorous enough to a teenager who really only wanted to be Steve Martin. But now that I had a Michigan-based problem I wanted to escape, my thoughts suddenly focused on the Mecca of show business, Hollywood. It had all the things I wanted—fame, fortune, opportunity, and, most important, it was about as far away from Nicole as I could get without having to go to another continent.

In short, it was the perfect plan.

A cowardly, extremely weaselly plan, but a plan nonetheless.

I asked my dad for the phone number of his friend who was our one connection to show biz in Hollywood. The guy was an artist's manager at the time whose claim to fame was that he represented Pink Lady from the now infamous TV disaster *Pink Lady and Jeff*. I called the man's office and asked if he had any info about where a fresh-faced young actor could find work in Tinseltown. He said he did and sent me in the mail a copy of *The Hollywood Reporter,* an industry trade magazine that once a week printed a listing of all the movies that were being made by the film studios, as well as all the studios' phone numbers. Upon receiving it, I started calling each studio and dumbly asked them if they had any movies they needed talented newcomers to star in. Every studio informed me that the only job openings they were looking to fill were those of lawyers and accountants. Undeterred, I kept calling and discovering that Hollywood seemed to be *the* place if you were an unemployed CPA or attorney but a pretty closed town if you were looking for acting gigs. However, when I worked my way down toward the bottom of the list and hit Universal Studios, lo and behold, they had a job opening that I actually thought I had a chance of getting:

A studio tour guide.

I had taken the Universal Studios tour during a family vacation to Los Angeles years earlier. There are home movies of my mother and me in a special-effects moving stagecoach in which we playacted that I was a villain kidnapping my mom as she pretended to scream and I pretended to drive the coach out of town. I remembered being in awe of all the movie sets and props we had seen, including a giant table and chair from *The Incredible Shrinking Man* that I thought was the coolest thing I had ever seen. And I remembered that the tour guide on our tram had been a funny guy who made lots of jokes and got lots of laughs as we drove through the studio back lot looking at old street sets that hadn't been filmed on in years. And I had recently seen at the end of Universal movies a title card that would pop up encouraging the audience, "When in Hollywood, be sure to visit Universal Studios." And now I suddenly saw there was actually a chance I could become part of this very, very faraway world.

A world without Nicole.

"Are you doing interviews?" I asked nervously, as if even thinking about taking a job in California would mean I was committing myself to completely changing my life.

"Yes, but they're next Monday," said the woman on the other end of the line. "Could you get out here that quickly?"

I did some fast math and realized that my last final exam at Wayne State was on Friday morning. If I finished that, came home, jumped in my car, and drove straight through, I could probably make it just in time for the interview. But what would I tell my parents? What would I tell my friends? And what would happen if I got all the way out there and didn't get the job? What then?

I looked down at my desk and saw written on my calendar that Nicole's parents and her little brother were going out of town this weekend and that she was expecting me to come over and spend "some quality time" with her.

The battle for abstinence would be taken to a new and unpleasant high. And I was too tired to do battle anymore.

"Please put my name down on the interview list," I said to the woman at Universal Studios. "I'll be there."

". . . what?"

Nicole stared at me in shock, then blinked her eyes, unable to comprehend what I was saying to her.

"I'm moving to *California*. I got offered a job there!" I said excitedly.

"*Who* offered you a job?" she asked in the same disbelieving tone one might use if their retarded brother had informed them he'd been offered a job at the Pentagon.

"A friend of my dad's. He manages Pink Lady. He's really cool."

"And so you're just going to leave?"

"I can't pass this up. I've wanted to work in Hollywood my whole life," I said, sounding like Mickey Rooney in a "let's put on a show!" movie with Judy Garland.

"You never told me that."

"I'm an actor. *Of course* I want to go to Hollywood," I said with a good-natured laugh that begged me to add the term of endearment "silly" to the end of the sentence.

She stared at me, looking hurt and confused, and I got the sinking feeling that this sad little scheme of mine was not going to save me from the blowup I was praying I could avoid.

"I can't believe you're just going to leave me," she said as she sat down heavily, looking shell-shocked. I sat down next to her and put a consoling arm around her shoulder.

"Hey, if I get discovered, then you'll have a famous boyfriend," I tried to joke.

Nicole glared at me and I took my arm back down.

I spent the evening trying to cheer her up, saying how I'd only be gone for the summer and about how we'd be back together by September. I knew I didn't want to get back together with her when I returned, but four months into the future seemed like an eternity. Something definitive would happen in both our lives by then, I told myself. The neediness for male company she displayed with me was such that I couldn't imagine her not getting another boyfriend the second my car crossed the state line into Ohio.

"I don't know why you're doing this," she blurted out suddenly in a tone of utter disdain that showed she was dropping any and all pretext of being the understanding girlfriend. "What are you hoping to be? *King* of the *tour guides?*"

Seeing that the situation was deteriorating rapidly, I decided it was time to get my cowardly ass out of there.

I gave Nicole a kiss good-bye, pretending to be as upset as she was, and walked to my car as I heard her begin sniffling behind me. I stopped and stared up at the night sky dramatically as I put my key into the car door, performing the "anguished boyfriend who must leave his gal to go off to war" sigh as I saw her start crying and run inside her house. I lingered for another few seconds next to my car, in case she was looking out the front curtains to see if I really was upset. After counting to about fifteen, I let my shoulders sag in defeat, sighed again, then slumped into my car and drove off.

As much as I hate to admit it, the farther I got from her house, the lighter I started to feel. By the time I was turning onto the main drag of Groesbeck Boulevard, I had the radio up full blast and was singing along loudly to the Pat Travers Band's live rendition of "Boom Boom Out Go the Lights," feeling better than I had felt in a long time.

And the next day, I took my final exam at Wayne State University, came home, put my bags in the car, gathered up all the maps and TripTiks my dad got me from the AAA to make sure I took the safest route to Los Angeles, and told my next-door neighbor Craig I was ready to go. He and I would be sharing eight-hour driving shifts for our nonstop car journey to the Golden State. (Craig wasn't moving out too—my dad bought him a plane ticket so he could fly home after helping me with my cross-country drive.) Craig loaded his stuff into the car, I said good-bye to my mom and dad, and we excitedly drove off into the Michigan sunset.

And after a harrowing three-day car trip that saw Craig falling asleep behind the wheel numerous times as I tried to nap, and which then saw the two of us arriving on Hollywood Boulevard the evening before my interview, deliriously tired and completely shocked to find this avenue of dreams that we thought would be teeming with movie stars was actually teeming with hookers, runaways, and homeless people, I lay in bed in the cheap motel we checked into across from Universal Studios and realized something interesting:

Even though I felt really bad about what I had done to Nicole, I was now in Hollywood, California, about to have a job interview at a major movie studio, and my future was suddenly wide open.

Hey, who says cowardice doesn't pay?

A Fun Feig Fact! Did you know . . . ?

. . . that "feig" means "cowardly" in German?
It's true! Look it up!

I Wish This Chapter
Was More Exciting

I really do.

You'd think that to have loaded up my car and headed
out to California with nothing more than a suitcase full of
clothes and a job interview to be a tour guide at a major Hollywood studio would have resulted in some madcap adven-
tures, a *Day of the Locusts*–like story of being seduced by
beautiful starlets, of nights spent out on the town prowling
for women with my wild new Los Angeles friends, and of
innocence lost like in that Bob Seger song "Hollywood Nights."
But this was *me* we're talking about, and even though I was
living in a major metropolis three-quarters of a country away
from the small town in which I had grown up, my innocence
was in no danger of being lost. It remained securely attached
to me the way my mittens used to be attached to the sleeves
of my coat when I was three.

Look, the problem is, as you have already seen, I'm just
not that exciting of a guy. I think I'm a decent guy and a
fairly nice guy, and I have on occasion been sort of exciting.
When I was eight and decided I wanted to be a stuntman and
threw myself off the garage roof onto a pile of empty boxes, I
was pretty exciting. When I decided in high school to enter

myself in a disco-dancing contest and danced around by myself on an empty dance floor to "Disco Inferno" while everybody watched me in disbelief, I was pretty exciting. (And I still think I would have won, too, if the guy after me hadn't started doing magic tricks like the Appearing Cane and the Silks from Thin Air while he danced to Heart's "Magic Man"—which, by the way, wasn't even a disco song!) And I know that when I got arrested for shoplifting because a friend of mine stuffed a package of Hot Wheels cars into his back pocket and then bent over to get some bubble gum out of a machine in front of the store right when the store detective was coming back from lunch, I was extremely exciting. Or at least I was to my retail store–owning dad, who refused to talk to me for days, saying, "I can't believe my only son is nothing more than a common criminal." But, in general, I'm really sort of a boring guy when it comes to my daily exploits. And so I also was in Hollywood, California.

Some of the highlights of my summer of nonlove were:

- Being told after my successful interview for tour guide that the only way they would consider putting me through the two-week training course was if I agreed to lie out in the sun every day in order to get rid of my terrible acne and, if possible, put even the slightest hint of color into my white, pasty Michigan skin.
- Lying out in the noonday sun like they told me to and accidentally falling asleep, thus getting a blistering sunburn that turned my pale midwestern skin bright red so that during the rest of my training, my peeling face made me look like Toxie from the Troma film *The Toxic Avenger*.
- Moving into a motel in one of the most dangerous parts of Los Angeles because it was near a doughnut shop I had once seen in a movie.

- Moving out of the dangerous motel after almost getting killed in the crossfire of a police sting while cluelessly walking back from an Arby's at eleven o'clock at night.
- Moving into a boardinghouse in a scary part of Hollywood that I shared with my landlady, a huge Mexican man, and a seventy-year-old dwarf whom I was supposed to walk to church every Sunday.
- Moving out of the boardinghouse after three days and moving in with a fellow tour guide trainee who slept in a waterbed and who wore a toupee even though he was only about twenty-five years old.
- Getting a crush on our other roommate, a pretty blond girl who used to scream so loudly whenever she'd see a cockroach in our kitchen that I got temporary tinnitus once while standing next to her trying to help her kill one.
- Passing my tour guide training course and working seven days a week in the hope that I would be discovered by a famous movie director as I was showing disappointed tourists where the house from *Psycho* would be if the studio hadn't moved it to another part of the lot that people on the tour weren't allowed to see yet.
- Watching numerous children pee off the side of the moving tram because their parents hadn't thought to make them go to the bathroom before taking a two-hour tram ride.
- Falling into Jaws Lake while trying to retrieve a woman's clog that fell off her foot while the tram was being attacked by the fake rubber shark.
- Almost getting killed by the Jaws shark because as I was trying to get out of Jaws Lake with the clog in hand, the underwater gears and mechanisms that made the shark move caught my pant leg as the shark was resetting and almost pulled my pants off.

- Falling in love with an older female tour guide with bleached blond hair and sun-scorched red skin who used to bake me cookies and kiss the back of my neck but who couldn't decide if she should go out with me or not because of my age and so played tug-of-war with my heart for the entire summer.
- Stumbling upon the older female tour guide making out with my toupee-wearing roommate behind a garage at a party that was being thrown in my honor.
- Watching the older female tour guide have a crying jag as she begged my forgiveness the next day in the tour guide break room and then *still* refused to go out on a date with me after I forced myself to start liking her again.
- Discovering only one week before I drove back to Michigan to start my sophomore year of college that my toupee-wearing roommate had the world's largest collection of *Playboy* and *Penthouse* magazines up in the attic over the garage, and
- Spending every free minute of my last week up in the attic over the garage.

At the end of the summer, I flew back to Michigan with my dad while my mom and uncle Jack drove my car back and reminisced about the time they had driven cross-country decades earlier, a trip that had seen my uncle Jack run off the road in the Mojave Desert by a truck and my mother flying headfirst through the windshield of Jack's Packard and almost dying.

Hey, at least *somebody* in my family did something exciting in California.

The Annotated Nancy

Keeping a journal always seems like a good idea.

It usually sounds like the perfect way to let out your innermost thoughts, a way to vent, to heal thyself through the uncensored recording of one's most private feelings writ down from pen to page, purging the soul of all its fears and insecurities through the catharsis of physicalizing the ethereal mind by making its activities permanent upon parchment.

And that would all be true if, after we wrote down these all-too-human musings that go through our heads on any given day, we then burned our journals.

But the sad truth is that we don't, and so what we're left with is the most embarrassing collection of stupid things we thought and felt and did that no one would otherwise know about if we hadn't made the enormous mistake of writing them down in the first place.

Case in point. My journal.

Specifically, the one I kept in the months after I came back from my summer of working as a tour guide at Universal Studios. I returned to my sophomore year of college at Wayne State and took a creative writing class. And in that class, we were told that we had to keep a journal, and that the teacher would be checking our journals regularly to make sure that we were writing in them every day. Which thus defeats the purpose of keeping a journal, if you know that somebody you've never met before is now going to be rummaging through the contents of your brain like a tax auditor at the Internal Revenue Service.

However, after a few weeks of making us turn in our journals and flipping through the pages to make sure we weren't just writing Xs and Os in there, the professor informed us that he was no longer going to check them and that he hoped we would now continue to write down our secret thoughts and feelings every night before we went to bed because it was "a good creative exercise."

The reason I bring all of this up is to let you know that the journal I'll be referencing in this chapter does not sound insane because it was written by someone who was trying to play a practical joke on his college professor, who he knew would be reading his words and judging them. No, it was written by someone who actually used to have thoughts and feelings and judgments that are every bit as embarrassing as they sound when you read them presently.

Just thought I'd warn you. Because my journal contains some of the most ridiculous, annoying, cringe-inducing entries ever written down in the history of journal-keeping.

Or at least they sound that way to me.

The following is an exact transcription of pertinent sections of my journal from the year 1981. All misspellings, word omissions, and errors of capitalization, grammar, and punctuation are reprinted faithfully as they appeared.

If you'd like to verify this, I'll show you the actual journal. You know, if we ever get a chance to hang out.

Enjoy.

9/15/81

I talked to Dave and he said that Mary, the girl I met at Bonanza, didn't come into Ark today. So, at least I can feel like she didn't go because she knew I wouldn't be there. You see, she asked me about getting a job and I told her to go down there today. Then, I remembered that I had my meeting at GPR and told her I wouldn't be there, but Dave would. So, if she didn't show up, I can assume she didn't because she wanted to see me. (Ha, ha, Don't kid yourself, Munster) So, tomorrow, I'll go over there and see her.

Okay, here's the story. I was working as a stock boy at my dad's army surplus store, Ark Surplus. Dave, one of my best friends since the sixth grade, was also working there as a stock boy. We would always take our lunch hour together and generally went to Pizza Hut, where we would spilt an extra-large pizza and drink an entire pitcher of Coke, thus ensuring we were completely wired on sugar, carbs, and caffeine for the rest of our workday. However, we had recently started going to Bonanza, the local chain steak restaurant, unwittingly adding heavy, sleep-inducing amounts of red meat to our midday diet. As we moved through the buffet line with our trays on this particular day, we met a beautiful girl who was working the cash register. Her name was Nancy. She was very friendly, and Dave and I immediately started joking with her. Both because of her beauty and my nervous energy over it, I was wittier than Dave that day, and as we all talked, I made both her and Dave laugh quite a bit. As I watched her laugh and smile at my comedy stylings, I was immediately infatuated. She was absolutely gorgeous, or at least she was to me. She had soft, wavy blond hair, beautiful blue eyes, flawless skin, and one of the most kissable mouths I've ever seen before or since. She was thin enough to be sexy without being thin enough to be scary and had dainty, perfectly shaped hands that moved gracefully over the cash register keys like Liberace playing Mozart. I could smell her intoxicatingly subtle and feminine perfume through all the odors of cooking beef and frying food that filled the lunchtime air, and my heart was pounding out of my chest.

In a nutshell, Nancy was my dream girl.

Big-time.

Feeling the impatience of the people waiting in line behind us, Dave and I thanked Nancy and moved off to a table. As we sat eating lunch, I kept looking over at Nancy. Occasionally I'd catch her looking at us, and my stomach would leap up into my throat. I couldn't tell if she was looking at Dave or myself but the fact that she was looking at all was encouraging. When we finished eating, there was no longer a line at the cash register and so I decided that Dave and I should say good-bye to her. In reality, I wanted to say good-bye to her myself, but I didn't have the nerve, nor did it feel right to ice Dave out of the scene.

We walked over and started joking with her again. After

a few minutes, I took the Dale Carnegie route to winning friends and influencing people and decided to ask her about herself (this is one of Dale's main rules for making people like you—my dad had given me this book years earlier when he was convinced I was the least popular kid in my school).

"So, how do you like working here?" I asked, trying to sound casual (so that she wouldn't think I was prying) yet interested (so that she wouldn't think I was just trying out a pickup line on her).

"I hate it," she said with a roll of her eyes. "I'd kill to get a job somewhere else."

"Well, hey, we work at Ark Surplus," I said enthusiastically. "You should get a job there. I think they're looking for a new cashier." I had made a quick decision not to say it was my dad's store so that I could avoid sounding like an underachiever who could only get a job working for his father.

"Yeah? Really?" she said, sounding interested.

"Hey, you should come over today and fill out an application," I blurted out, a bit too energetically.

"Maybe I will," she said. "I get off at four. I can come by after that."

"Great," I said, excited that I was going to get to see her on my home turf. But then I remembered something. "Oh, wait, I won't be there after four. I've got a rehearsal to go to."

She asked me what I was rehearsing. I took the opportunity to try to impress her with something that sounded impressive but wasn't. "GPR" was actually WGPR, a Detroit TV station that was owned and run by the African-American community. It was relegated to Channel 62 on the UHF dial (if you're under thirty, chances are you won't have any clue what UHF and VHF mean—ask your parents about it—it's far too boring to explain in a book), and they had been developing a soap opera for over a year. My friend Pete and I were playing the various white-guy roles in the scenes they were preparing to showcase for potential financial backers. My characters tended to fall into two categories—mean white guy who wonders aloud with his friend what it'd be like to sleep with a black woman, and goofy white guy who completely misunderstands black culture. The whole soap opera wasn't very impressive if you knew all the circumstances surrounding it, but I figured it was a good way to sound like a big shot in front of a girl with whom I was now head over heels in love.

I finished my explanation by dropping in the fact I had just spent the past summer working in Hollywood as a studio tour guide, hoping to seal my persona as a big shot in the making, when I noticed that Dave had been forced into the role of "guy who has to stand there and say nothing because he has no way into the conversation." And so I ended my dissertation with a selfless, "But Dave'll be there after four. He can help you out."

Nancy smiled and said she'd stop in, and then Dave and I said good-bye to her and headed back to work. As we walked out the door, I made sure to let Dave go through first so that I could take one final look back at her. When I did, I saw she was watching me. I gave her a friendly wave, and she gave me a big smile back.

I wasn't at all certain, but I had a feeling that I might be in.

And so that's why when I heard from Dave that Nancy hadn't shown up at the store that day, I tried to take it as a sign that she decided not to come by because she knew that I wouldn't be there.

As for the "Don't kid yourself, Munster," I think that

was a line from an episode of *The Munsters* that I had added to my ever-growing lexicon of memorized bits of dialogue from favorite movies and TV shows.

Hey, I *told* you I was a geek.

9/16/81

Well, today has turned out to be a terrific day! School was okay and, as usual, I fell asleep studying German (I've got to stop studying in the recliner). But the real reason today was so great was because of Nancy. Here's what happened—Dave and I went into Bonanza for dinner and to see Nancy, like I told her we would,[1] but when our food came, I asked one of the hostesses where Nancy was. She said Nancy wasn't working today. I was rather upset.[2] Then she asked, "Is your name Paul?" I told her yes and she said that Nancy had left me a note. She brought it over and it was addressed to me! Not Dave, but me![3] It said that she was sorry for not being there but she changed her schedule (or they changed it on her. One of those.) It then said that she worked tomorrow and she hoped I would come in to see her. Well, that note made

1. I'm not sure when I told her this but I must have said something when we were talking at the register the previous day. I have no recollection of doing this, though.
2. I guess I must have made quite a point of our returning for this dinner the previous day in order to have been "rather upset." That or I was just showing my journal what a hard-ass I was, because I can guarantee that I didn't act upset to the hostess, who I remember was also quite pretty. By the way, why didn't *Playboy* ever do "The Girls of Bonanza"?
3. One of the most embarrassing and annoying things about my journal was this constant use of exclamation marks, which I believe made whatever goofy-ass thing I happened to be saying seem ten times goofier. *I* want to punch myself when I read them, so I can only imagine how you must feel. And there's a lot more of them, friends. Prepare yourselves.

me extremely happy. As Dave and I were eating, Dave noticed that the manager was talking on the phone and looking at us. All of a sudden, the manager (who is a girl[4]) came up to me and said, "Nancy wants to know if you're coming in tomorrow." I asked when she was working and finally, the manager let me use the phone. I told Nancy that I had my birthday party tomorrow night,[5] so I couldn't come in after seven. After a lot of deliberation, I nervously asked her to go out with me Friday. She said she'd love to but she's grounded. However, she's going to try to talk her parents into letting her go. So, she told me to come tomorrow about five and see what's happening. Then she wished me 'Happy Birthday.' She has the nicest voice. It's really beautiful, and so is she. She's gorgeous and, from our talks, we seem to have very compatible personalities. I really hope this works out. I really have a good feeling about her. I'll keep my fingers crossed.

What it was about me falling for girls who were grounded, I have no idea.

9/17/81 HAPPY BIRTHDAY!

. . . This was the best birthday present! I went down to see Nancy today at five. When I went up to her, she had that beautiful smile on her face and she said, 'Can you still go out tomorrow night?' That's right! Her parents are letting her go. She can only stay out until eleven, but

4. Who knew a steak house would be such a lady-fest?
5. To be held at Farrells ice cream restaurant, former home of the Zoo, the Gibson Girl, and the Pigs Trough. If you remember this place and these dishes, then you remember what UHF and VHF are. Hello, fellow middle-aged person!

who cares!? She's supposed to call me tomorrow (that's a switch!⁶) and we'll decide what to do. We've already decided that at 9:30, we'll go watch the fireworks at farm city week.⁷ Hope it doesn't rain! So, I can't wait until tomorrow night! I hope everything goes perfect. Well, keep your fingers crossed for me and know the Truth. Gute Nacht!

You're probably wondering why I capitalized *Truth*. The thing is, I was still pretty religious back then, despite my anger at God for the whole *National Lampoon* incident, and still felt the Guy was watching my every move. And in Christian Science, saying things like "know the Truth" meant that you believed God would give you whatever you wanted, as long as it was right and meant to be. So, by telling myself to "know the Truth," I was correcting the part of me that wrote "keep your fingers crossed" by reminding myself that luck had nothing to do with anything; that I believed only God had the power to make things work out between Nancy and me.

The reason I bring all this up is not to give you a lesson in the secret workings of obscure religions, but to make you aware of a couple of things:

- The first is that back then, not only did I have to worry about trying to get dates, but I had the added pressure of worrying that the women I fell in love with might not be

---

6. From what?
7. An event in downtown Mt. Clemens where all the streets were closed, and vendors and food sellers set up booths. It was a big deal and was always packed with people. I'm sure you could have figured this out for yourself but, hey, doing these footnotes is kinda fun. Makes me feel like my book is actually smarter than it really is.

approved by God. Which means that I had told myself I could conceivably get into a situation in which I was in love with a girl about whom The Ruler of All Space and Time would say, "Hey, what are you doing? That's not the girl you're supposed to be with! I do not approve of you two dating!," thus turning Him into a hotheaded, nonunderstanding father from a *Sweet Valley High* teen novel.

- The second and more disturbing thing to me was that I provided myself with no place in the world where I could write down my most private thoughts. Even in this sad little blue spiral notebook I kept under my bed, I had convinced myself that God was always going to be reading over my shoulder, clearing His throat loudly to let me know every time I did something that wasn't approved of by Him.

And you wonder why I was so neurotic?

9/18/04

Well, what can I say? Getting right to the subject of the day, my date with Nancy went <u>great</u>! I must admit that I was quite worried this afternoon because of our phone conversation. You see, she called me (as expected!) and we tryed to decide what we were going to do. We would be going with another couple that works at Bonanza, Scott and Kelly. (Scott is a good person. He laughs at my jokes.[8] Kelly looks just like Rob Radkoff's sister[9]). Anyway, as we talked, she started saying how Scott was

---

8. Clearly, this was also my criterion for being friends with guys as well as women. Good to know I couldn't be too easily manipulated in life, eh?
9. This was a big compliment, trust me.

going to get some beer (oh, brother!), and did I mind girls who smoke. Well, that kind of worried me and depressed, because I was hoping she was a fellow "straight" person.[10] We decided on the fireworks at Farm City Week, but I faced the date almost with dread, seeing it as one Christian Scientist versus a carload of freaks.[11] Well, I went to pick her up and she looked <u>beautiful</u>!!! She was wearing a fuzzy light blue sweater (V-neck), nice jeans, and a cute little pair of white moccasins/docksiders (that's the best I can describe them, but they were cute). She looked the way I always wanted a girlfriend to look. I really felt proud. Then, her stepfather walked in. GULP![12] The guy's a little taller than me, but he's got a voice that makes Paul Robeson sound like a soprano.[13] I tried my best to sound intelligent and impressive, but who can tell what he thought? So, we left there and went to Bonanza to pick up Scott and Kelly. We sat around there for a while and I became a little worried again, because I felt like I was back in the high school cafeteria in my Freshman year.[14] But the girls were nice. We left there after a while with our other couple and headed into Mt. Clemens. After we parked, we walked around Farm City Week, looking at the booths and talking. I still hadn't even attempted to hold her hand or anything. Finally, we found a place on the grass to watch the fireworks. Scott and I went back to my car and got a blanket

10. Just so you know, that sentence makes me cringe so much today that I practically hurt myself.
11. Cringing again. Ow.
12. Yes, I actually wrote that.
13. The guy who sang "Old Man River." These are the obscure references you get when your parents give birth to you when they're both thirty-nine years old.
14. That comment confuses me as much as it confuses you. Let's just let it go.

to sit on. The fireworks didn't start on time, but Nancy and I started talking and joking. We were pretty cold, so I put my arm around her and she then took my hand and snuggled up next to me. The fireworks began, not only in the sky, but in my head,[15] because we kept holding each other closer and tighter. I was in heaven. The half hour seemed like a minute all too short. After the show was over, we decided to go to Big Boy for something hot to drink.[16] We walked over, first hand in hand, then with our arms around each other. She held me tightly and gently massaged my hand.[17] I really felt special. I never felt that feeling of affection and embrace as I did tonight. In Big Boy, we held hands under the table, even though I was doing funny things in excess[18] (nervous energy, I guess). After that, Nancy and I went to get the car to pick up Scott and Kelly. (Scott was still eating.[19]) In the car, Nancy sat right close next to me and held my hand. I had always wanted to have a girl that would sit next to me while I drove[20] (high aims in life, eh?). We picked up Scott and Kelly, dropped them off at their car, and I rushed Nancy right home, because she had to be in by

15. This sentence was heavily influenced by an episode of *The Brady Bunch*, in which Bobby Brady would see fireworks whenever he'd kiss a girl named Millicent, thus showing you the caliber of my sexual references. Thanks, Mike Lookinland!

16. The same restaurant I met Stacey in. Who knew the place I used to eat with my grandma would turn out to be such a love shack?

17. Not quite sure how that worked, but I remember it was nice, despite how odd it sounds. My descriptive skills were a bit lacking back then. Hey, what'd you expect me to be when I was nineteen? Saul friggin' Bellow?

18. The moral here is that it's not easy to be funny with only one hand. Any amateur comedians among you might want to write that down somewhere.

19. In case you were wondering.

20. I guess she sat next to me better than Nicole did. I didn't realize it was such a specific skill.

eleven (futile![21]*) and it was ten to. We arrived at her house and I walked her to her door. We stood their, holding each other, talking for a long time about when we would meet again. She's still grounded, so I don't know how soon our next date will be (as soon as possible!). However, tomorrow, I'd supposed to go see her at work between 3 and 4. (After my WGRP meeting at eleven). She said she was going to talk to her mother about lifting the grounding. Please lift it! I can't wait until our next date! Finally, I had to let her go. I kissed her goodnight about three times (lost control for a moment!*[22]*) and she went in. I bounded back to my car, bursting with good feelings. I hope this works out, but in moderation. I'm not going to let myself get like I did with Nicole and Stacey (the only other girls I've even dated more than once). I can't go crazy and forget about my career advancements.*[23]* I at least feel that God is helping out by putting this grounding on her.*[24]* This should help moderate me. But, PLEASE, let it work out!*

I have to say that it really *was* a magical evening, despite the embarrassing way in which I wrote about it in my journal. There was something very gentle and tender about Nancy that night that really made her seem like the perfect girl for me. Even though she had freak chick–like outbursts when she was with her friends (swearing, drug and alcohol talk, love of bad heavy metal bands), she could also come off very sweet and innocent when it was just the two of us. I

21. ???
22. Yes, what a wild man I was.
23. Advancements like working at my dad's store cleaning toilets and being in a bad local soap opera that would never see the light of day.
24. There's nothing worse than one of those God-sanctioned groundings.

really, truly did believe I had found the perfect woman. But don't all of us, male and female alike, believe just that in the early stages of any relationship? It's that wonderful period of bliss in which anything can happen, in which yours can become one of the world's greatest romances, the one that reaches the heights of both passion and commitment, the one that inspires poets and young lovers, the fabled "Match Made in Heaven." These times are so profound and so inspiring that we wish we could simply stop time and not let anything change—that we could entomb ourselves and our new loves in amber and create a never-ending moment of perfection.

But, as we all know, we can't. And Time, that heartless bastard, keeps ticking forward and has a tendency to ruin everything.

You can just never tell if Time's going to ruin things quickly or slowly.

9/21/81

Today was the kind of day that you never expect when you wake up. I went to school and it rained, so I got rather wet. (Incidentally, I received a 98% on my first German quiz. Hooray!) I came home after school and, after some guitar—and drumming,[25] I settled down to work on my Astronomy lab report. I hadn't worked on it

25. I was a budding musician back then and had taken years of guitar lessons, which resulted in me being a very mediocre guitarist who fancied himself to be quite good. And so I would daily go into my bedroom, turn up my electric guitar extremely loud, and play along with rock albums. I also had recently started playing the drums and had a small Slingerland jazz kit in my room that I used to pound on for hours. It was all great stress relief, although I'm sure my neighbors wanted to shoot me. And now, back to our story.

for more than a few minutes when the phone rang. It was Nancy and she had gone into work about an hour and a half early so that I could go over and spend some time with her. Well, I rushed right over, after pulling my lunch out of the microwave,[26] and met her in the break room/banquet room.[27] Becky was there also and we all talked and joked around. Then Nancy gave me a stuffed Donald Duck to put in my car, because she knew I liked Donald Duck[28] and she always told me my dashboard was too empty. She also gave me two tapes (Def Leopard and Ozzie Ozborn[29]) to listen to, and two notes she had typed up in school.[30] We then all went over to NBS (Paper Supplies) to pick up some supplies for Bonanza. As we got up to leave, she held my hand and we walked out of Bonanza that way. I felt pretty great. When drove there and back, she sat real close to me and held my hand or my arm, and inside NBS, we walked around with our arms around each other.[31] After that, we came back to Bonanza and it was almost time for her to start work. She told me that her brother, Mike, who is Becky's fiancé, would be at Bonanza tonight and she wanted me to meet

---

26. Don't know if that means I pulled it out and ate it, or just pulled it out. I guess you could probably care less. But I care. Hate to think I wasted food, even in the cause of love.

27. Because there's no better place for a banquet than at a cheap steak house.

28. Yeah, that's right. I liked Donald Duck. What's it to ya?

29. I was never a fan of these bands. I was more of a Ted Nugent fan. I liked bands that did great guitar solos that I could pretend I was playing along to. Bands like Def Leppard and Ozzie weren't garage band enough for me. I liked music that I thought I could play, like the Ramones. Did you really want to know all this? And in a footnote, no less?

30. Now lost to both memory and history. I have no recollection of what they said. Alas.

31. Because what's more romantic than office supplies? Seriously. What is? *Nothing,* that's what!

him. I agreed and kissed her goodbye a few times (Right in the Bonanza![32]) I then went home and polished off a lot of homework. At 7:20, I headed back to Bonanza. I was expecting to stay only 15 minute, while Nancy had her break, but ended up staying almost two hours! You see, it wasn't busy and she didn't have a lot to do, so I was able to stay and talk to her. I even helped her clean up tables and straighten the place up. (I expect a check from Lorne Green[33]) Her brother, Mike, is a nice guy, although I think he had trouble figuring me out. At one point, when Nancy was doing something, I was talking to Mark, a guy who works there. He told me that Nancy really liked me a lot and always talked about me. He said, "You've got nothing to worry about with her." That made me feel great! I've never had anyone tell me that someone feels that way about me. It really seems too good to be true. I keep finding myself saying, "What's the catch?," or, "When am I going to wake up?"[34] When I was leaving, we went out into the little vestibule and, for the first time (ever, I think) I really truly kissed her. It wasn't like Nicole used to give, the ones in which she'd dive at your mouth and lustfully try to eat your face. This one was a slow tender kiss that seemed to make all time stop. It was the perverbial 'fireworks.'[35] For the first time, I was actually kissing somebody, not because I felt I had to or because I had to prove myself, but because I wanted to show someone I truely like very much my true

32. I don't know why that sounds obscene to me now.
33. He was a spokesman for *Bonanza* back then. Ironically, he was also a spokesman for the dog food Alpo at the same time. Write your own jokes.
34. Very soon.
35. Two *Brady Bunch* references in one chapter? I really am a child of the seventies.

feelings. It was a lustful feeling kiss.[36] It was natural. And it was someone who was feeling the same way I was feeling. That was the difference. It was a mutual expression. I came out of it feeling alive and <u>full</u> of happiness and <u>true</u> affection for Nancy. I just hope this isn't a passing thing. God, I hope not. I've decided to give her my class ring next time we see each other.[37] One problem's arisen. She can only go out with me once a week. This may be good right now, though, because this way my productivity shouldn't drop and I should be able to do all my homework successfully. I hope so. Goodnight, Nancy.

Let it be known here that I've always had a very strong Protestant work ethic that was drilled into me by my father. One of the biggest reasons for this is that my mother's youngest brother, my uncle Bill, was the black sheep of our family because he was never able to keep a job. This was basically because he didn't want to. He was what my dad would occasionally refer to as any of the following: A Man of Leisure; Lazy; A Little Off; A Bum; A Schnook; Very Sad; Driving Me Crazy; Someone Who Needs to Meet a Rich Widow; An Expert on Classical Music Because All He Does Is Sit Around All Day and Listen to It; and Someone You *Don't* Want to Become Like. And so I've lived my entire life since childhood afraid that I had some dormant Uncle Bill gene in my DNA that was going to kick in and turn me into a guy who decided it was easier to sponge off relatives like my father (who always gave Bill money because "like it or not, family always takes care of family")

36. I'm pretty certain I meant to write "It *wasn't* a lustful feeling kiss." But who knows? I was a bundle of contradictions back then.
37. No, this was not the 1950s. I actually thought that guys still gave their girlfriends their class rings back then. I think I had watched one too many episodes of *Happy Days*.

than to hold down an actual job. And so phrases like "because this way my productivity shouldn't drop" were a big part of my vocabulary back then.

And this was something that Nancy didn't know about me.

Sorry about not writing last night. I've started doing exercises before bed and last night they tired me out.[38] *Well, things are pretty much the same. Nancy and I are getting along better each day, although yesterday I thought I had lost her for sure. For some reason I can't explain (besides pronounceation problems), I called Nancy "Nicole." I almost died. She was very upset and I think I was more upset that she was. For a few minutes, I had the terrible feeling that everything we had toward in our relationship would come crashing down before me. I'll never forget that feeling as long as I live.*[39] *I broke out into a cold sweat and felt suddenly dizzy and nauseas, as if I was about to loose an important part of myself. Thankfully, she finally forgave me, although I've got this sinking feeling that it hurt her bad. I felt a little uneasiness when we were together today. I hope to God she forgives me. The honest fact of the matter is, I don't even know why I said it! Ever since I met Nancy, I've subconsciously been mixing it up with the name "Nicole." I guess maybe I said the name Nicole so much before Nancy that the fact that the first letter and the meter of the word automatically slip my mouth into a*

----

38. I believe I used to do 20 push-ups and 20 sit-ups. Please feel free to draw your own conclusions about my athletic stamina from this.
39. And I haven't. Seriously. It was awful.

familior word. I don't know but I've got to make sure it <u>never</u> happens again. If it did, it'd be the end, I know it. Now, Nancy thinks I've still got feelings for Nicole when the absolute truth is that I never want to see Nicole again after the things she said to me on the phone that day.[40] Oh, Nancy, the things I put you thru! Please, don't let me mess this one up!!!!!!!

Today, I went up to Bonanza to see Nancy twice. Neither time did she sound too well—she says she's sick. I think she's just very nervous about her job interview tomorrow. She's interviewing to be a secretary at a Law firm. If she gets it, her hours will be during the week only and she'll probably get more money. I know she'll get the job. She's got want it takes. (And extra to burn). If it's right, she'll get it. I want only the best and right things in the world to happen to my little girl. God guides and watches over all. Today, I gave her my ring.

These last six sentences make me want to get in a time machine, set it to 1981, go up to the nineteen-year-old Paul Feig while he was writing this, and slap the shit out of him.

I can only imagine how you must feel.

9/27/81

Howdy! Quite a change from the last entry, eh? I feel a lot better now, a whole lot better. Things are going just great between Nancy and myself. We went out last night

---

40. It was an angrier rehash of Nicole's "What do you want to be? King of the Tour Guides?" speech, albeit with more mocking of me, since I had returned to Michigan after a summer in Hollywood no more famous than I was when I left. By Michigan standards, if you go to Hollywood and don't get discovered within a few days, you're a show biz failure.

and it was <u>GREAT</u>! (Wow!) I was a little worried when it started off, because we went to Lakeside, and Nancy got rather upset because I didn't want to look in the jewelry stores. She called me a 'cheapskate,' although she was just kidding. (She better have been. I bought her eight dollars worth of buttons, a leather tie for 12.50[41] and we went to the movies. For someone who's unemployeed, that a pretty expensive night.[42]) Then, after Lakeside, we drove around trying to decide what to do. We went by her brother Mike's house but he wasn't home. (Thank goodness! We never would have ended up where we finally did!) So, we finally decided to go to a movie. She suggested the Drive-in and I reluctantly accepted (Are you kidding? I had us there in two seconds![43]) The movies were the 'Blues Brothers' and 'Contenental Divide.' Good thing I'd already seen them, because I didn't see more than three minutes of movie the whole night. (Whoa!!![44]) It was great! The whole way home, she sat right next to me and kept kissing me. She calls me "Pumpkin", "Sweetheart" and "Honey" and I just melt like butter at any one of them.

41. There is no more 1981 of a comment than this reference to a leather tie. Yes, friends, I too used to wear one. We thought they were cool back then. All because of a band called the Romantics, who wore red leather suits and ties on their album cover.

42. I was working at my father's store during this time, so I have no idea why I wrote this. Probably just to add to the drama of all the money I spent. Who I was adding drama for I have no idea. God, maybe? No, He knew I was working for my dad. I guess it'll remain one of those mysteries of history. Just not a very interesting one.

43. Comedy!

44. My best friend Craig and I used to do constant imitations of Popeye the Sailor, and our favorite thing to say was "Whoa!" in a Popeye voice, in the same way that Popeye would say it when he'd see something surprising. Just thought you should know.

It's here that I have to get into the whole issue of censorship. Or namely, my censorship of myself.

This takes me back to one of the reasons that I think journals are by nature sort of a bad idea. Because, unless you really don't care what the world thinks of you or you really plan on never letting *anyone* see your journals, even after you die, then you tend to censor yourself when you write in them. You have to. Because you have to figure that at some point somebody you know is going to read them. And, most important, you have to assume that the love interest about whom you write your most private thoughts is going to be the very person who will end up sitting down with your journals after you've been together long enough and go through them to trace the history of your wonderful relationship together. And because of this, you tend to create a rosier picture of your feelings toward that person and your descriptions of your times together than you would if you thought you would eventually be breaking up with that person and removing any chance that he or she would ever have access to this record of your innermost thoughts.

Or at least I did. What I failed to mention about Nancy in my journal was that she was a smoker. I made reference to her asking me what I thought about girls who smoked in my euphoric 9/18 entry but never made any mention of it again. This was because I didn't want her (or myself) to know that I disapproved of it, and I also wasn't sure if God was checking in on me when Nancy was smoking or just reading the CliffsNotes of my relationship with her via my journal. I was sure that He wouldn't approve, and I didn't want anything to get in the way of my love for Nancy.

But she was a whole new experience for me. I had known plenty of girls in school who smoked, and I always tried hard not to show my disapproval of this for fear of looking uncool. But I had never dealt with a smoker up close and personal, and I had definitely never kissed a girl who smoked before. At first, Nancy would try to mask it from me by chewing gum or eating Lifesavers. But as the days went on and we got closer and closer, she started caring less and less about hiding it. Very soon she was smoking the entire time we were together. There was a short period where I found this slightly appealing, as if I were a worldly, sophisticated guy who had a worldly, sophisticated girlfriend.

But very quickly her smoking lost its appeal. Her mouth tasted steely and cold whenever we would French-kiss, and my car and clothes were starting to reek of secondhand smoke. What was worse was that she was a smoker who had no concept of the migratory patterns of smoke and ash and how these were affected by drafts and wind directionality. Hence her smoke would usually be wafting straight into my face no matter where I sat or how much I tried to secretly blow it away from me. I soon started making comments about it, and she would apologize and switch the cigarette to the opposite hand in order to keep the smoke away from me. But quickly she'd forget and I'd once again find myself feeling as if a farmer was burning a pile of leaves in front of my face. I eventually started making a bigger deal out of it, giving speeches about the unhealthy aspects of smoking, and she'd give me a condescending kiss and say, "I love that you care about me," and then continue chain-smoking like an ex-hooker at an AA meeting. Soon, my sermons about the dangers of cigarettes elicited only one of two responses from her:

1. She would roll her eyes and sigh impatiently, as if I were her squaresville father and she was a bratty teenager in a 1950s sitcom, or
2. She would yell, "Get off my back. God! Who are you? My fucking mother?"

I didn't know where the sweet and tender girl I thought I knew would go in those moments, but it was becoming more and more apparent that she was fading further and further into the distance after each outburst. It wasn't that Nancy was getting meaner. It was just that she was getting more and more comfortable with me, which meant that she was trying less and less to cover up her true personality, which was looking less and less compatible with mine.

Which is usually when the problems begin.

9/29/81

Yawn! Boy, I'm bushed! I'm not talking about being tired because of staying up too late (although I am). I'm talking about everything. School is loading me down terribly. My last two semesters weren't half this bad. This semester's terrible. (Workwise, that is. I still enjoy the classes.[45]) I finally finished my short story for English. 16 typed pages! I did it again! Just like last year in script class when we had to write part of a movie script. We only had to do fifteen pages. I go and do fourty five.[46] Oh well, at least I'm ambitious. (Masocistic is more the word[47].) Now, something in my life is contributing to my lack of homework time. I'll give you a hint—she's beautiful and swears a lot. Congratulations! You guessed!

45. Self-censorship again. I didn't want the eternally kibitzing God to think I was being ungrateful for the college education I was getting.
46. Fortunately, this script, about a guy who moves to the big city to make a name for himself and ends up becoming a bellhop, has never seen the light of day.
47. Actually, neither word is right. I'll get back to you when I think of a better one.

Nancy. Boy, I tell you, this has got to stop.[48] I'm falling behind. Everyday, she calls up. 'Come and see me at work.' 'Well, Nancy, I've really got a lot of homework.' 'Oh, just come up for a little while.' 'But, honey, I've really got a lot of work.' 'Well, piss on you!' 'Alright, I'll be up in a minute.' The story of my life. This can't go on. I feel like I'm bloody married.[49] Oops, don't say that word.[50] She is actually talking about marriage, or at least living together. Hold on! I'm only 19, she's only 17, and I have absolutely no intentions of even thinking about getting married until I'm at least 25. (And even that's too soon for me) She gets upset, really upset, every-time she mentions living together and I don't say any-thing.[51] Brother! I'm still a kid.[52] I'm not getting married yet. I'm not even toyying with the idea. I don't know what I'm going to do. I like her a whole lot, but I don't even want to be serious. I've got to do something. She wrote me a letter today that said she would literally die if our relationship ended. Oh, great! How do I get myself into these things?! I went over her house tonight for what I thought would be about two minutes. Ha! I ended up staying an hour and a half. She was wise to my feelings, though, because she kept saying "You don't like me as much as I like you." It's not that. I like her alot. I'm just afraid to do anything to make her more serious

---

48. Uh-oh.
49. Note the influence of the Monty Python comedy troupe in my anachronis-tic-for-Michigan use of the word *bloody*.
50. "Married," not "bloody."
51. Before you judge me too harshly, keep in mind that I had only known her for two weeks.
52. Yes, a big voting-age, draft-age, old-enough-to-drink-in-Canada kid.

about us. What happens? I come home with two hickeys!
My first! How embarrassing! I forgot about them, and
Mom and Dad saw them. Boy, did I get razzed! Brother!
I'll have to figure something out. Maybe I'll go back
to CA.

The "Evening of the Hickeys," as I like to refer to it, went something like this:

I went over to her house even though I had tons of homework to do. When I got there, Nancy wanted me to sit and watch TV with her. As I begrudgingly did, she sat next to me and tried to get me to make out with her, despite the fact that her mother and stepfather were visible in the very next room. For obvious reasons, I wasn't comfortable with that and so, as a "joke," Nancy slapped me really hard across the face. She thought it was funny but, I'm ashamed to admit, it was the only time in my life that I almost hit a girl. It was such a shock and it hurt so much that I had a moment where all the angst I had ever built up inside me from all the bullying I put up with in school almost burst out of me. Of course I didn't do anything, but I was really mad. And the fact that she was laughing at my anger made me even madder. As I sat and stewed, Nancy tried to make it up to me. She did this by softly kissing my neck, which definitely had the desired effect of diluting my anger. However, I soon felt a stinging sensation on my jugular vein and quickly realized that I was getting the first hickey I'd ever received.

A jolt of panic ran through me as I suddenly had visions of walking around my college campus with a mark on my neck that would tell strangers far more about my private life than I wanted them to know. Plus, a hickey just seemed like such a stupid thing for a nineteen-year-old to have. And so I tried to pull away.

However, Nancy held the back of my neck in order to keep her mouth locked on my jugular like a vampire. I tried to get her to disengage but she wouldn't. The stinging on my neck where her lips were sucking was becoming quite painful, and I could tell that she was going to give me the biggest, darkest hickey ever unless I did something quickly. And so, in a panic, I placed my hands on her forehead and ignominiously pried her face away from my neck as if I were Superman trying to pry a killer octopus off my body. It was a real struggle and she fought against my hands so hard that I was worried I was going to break her neck. Finally, I found the strength to overpower her and she fell back onto the couch, surprised.

"God, thanks a lot!" she said, indignant. "Real romantic!"

"I just don't want a hickey, that's all," I said, just as indignant.

"Why? Are you ashamed of me or something?" she shot back.

"No! I just don't want one. It has nothing to do with you."

And this was when she got a very hurt look and said, "You don't like me as much as I like you."

I, of course, folded immediately, not wanting her to be mad at me, and so fell all over myself to prove that I liked her as much as she liked me. I then gave in to making out with her, once her mom and stepdad headed off to bed. By the time I left, Nancy thought everything between us was better than ever.

When I got home, I had forgotten about the hickey incident and so came in and said hi to my parents, who were watching the news. My mother saw me, gasped, and then started laughing. "I know what you've been doing," she said in a singsongy voice that immediately creeped me out. My dad looked over, said, "Have a good evening, Romeo?" and then also started laughing. I dashed off to the bathroom as my parents' hysterics drowned out the television. When I looked in the mirror, I saw exactly what I had been afraid of—a huge, dark red hickey the size of a walnut on the side of my neck.

I was branded.

The next day, I got up early for my classes and cautiously looked in the mirror. Having never had a hickey before, I was hoping that maybe it went away overnight. Unfortunately, if anything, the hickey had gotten even darker. The idea of walking around with a huge hickey at my college, where I was surrounded by smart people and where I was trying to reinvent myself as an intellectual to those who didn't know my nerdy past, was as abhorrent to me as walking around campus wearing a Snuggles the Bear T-shirt.

And so I pulled the only turtleneck sweater I owned out from the bottom of my dresser drawer. And despite the fact that the temperature that day was in the upper seventies, I wore it to Wayne State University, my blood-red hickey hidden beneath a double-thick layer of sweat-inducing wool.

After classes, I drove over to Bonanza, since I had promised Nancy I would stop by to say hello. When I walked in the door and she saw me from the register, her face fell. She then ran into the back of the restaurant. I saw her friend Kelly run after her as I stood there, completely confused. After a minute, Kelly came out of the back and said to me, "Nancy's really upset with you."

"Why?" I asked cluelessly.

"Because you're wearing a turtleneck," she said, looking at me like I was the most thoughtless man who ever walked the earth. "You're covering up the hickey she gave you."

The fact that Nancy had told Kelly and probably everybody else in the restaurant about my hickey made me feel like storming out of the place.

"I was cold this morning," I lied, hoping to end this ridiculous discussion. Little did I know that it was about to get even more ridiculous.

"No, you weren't," she said accusingly. "You were trying to hide it. I mean, how would you feel if you gave Nancy a diamond ring and she didn't wear it?"

There's a type of logic where, once you're confronted with it, you realize that it's so absurd and so outside the realm of rationality that you immediately know you're better off extracting yourself from the argument altogether than getting drawn into its futility.

And so I ended up going into the break room and apologizing to a tearful Nancy for the sin of having worn a turtleneck sweater to college that day. As she sniffled at me through red eyes and said that she was only trying to show the world how much she cared about me by giving me the hickey in the first place, we hugged and she forgave me. And I spent the rest of the day realizing that I was no longer enjoying this relationship.

Things started going downhill from there. Nancy was trying harder and harder to use her sexual attractiveness to lure me deeper into a committed relationship. I now believe she was simply desperate to move out of her house and into an apartment with me, her boyfriend whose father owned a successful army surplus store. We continued making frequent visits to the local drive-in theater, but these sessions were starting to become more and more uncomfortable as Nancy began to lobby for us to go "all the way." But knowing that this would only make it even harder to extract myself from our failing relationship, as well as the fact that I was still too afraid to have sex, I of course refused to give in. The furthest sexually I had taken our make-out sessions was lying on top of her fully clothed as we kissed passionately on the front seat of my car. She started trying to convince me that we should undress each other but, alas, this only resulted in her becoming the recipient of my tried and tested "virtues of abstinence" speeches I had perfected with Nicole a half year earlier.

However, Nancy was in it for the long haul, clearly figuring that I could be broken down if she invested enough time and pressure on my libido.

And I again started becoming more and more obsessed with getting out of the relationship.

10/22/81[53]

Well, today I talked to Nancy. I broke the four day avoidance period. She caught me when I got home from the library. It was nice these last few days, not thinking about or talking to her. I like being on my own. (In the girlfriend sense) . . .

Lest you think me a terrible person (as opposed to the annoying, immature one I was), there was a very good reason why I wanted to avoid Nancy:

Our last date had not been a good one.

Another Farm City Week–type event was taking place in downtown Mt. Clemens, and I wanted to go. I had a sincere

53. Notice that almost a month has passed since my last entry. There's no better indication of a waning romance than the loss of desire to write about it. Let the downfall begin!

desire that maybe Nancy and I could recapture the magic that occurred between us the last time we went to a festival downtown. Perhaps another display of fireworks could reignite the fireworks I had felt for Nancy our first evening together. The problem was that Nancy didn't want to go. She wanted to go back to the drive-in. However, I was able to guilt her into attending the downtown event by making a big deal about how I had taken her to an intolerable Triumph concert the week before and so she "owed it to me" to do something I wanted to do. She huffily agreed and I immediately knew things were not going to go well.

We parked our car and walked into downtown Mt. Clemens. The place was absolutely packed, food stands lining the streets and crowds of happy, laughing people sardined into the main drag. We started to work our way through the crowd, which was clearly beyond legal capacity. It's here I have to tell you that Mt. Clemens has a large African-American community and at that moment the throng around us was mostly black. I could feel Nancy's growing anger at the difficulty we were having getting through the crush of people around us, but I had no idea that what was about to happen was about to happen.

We hit an impasse of people and suddenly I felt Nancy jerk her hand out of mine and give a loud, annoyed sigh— the kind of sigh you give when you want everyone within earshot to know you're upset. I turned to look at her and tell her not to lose her temper when suddenly Nancy screamed out at the top of her lungs, "GOD, I HATE NIG—"

BOOM!!! A huge firework went off in the sky above us, miraculously covering the final syllable of Nancy's horrific racial slur. However, I saw a sea of faces turn and look at Nancy in disbelief. And then slowly I saw those faces turn and look at me, the only other white person within twenty feet of her. I was so shocked and unprepared for what Nancy had just done that my stomach couldn't even drop into my shoes like it normally did when something terrible happened. All I could think was that I had to immediately disown Nancy, who had made her own bed with this hateful and ill-advised moment of prejudice, and get the hell out of there. And so I immediately looked away from Nancy as if I'd never seen her before in my life, shrugged a "What's *her* problem?" look at the people in front of me, and continued out of the crowd.

When I reached the end of the street, miraculously Nancy was still behind me. Either people hadn't really heard what she said or they simply figured she was some trailer trash girl whom it wasn't worth confronting. I was so angry with her and so desperate to get away from her for fear that she'd do something else just as stupid and awful that I kept walking. She yelled for me to wait up and I proceeded to go on a tirade about what she just did, and she yelled back at me that if I had just agreed to go to the drive-in like she wanted to, it never would have happened. I ended up driving her home early. She attempted to save the evening, moving over close to me as I drove and telling me that she was sorry, that she didn't know why she had done what she did, that she really wasn't prejudiced, and that it was all probably because it was "that time of the month." (I wasn't aware that racism was a side effect of menstruation.) When we reached her house, I gave her a terse "good-bye" and drove off into the night. And that was why I started avoiding her calls. Why I didn't break up with her is just more proof of what a huge wussy I was. But that was about to change.

The breaking up part, that is. Not the wussy part.

Boy, oh, boy. What a weekend! (That doesn't mean it was good, incidently) It happened! I didn't think it would, although I wanted it to, but it happened! I broke up with Nancy. That's right. I felt great right after it, free at last. Now, though, I feel lousy. Terrible. I don't know why. I guess I feel bad. Nancy was so upset. I didn't want to make anyone mad. But it had to happen. For her sake as well as mine. She wouldn't have been happy with my avoidance antics and I just plain wasn't happy. I'm sure I'll get over this depression. One thing's for sure. I'm staying away from girls, at least for a few years (if not longer).[54] You think I would have learned my lesson with Nicole. But NO![55] I had to go and get involved again. Gosh,[56] I've only had two girlfriends and I haven't had a healthy two way relationship yet. I'm not sure what my idea of a perfect relationship is, but I think it's lots of love, a common intellectual level, and a lot of freedom. Call me a dreamer, but that's it. I'm so sorry if I hurt you, Nancy.

I finished my short story yesterday and I love it. It's called <u>A</u> <u>Grain</u> <u>of</u> <u>Sand</u> and it's about a comet hitting the earth and starting a nuclear war.

Good that I was able to funnel my angst over the breakup with Nancy into global destruction.

I wish I could say that this final Nancy entry was the

---

54. And the collective sigh of relief from womankind was deafening.
55. Credit John Belushi for this comment. Yet another pilfered catchphrase from my old lexicon of other people's comedy.
56. Notice attempt not to take the Lord's name in vain.

result of me making a mature decision that our relationship was unworkable, which then motivated me to go directly to her house and tell her it was over between us.

But, of course, I can't.

I can only tell you what really happened.

Nancy and I headed to the drive-in for yet another evening of making out and sex avoidance, and I was miserable. However, Nancy had clearly made up her mind that on this night, no matter what it took, we were going to have sex. She had apparently been fighting with her mother lately and was desperate to move out once and for all, and I was still her only ticket to housing freedom. I, on the other hand, had decided the exact opposite—that *nothing* sexual was going to happen between us. I wasn't even going to make out with her. My angst about our failing relationship had driven me to become even more moralistic than usual and so I was as ready as Billy Graham in a revival tent to make a religious case for abstinence that would make all my past temperance speeches pale in comparison. So adamant was I that this evening was going to have nothing romantic about it that I brought along my Star Tracker night sky map, which was a rotating cardboard wheel from my astronomy class about the size of a Frisbee that allowed the amateur stargazer to find all the celestial bodies in the autumn sky. It was hidden under the driver's seat, and I was determined that tonight Nancy would simply watch the movie and I would watch the nebula in Orion's Belt.

Once we pulled into our usual spot and the movie started, one of the strangest hour-and-a-half periods of my life took place between Nancy and myself.

Nancy kept trying to start a hot and heavy make-out session, and I was doing everything under the sun to stop her. But in order to keep her from getting mad, I kept going into joke overdrive, making goofy faces and doing voices and imitations of her trying to seduce me, for the express purpose of killing the mood. For the first half hour, she thought it was just me being cute and entertaining, as if part of my foreplay was to soften her up by tickling her funny bone (which, in happier times between the two of us, it actually was).

However, she slowly began to catch on that my nonstop vaudeville act was truly the most attention I intended to give her that evening. She finally sat back up in the passenger's seat, crossed her arms, and huffed an angry sigh, pretending she had decided to give up on me and watch the movie. This was when I ill-advisedly turned up the knob on the confrontation index by pulling out my Star Tracker sky map and looking up and out of the driver's side window at the heavens. This was the final blow for Nancy, and so, at long last, began my very first actual breakup.

I quickly decided, as most nonconfrontational people do in situations like this, to blame the entire failed relationship on myself. When she asked me why I didn't seem to like her anymore, I went on a grand dissertation about how I didn't know what was wrong with me, about how stupid and confused I was, and about how Nancy would probably have to suffer through endless years of my indecision and immaturity and selfishness if she and I were to stay together. At first, she took everything I was saying as a cry for help, as if I was asking her for assistance in fixing a personal shortcoming I desperately wanted to change. When she moved close and said, "We'll work through all your problems together," I knew that this strategy wasn't going to work.

And yet I didn't know what else to do.

And so I simply ratcheted up the bad-mouthing of myself, eventually saying that I was nothing short of a mental patient who was psychologically incapable of having any kind of relationship with a woman. I became so convincing, at one point even bringing up the history of mental illness that has appeared from time to time on my mother's side of the family, that I was sure I could see in Nancy's face a fear that she was with someone who might actually be dangerously unstable.

However, as luck would have it, Nancy wasn't buying a word of it.

She gave me a long, angry look and said, "Why won't you have sex with me? Even crazy people have sex, you know."

I tried to go into the "virtues of waiting" sermon but she abruptly cut me off.

"Don't you know it's not even good for you to not have sex?" she said indignantly. She then pointed at my groin and, making a vague circular gesture that I knew was meant to indicate all things relating to my sex organs, said, "That stuff gets all backed up in your balls if you don't let it out and then you get cancer." And then she added, with great disdain, "Unless you play with yourself or something."

The turn of the conversation left me feeling embarrassed, trapped, and out of ammunition, like when you try to argue politics with someone who has a million facts and statistics that you've never heard before. But it was her indignation at the idea that someone would "play with" himself that threw me the most. I wanted to become indignant back at her, asking if she believed guys were never supposed to masturbate and hence only vent their pent-up sexual energy by having casual sex with women, whether they liked them or not. But to say that would be to admit to Nancy that I did indeed "play with" myself, and she had suddenly made me wonder as much as the Jamaican deejay did years earlier if my history of self-love was perverted and wrong, and if it had killed my desire for a normal sex life. However, I quickly realized I could use this debate to my advantage.

"Look," I said, as if making a huge admission. "I'm just not that interested in sex."

This seemed to stop her cold in her tracks. "What do you mean?" she asked, brow furrowed. "How can you not be interested in sex?"

"I'm just not, that's all." And suddenly I saw my way out of the relationship.

I was going to be the guy who loves life so much that he's transcended the physical world.

I launched into a variation of my abstinence speech, but this time it was from the artist's point of view. I talked about all that the world has to offer, about all the spiritual energy that was around us but which was going undetected because we as humans were so centered on the confines of our bodies that we were unprepared to receive the higher planes of thought that were there for the taking, if only we could dig ourselves out of the material world. Truth be told, everything I was saying was a simplistic fusion of things I had learned in Sunday school, coupled with a heavy mishmash of ideas I had learned when we studied Eastern religions in my old high school sociology class, along with themes from the speeches Ruth Gordon's character had made in the film *Harold and Maude*. Whether the actual concepts I was putting forth were convincing her of my advanced spiritual state or simply making her realize the guy she thought was her boyfriend was clinically insane, I could tell that this strategy was going to work. After what seemed like an endless monologue from me, Nancy sat back heavily in the passenger seat of my car, sighed loudly, and said, "So . . . you're breaking up with me?"

I wasn't looking for it to be put so bluntly but, seeing

the escape hatch wide open and beckoning me to jump through it, I looked at her and said, "Uh . . . yeah. Kinda."

She stared at me for what felt like several years and then said, "Take me the fuck home."

We drove back in silence, her hurt and angry energy filling the car as if someone were pumping poisonous gas into my Dodge Coronet. But I knew that if I could just get her back to her house and out of the car without her killing me, I would be free.

We pulled into her driveway and I expected her to bolt out of the car. However, she didn't. She just sat there. Very quiet. And very upset.

I got out of the car and opened her door. She put her hand over her face as if she was going to cry and then sighed painfully, as if the reality of the breakup was finally sinking in. She then put her hands back down angrily, mad at herself for showing me that she was sad. She got out of the car and started toward her door.

I was compelled to try to make things better before I left. I just couldn't dump her and drive off into the night, not after all the romantic energy we had expended on each other since we'd met. And so I stopped her at the door. Trying to be like the actors I had seen in TV shows and movies, I took her hands in mine and faced her. She looked off to the side, avoiding eye contact, shifting uncertainly. I stared at her, trying to get her to look at me. I said her name gently, kindly, trying to show her how sincerely I wanted to say something nice to her. After I said her name a second time, she looked at me. I could see in her eyes that she was hoping I was going to say I was reconsidering, that this was just a weird evening that had gone wrong but which I was now going to repair. Don't crack, I told myself. Just get her to not hate you.

"Nancy," I said softly, "I care about you. Very much. And you'll see. This is all for the best." And then, wanting to send her off on an inspirational note, as if I were the kung fu master and she were one of my prized students heading out into the world, I did something that even today I cringe at.

I gave her the moon.

No, I didn't pull my pants down and show her my bare ass. I gave her the moon that was hanging above us in the night sky.

The irony is that I hadn't seen *It's a Wonderful Life* at that point in my life, which would at least provide an excuse for doing something so misguided. Unfortunately, this was something I thought of all by myself. And while it's a really romantic moment in the Jimmy Stewart–Donna Reed holiday classic, I'm here to tell you, as a friend, that it's a really bad idea to do in real life. Especially when you've just broken up with someone.

It went like this:

Nancy had said, "So, you're just going to leave me and that's it? That's it between us?"

I said, "It's just the beginning for both of us. We have our whole lives ahead of us. We can do whatever we want. The possibilities are endless."

She said, "But I'm supposed to do it without you? You're just going to go off and I'm supposed to be all happy for you? That's fucked."

I once again went into spiritual guy overload when I saw that she was on the verge of yelling at me. I looked up into the clear Michigan night sky. It was there I saw the full autumn moon. I was certain this would be the perfect thing to say, and I couldn't imagine that my poetic words wouldn't leave her affected, moved, changed.

I gave her a beneficent smile, my love of life and everything within it beginning to swell like the Grinch's heart when he decides to pull the sled filled with toys back up from over the edge of the cliff and save Christmas. "Nancy," I said, gesturing grandly with my hand toward the moon in one fluid, graceful motion, "I give you the moon."

She looked at me and her eyelids went to half-mast, the kind of look that a woman gives you while she's trying to decide if she's going to kick you in the balls or not. But I pressed on, convinced that I could make her see the greatness of my magical gift to her.

"I give you the stars," I continued, sweeping my hand across the heavens and then down to show her the neighborhood she'd never noticed until this night. "I give you the trees, the grass, the people, the wind, the air," I intoned mystically, looking around as if seeing the world for the first time. "I give you life, and everything within it. I give you the chance to do whatever you want, to be whatever you want to be, to discover all that is out there. To live this life to its fullest. Go out and make the world yours." I looked back at her, expecting that she would have tears of joy in her eyes. However, all that was there was the look that said she was now certain I was the biggest jackass who ever walked the earth.

"You know what?" she said in a tone that sounded like she wanted to kill me, as all the air seemed to deflate out of her body. "Forget it. Just get out of here. Good night, good night." She said these final good nights in that sarcastic, dismissive tone you use when you realize you can't reason with someone and so are telling them to go fuck themselves. And, with that, she turned, went into her house, and slammed the door.

Once again, like I had with Nicole, I made a big show of standing and staring up at the stars in a spot in which I knew she could see me if she peeked out her front window. I sighed grandly, hoping to show her that the breakup was hurting me as much as it was hurting her. I then walked slowly over to my car, got in sadly, and pulled away, feeling pretty certain that she hadn't bothered to watch any of my pathetic performance.

Unlike the moment when I had happily left Nicole in the dust for the green pastures of Hollywood, this time I suddenly felt really terrible. I was relieved that I had broken up with Nancy, but I also realized that I had *actually broken up with Nancy*—that there was no going back, that all the things I had enjoyed about our relationship were as gone as the things I couldn't stand about it. All those moments of excitement, of helium-filled chests and butterfly-filled stomachs that occur when you first fall in love, they were all gone. They might as well have never existed. All the things I found attractive about Nancy, all the energy I spent hoping she would fall for me, all the energy I spent praying that she would be the perfect mate I had dreamed about since I was little—they all meant nothing now. Nancy hated me.

By the time I pulled into my driveway, I felt absolutely awful.

As I walked down the hall to my bedroom, I passed my dad's den. He was working at his small desk as he did every night, going over the balance sheets and accounts for his army surplus store, his reading glasses sitting halfway down the bridge of his nose as he went over columns of numbers that I never understood my entire childhood. I slowed down as I passed his doorway, hoping that he would notice me and ask me how my evening was and that we'd play cribbage. He was staring intently at a number he had totaled up and let out an aggravated sigh. I saw this as a signal that we wouldn't be sharing any father-son moments this evening and kept walking.

"How was your evening?" he said just as my hand was reaching out to open my bedroom door. I thought about simply saying "fine," as I had done on so many other occasions when my father had asked me that question, figuring that my moment of wanting to tell him my problems had already passed. However, I suddenly found myself standing in his doorway, leaning awkwardly against the frame, trying to act cooler than I wanted to be at that moment. He stared at me over his reading glasses, and I immediately felt a wave of sadness.

"I broke up with Nancy," I said with a shrug that attempted to relay a casual attitude. Apparently it wasn't working.

"I know what you're going through," he said, taking off his glasses and setting them on his paperwork. "I remember breaking up with an old girlfriend of mine once. I really felt awful afterward. I think I even cried when I got home."

Suddenly wanting to tell him everything, I simply said, "Yeah, I know. I feel terrible."

"Well," he said with a small exhale, "you're young. Better not to tie yourself down. Not if it doesn't feel right."

"It didn't," I said. "I really liked her for a while, though."

"Well," he chuckled supportively, "that's why you date."

"Yeah," I sighed. "'Night."

"You'll get over it. And so will she."

"Thanks." Then I gave him a look. ". . . I think."

He laughed and I went into my bedroom. And that night, as I lay awake until about four in the morning, I wondered how much Nancy was hating me at that moment. And I wondered how long I would feel as bad as I did.

It was only many, many years later, when I was living in California and received a call from Nancy, who had called my aging parents to get my phone number, that I realized I had ultimately made the right decision in not staying with her. When I answered the phone and was momentarily happy to hear from her, she said in a teenage tone that was filled with the incredulous judgment of someone who still didn't understand how life worked, "God, your parents sounded so *old*." And after a few minutes of meaningless chatter, and after telling her I had to head out to a meeting that I didn't actually have, and after hanging up the phone, I was happier than ever that I hadn't given in to my teenage hormones way back when at the Macomb Drive-In on Gratiot Boulevard in Mt. Clemens, Michigan, in the fall of 1981.

BOOK FOUR

The Ballad of the Homesick Virgin

The First Verse: Geek in Crisis

Things were going well, post-Nancy.

I had made it through the rest of my sophomore year of college without one date or failed romantic entanglement, and I had kept my nose to the proverbial grindstone, managing not only to ace all of my classes but also to get accepted to the University of Southern California's film school, a place I had found out about during my previous summer as a tour guide.

As I took my final exams in downtown Detroit, I had my future completely figured out:

- I was going to drive back out to California with my mom the day after I finished my exams;
- Move in with a fellow tour guide friend, Will;
- Go to all the movie and TV studios to see if they had any job openings for someone like me and, if not, rejoin the Universal Studios tour guide squad;
- Spend the summer working and saving my money;
- Move into my college apartment at the end of the summer to start my final two years of undergraduate work;
- Do my two years of undergraduate work;

- Graduate;
- And then become a famous actor/writer/director, just like my hero, Woody Allen.

It was the perfect plan.
Which was why it was bound to fail.

It's hard to say why what happened next happened next. Granted, I've always been a sensitive person and was quite a homebody when I was growing up. I seldom went to sleepovers because I liked the safety and comfort of my house and bedroom too much. I even started crying once when I was eight upon hearing the Crosby, Stills, Nash & Young song "Woodstock," because I thought it was about kids leaving their parents and it upset me to think I too might someday want to leave my parents forever (and the thought of having to be a hippie on top of it made the thought all the scarier). But, however neurotic my past was, my emotions still caught me completely off guard this time.

I honestly don't know where the following onslaught of angst came from. It may have partly been that my father and I had recently grown closer, since I was working at his store so often and because we had begun watching *Benny Hill* and Laurel and Hardy shorts together every night on TV and having a great time as we laughed and bonded. It may have partly been that my childhood cat, Tirzah (named by my grandmother after some princess in the Bible, but whom all my friends referred to as "Turds-ah"), had just turned fifteen and was clearly in her final years of life. Or it may have partly been due to the fact that I was now face-to-face with what I knew was the official end of my childhood. It was one thing to graduate from high school and simply commute to college while still living at home, and it was one thing to move away to California for the summer to work as a tour guide, knowing you would be returning in a few months to your old bedroom. But it was a whole other slap of reality to realize that you were heading off for what you knew in your heart was going to be the rest of your life. And this, as I was about to find out, was more than my immature nineteen-year-old brain could take.

As the day of my departure approached, everything I saw made me uncontrollably sentimental and sad—the town where I grew up, the stores where I used to shop, the schools where I used to learn, the streets where I used to ride my bike, the neighbors I used to see every day, my old toys, the cracks in our driveway, the trees in our yard, the wallpaper in our dining room, the plates and cutlery in our kitchen, the freezer filled with ancient ice cream and leftover food, the heater I used to lie in front of to warm my feet in the winter, the old lime green beanbag chair that none of us except Tirzah ever sat in, the closet full of my dad's old coats and hats, the piles of folded grocery bags my mom hoarded in the laundry room, the faded tan aluminum siding on our house, the plaid recliners in our living room, the turquoise blue lamp my mother bought on a public television auction and my father hated, the kitchen stool with a retractable stepladder inside it that I used to pretend was a spaceship with a gangplank, the mustard-yellow princess telephone on our kitchen counter, the vase I broke when I was eight and sloppily glued back together, my parents' bedroom, my dad's den, the laundry room, Tirzah's bowl, the Wacky Packs stickers on my bedroom door and headboard, my grandma's abstract paintings in our living room that nobody but my dad liked, the noisy furnace behind the door in the hallway, the bathtub, the sink, the crocheted toilet paper cover with a fake Barbie doll in the center that was supposed to make the covered roll look like the doll's dress, the Avon bottles shaped like old cars and sports equipment, even the lime-green shag toilet lid cover—it all made me want to burst into tears. It felt like the minute I left the house for California, everything was going to be incinerated or ransacked by looters who would leave these sentimental items broken and scattered all over the street in front of our house.

By the time the day of departure rolled around, I was an emotional wreck. The only person who seemed to be excited about me moving away was my mother. She had loved having me out in Hollywood the previous summer, being her connection to excitement and travel and new things in a world she could only watch on TV, and she was over the moon at the prospect of a cross-country car trip to Los Angeles with her nineteen-year-old son who wanted to be in show business. Alas, her enthusiasm refused to rub off on me, because when it came time for her and me to get into my car, which was packed with my suitcases and guitars and anything else of mine that I thought could make whatever new place I would be living in feel like home, I was a mess.

I walked through our house for the last time like a person preparing to commit suicide. I took in every room, every piece of furniture, every memory that had occurred at any place in the house, whether good or bad—the headboard on my parents' bed upon which I had cracked open my seven-year-old skull while pretending I was on a trampoline; the kitchen table at which my mother had sat my bad-seed friend Randy and me down and lectured to us after we were caught shoplifting; the back door to our house where my father had slipped on the ice when I was five and I saw him lying unconscious and thought he was dead. All these things waved good-bye to me, telling me that the minute I was gone they were going to lose all meaning and become mere objects that had no history and no sentiment—that they would simply return to being the inanimate objects that they in reality were, as if I had never existed with them.

I climbed into my car like I was climbing into the electric chair.

"California, here we come!" my mother said joyfully, as if we were Lucy and Ricky on our way to Hollywood.

I looked out the windshield and saw my father standing and waving merrily. Was he just good at hiding his sadness at my departure or was he actually happy to be getting rid of me? I couldn't tell, but it didn't matter.

I didn't want to leave.

I put the car into reverse and started to back out of the driveway. Raw emotion flew up from my stomach into my throat like vomit and I was suddenly strangled with grief. I stopped the car and started weeping uncontrollably, hiding my face in my hands, embarrassed by my emotional outburst in front of my mother, who seldom displayed emotion of this sort, except when she would burst into tears while talking to Aunt Sue about how terrible Grandma Feig was to her. I was racked with sobs as I sat in my idling car filled with my most essential possessions and my mother sitting in the passenger seat next to me. Looking for help, I forced myself to peer through my fingers to see what my father would think of this outburst. I saw him walking slowly toward the car with a perplexed look on his face that showed he didn't know what was going on. I glanced over at my mother. It was then that I saw her do something that has been seared into my brain ever since: she was doing a charades-quality pantomime of me crying to my father, which involved balling her hands into fists, putting the knuckles of her index fingers into her eye sockets, holding her elbows up and out, and then flapping her bent arms like wings while sticking her bottom lip out and frowning, in order to demonstrate to my father that I was crying like a five-year-old girl. I'm sure my mother didn't mean it to be insulting and yet it was the most disparaging imitation of me I've ever seen before or since. And this is coming from someone who was mercilessly imitated by his peers because of the horrible lisp he had until eighth grade. My mother's performance to my father seemed to be saying, "Your son is having a girly little breakdown. Don't worry about it."

I saw my father give a half-nod, which showed that he understood why I had stopped the car but that he still couldn't quite get his head around the fact that his almost-twenty-year-old son was crying hysterically. And who could blame him? It was exactly one year earlier that Craig and I had backed out of that same driveway in the jolliest of moods, making jokes and waving good-bye as if we were heading off on an ocean voyage like you see in all those old black-and-white movies where people on the dock throw streamers and confetti as the ship pulls out. To him, this departure shouldn't have been any different than that one had been, and yet now his only son was a Water Willy of tears.

The shock of seeing my mother doing such a crude and heartless imitation of me made me find some halfhearted inner strength, and I took my foot off the brake and continued backing out of the driveway. I saw my father wave good-bye again through my tear-blurred eyes. I waved good-bye back, took one last look at the house I grew up in, put my car in drive, and headed off with my mother to California.

Whereas the trip with my pal Craig had been a fun-filled romp—a veritable orgy of Monty Python, Bugs Bunny, and *Star Wars* recitations, offset by in-depth discussions about Craig's newly existent and my nonexistent sex life—it quickly became apparent that a four-day car trip with my mother was going to be something less than fun. Or at least that was what my brain had decided after seeing her Kabuki-like imitation of me crying in our driveway. My mother bravely tried to be merry and act like one of my pals, pointing out funny billboards and turning up the radio and saying horrifying things like "Let's have a singalong" and "What would you and Craig be talking about right now if he were here instead of me?" I, however, was having none of it. It wasn't fun to listen to my favorite music with her in the car, it wasn't fun to joke around with her because she was my mother and so I couldn't talk about anything that I found interesting or amusing, and it wasn't fun to sing songs or play "I Spy" games with her, once again because she had committed the inexcusable act of being my mother. I was angry and depressed and gripped with sadness as I felt the house I grew up in becoming more and more of a distant memory. And by the time we reached our first motel, somewhere in Missouri, my sadness hadn't abated. If anything, it had grown.

We went down to the dismal motel restaurant to eat dinner and my bottoming out continued. As we were eating in the plywood-walled dining room with the glowing salad bar in the corner, I saw a large painting of a leopard on the wall. The jungle cat was lying on a bed of grass in a field with its arms stretched out in front of it and its head up, ears back, staring impassively off into the distance and looking exactly like my cat Tirzah when she'd lie in front of our family room window. I was once again overcome by grief as I stared at the painting and immediately started crying again, my face buried in my hands. The surrounding tables were filled with large older men who looked like they had all served in some arm of the military during World War II, and I could feel their eyes burning into me as they wondered who the faggy nineteen-year-old guy having dinner with his mother and weeping uncontrollably was. My mother, unaccustomed to emotional outbursts from me beyond the age of twelve, made vague attempts to cheer me up by joking, "If you really miss Tirzah that much, I'll put her in a box and send her to you." Knowing that my mother had always hated Tirzah because she had been forced to take care of her all these years, the comment just made me angry. I snapped loudly through my tears, "Fine! Do it! I know it's what you've always wanted!" My regression to being a bratty eight-year-old didn't play any better with the WWII veterans than my crying did, and I looked up to see two of them exchanging eye rolls and head shakes that said if my mother wasn't there, they would probably take me out back and give me something to cry about.

As the trip continued and my mother and I got closer to California, I tried to get myself excited about my new life, but a deep feeling of dread poisoned my every thought. I phoned my friend Will to let him know we were almost there, hoping that talking to my future roommate would generate a fresh vein of enthusiasm but, alas, it only made me sadder as I remembered the rather depressingly dark interior of his apartment that I would now be living in. Will was a vegetarian and so used to steam broccoli for dinner every night, and the whole apartment constantly reeked as if someone who had eaten a plate of asparagus had just peed in the sink. The only thought that had the power to cheer me up was my recently hatched plan of getting a job as a page at one of the television networks. I had seen NBC pages standing in the aisles of *The Tonight Show* for years whenever Johnny Carson would go up into the audience to do a "Stump the Band" segment, and I always noticed that the pages were generally young people. So I was certain that I could go right to NBC, especially being a guy who had just been accepted to the prestigious USC film school and who had previously been a mass communications major at Wayne State (not to mention an amateur stand-up comedian and an actor in school plays), and immediately procure a job as one of the people in the blue blazers who got to hand things to Johnny Carson. Getting a gig like that was my pot of gold at the end of the asphalt rainbow we were driving on, and the more I made myself think about it, the more it made me feel that coming back out to California months before I would be starting college was a good decision after all.

But I was still feeling weird.

My mother and I arrived in Los Angeles, and before even calling Will, we immediately set out to land my job as a page. We drove directly to the NBC studios, which were right down the street from Will's apartment, and went to the reception desk.

"Hi," I said to the receptionist as my mother watched me proudly, excited to be standing in the lobby of the same network that broadcast her favorite soap opera, *Days of Our Lives*. "I was wondering if you have any job openings for pages."

"Pages?" the woman asked with a little laugh that said she was amused at how clueless I was. "I think there's a waiting list. Just a minute."

She then picked up the phone and had the guy in charge of the pages come out to deliver the bad news.

"Look, here's the deal," the man said as we sat on a couch in the lobby, my mother sitting next to me, leaning forward and nodding and saying "Uh-huh" and "Ooooh" in a way that made me want to have her removed by security guards for putting her nose so far into my business. "In order to be a page, you have to have a college degree in either mass communications or television production or business. Then we put you on a waiting list, which at this moment has hundreds of names on it. Then we conduct interviews and hire people accordingly. So, if after you graduate from USC you still want to put your name on the list, we'd be more than happy to have you."

We got up and my mother thanked the man profusely and talked about what a huge fan of Johnny Carson's I was, as if I were her retarded son who hadn't been blessed with the power of speech. I made a big show of thanking the man and saying how I'd see him in two years and said good-bye to the receptionist and smiled at everybody in the lobby and was absolutely dying inside. As I pulled out of the parking lot and my mother consulted the map to figure out how to get to ABC Studios, I felt the icy hand of grief crawling up my throat once again. Everything felt wrong, and everything I saw seemed to be telling me that I shouldn't be in California. My mother asked if I was going to call Will to let him know we had arrived and at what hotel we would be staying, but I told her I would call him later. The truth was that I didn't want to call him because I didn't want to do anything that was going to commit me to staying in Los Angeles at that moment. As we drove through the many depressing, sun-baked parts of Los Angeles trying to find the studios of the American Broadcasting Company, where there would hopefully be much laxer standards for hiring pages, everything I saw pushed me into deeper and deeper depression.

If you've never been to either southern California or Michigan, you have to realize something: the two places couldn't look less like each other. Partly because of weather and climate, and partly because of architectural differences inspired by the preponderance of earthquakes along the West Coast, many parts of Los Angeles tend to be a rather burned-out-looking wash of stucco and concrete, of smog-choked palm trees and dirty sidewalks used primarily by those who can't afford cars. In Michigan, despite the fact that the failing auto industry of the 1970s and early 1980s created a lot of urban and suburban decay, you were always surrounded by the deep green of grass and trees and foliage, as well as the spirit-lifting deep reds of the midwestern brick buildings. Or at least the red bricks had the power to keep *my* spirits lifted, since it was how the place in which I was born and raised looked. The sight of the washed-out, sun-drenched blight that is downtown Hollywood was enough to depress me during the previous summer when I was excited about being a tour guide, but now that I was already unhappy to be back in the Golden State, seeing it all at this moment was driving me into the lowest depths of melancholy.

By the time we arrived at ABC, which looked like a prison compound with a guard gate that I could tell was going to be impossible to talk our way past, I had made up my mind:

There was no way I was going to stay in California this summer.

I simply wasn't ready. I was a victim of my immaturity and I was ashamed of this fact, but I suddenly didn't care. I knew that I had to come back for film school at the end of August, but that was months away and I figured I would just deal with it when the time arrived. There was no way I would be staying in Hollywood again this summer.

And so I informed my mom that I wanted to go back home immediately. She seemed surprised and yet not surprised. I guess the surprised side of her seemed that way more because she was so excited to be out in what she called "La-La Land," a phrase she had heard Merv Griffin use on TV once, and so she had a hard time understanding why I wasn't as excited as she was. I knew she was also thinking, "If he already lived here the previous summer, why isn't he drawn to its show-bizzy charms again?" But the not-surprised side was both the part of her that had watched me cry and be depressed for the past four days and the part that was shocked to find that Hollywood did indeed look like a huge shithole in certain places. And since she was my mother, she supported my decision wholeheartedly. Or so she thought at the moment.

The next day, we set off on our journey back to Michigan. As we were heading out, my mother asked me if I had called my friend Will to tell him that I wouldn't be living with him this summer. I told her I had.

I hadn't.

I couldn't. It was just too embarrassing. I knew that I had to have a better excuse than "I got depressed and missed my dad and my cat" and so figured that during the car ride home I would think of something. Besides, the longer I didn't call, the better chance I had of getting away with some story about a family emergency that had forced me to hurry back to Michigan without time to call the person who was waiting for me to be his roommate and help him with half of his rent.

If the ride out wasn't much fun, the ride home was ten times worse. Even though I was happy to be heading back home to another summer surrounded by family and friends, I was plagued by guilt and embarrassment over my chickening out. On top of this, the excitement of Hollywood at the end of the line that had kept my mother so buoyant and resilient during the trip out west had been replaced by her own depression at knowing her summer was no longer going to be exciting. Instead of getting my phone calls from Universal Studios telling her what stars my tram happened to drive past that day, she would now be treated to the three more months of getting to see me roll out of bed grouchy and disheveled at ten or eleven in the morning. We barely talked the entire four days of driving, and when we did, it was to snap at each other; I in response to her trying-to-make-conversation questions about things I either knew she knew the answers to or things that were not her business to ask me about; and she in response to my snippy one-word responses and grunts. My only desire at that moment was to be driving by myself, alone with my thoughts and music, and her only desire was to have a more exciting life than the one she was now very much aware she had. The four-day trip home hit its lowest point when, on an endless stretch of flat road somewhere in Texas, the song "Danny Boy" came on the radio and my mother started crying uncontrollably over my grandmother who had passed away years earlier. She kept burying her face in her hands and bawling, "Mother used to sing this to me" in a high-pitched wail that broke my heart and also made me want to throw her out of the car. It was one thing for my mother to have to see me have a breakdown, but it was a cardinal sin to force me to watch one of hers.

I arrived back in our house to a father who had figured out that our late-night TV-watching time together had been one of the sources of my homesickness and so now refused to watch anything with me after the eleven o'clock news. He would always say he was tired or that he had reading or work to do and would disappear into his den. I tried to re-create the fun by watching our late-night shows and substituting Tirzah the cat for my father, but she proved to have lost whatever mellow edge old age had given her and refused to sit on my lap to watch *The Benny Hill Show,* instead taking several chunks out of my thigh with her back claws as she fought to free herself from my desperate grasp. Yes, Thomas Wolfe had it right when he said "You can't go home again," and I realized that even though I was glad to be back in Michigan, I was going to have to find something interesting for my embarrassed and immature brain to do that summer.

The Second Verse:
Performance Anxiety

I decided to join the Macomb County Community Theater in my hometown of Mt. Clemens.

I found out that several of the people who had been in *Grease* with me had joined the Macomb troupe and so I figured it would be fun to rebond with them and re-create some of the brilliance we all made onstage together a year and a half earlier. I was certain that news of my bravura performance as Vince Fontaine would have preceded me and that plum roles would be thrown at my feet by the overjoyed directors and producers of this local repertory company. However, when I arrived to grace this band of performers with my talents, they had already cast all the parts in their three musicals and were deep into rehearsals. And so I was offered a lowly place in the chorus of the only show that needed more bodies onstage, *Guys and Dolls*. I was shocked at the squandering of my generous offer to join their theater and quickly told myself I would punish them by withholding my services. However, my indignation lasted about five seconds and I happily agreed to lend my limited singing and dancing skills, despite the fact that I had joined the company so late that the programs had already been printed up without my name in the credits.

Yes, I thought, being in the chorus in Mt. Clemens is *much* better than living in Los Angeles and being a tour guide at a major Hollywood studio. Maybe I can get a job as a paperboy too.

It was that same night I received a call from a person I had completely forgotten about: Will in California. He sounded breathless when I answered the phone. "Where *are* you?!" he said, sounding like he had just run a marathon.

"Oh, hey," I said, immediately kicking myself for having picked up the phone. "I'm back in Michigan. I . . . uh . . . I decided not to stay out there this summer. I got offered a really great part in a play back here."

"And you didn't *call* me?!" His breathless tone was suddenly gone and was now replaced by an anger I had never heard from him before. "I was calling all the hotels, and then when I couldn't find you, I started calling all the hospitals and police stations. I thought you and your mom had gotten kidnapped or killed or something. Why didn't you call me?!"

A hot, prickly heat ran down my back, the kind you feel when you know you did something terrible and now there was nothing you could say in your defense. "Oh, man, I'm sorry. I got so caught up in everything I forgot."

"Yeah? Well, thanks a lot. Have a great time in your little play this summer, *asshole*."

He hung up. I felt awful. The tone he used was the same tone I had worked so hard to avoid having both Nicole and Nancy use when I had broken up with them. Now I felt like I had just experienced my worst breakup yet and it was with a *guy*. I wanted to call back and apologize but the thought of getting yelled at again by a friend I used to joke around with was more than I could take, and so I simply told myself that I would have to get used to the fact that I could never talk to Will again as long as I lived.

It was here that I had to wonder how I could think I was such a nice guy in life and yet have people in two states that hated me. Maybe I was much more of a prick than I was willing to admit to myself.

Needing to convince myself that my return to Michigan was a good idea and worth the loss of a friendship, I immersed myself in my chorus boy duties at the theater. However, there simply wasn't that much to immerse myself in. My choreography consisted of standing off to the side of the stage during each musical number, leaning toward whoever happened to be singing while resting one hand on my bended knee, and putting my other hand on my hip as I bounced up and down in time to the music, the way animated characters used to bounce up and down to the soundtrack in those creepy old black-and-white Mickey Mouse and Popeye cartoons. The extent of my vocal responsibilities consisted of singing *"For it's good old reliable Na-than, Na-than, Na-than, Na-than Dee-troit!"* and *"The people all said sit down, sit down you're rocking the boat"* over and over again. For a guy who had received a large ovation at the end of every performance of *Grease* for his over-the-top portrayal of an overconfident deejay, this was something of a massive comedown. It also meant that I had a lot of free time in which my ever-wandering eye could possibly get me into another bad dating situation.

I found myself trying very hard not to become attached or attracted to any of the girls in the cast, trying to keep my vow of avoiding romantic entanglements in the wake of the Nancy debacle. But it wasn't easy. There were lots of pretty girls in skintight leotards undulating around me every day, and each rehearsal became a head-spinning exercise in trying not to get a boner that would show through the polyester gym shorts I was dancing in.

But my real lust and longing was aimed exclusively at Maura, a stunningly beautiful blond dancer whom I had met in one of my classes the previous year at Wayne State. Maura was a ballerina, thin and toned, tall and graceful, willowy and heart-stopping to watch. And watch her I did. For all my vows to avoid another girlfriend, I would have jettisoned that rule faster than it takes to complete a *TV Guide* crossword puzzle if Maura gave any indication that she was interested in me.

It's here that I have to introduce the one person who connected Maura and me together into one odd little dysfunctional family—my friend Matt. Matt had been in *Grease* with me a year and a half earlier and had a habit of beating me out of parts I was certain were perfect for me. He had gotten the role of Kenickie that I had wanted in *Grease,* and now was portraying Benny Southstreet in *Guys and Dolls,* Ali Hakim in *Oklahoma!,* and The Old Man/Henry in *The Fantastiks,* also roles that I had wanted. The ridiculous reason I was so unfairly passed over for all these parts was that Matt was simply *way* more talented than me. The guy could do anything. He could sing great, he could dance great, he could act great, he was funny, he was dramatic, he was good looking, and he was nice.

He was also Maura's boyfriend.

It all felt so unfair, Matt dating the woman I was lusting after as he played the roles I wanted. It felt like a famous playwright had written a character for me to portray named Paul Feig and yet for some reason had decided to cast Matt in the role. Both Maura and Matt were very demonstrative with their affections, and I found myself day after day in situations with them in which I had to smile and pretend that I wasn't going out of my mind with jealousy as they kissed and cooed all over each other. But I enjoyed being around Maura so much that I decided to relegate myself to what would eventually become the most recurring role in my life, and that was The Funny Third Wheel. I tagged along when Matt and Maura would go out with the cast, and I would sit next to them whenever I could. Matt was always very nice to me and laughed at my jokes as much as Maura did, and as the weeks went on, Matt and I became friends and started hanging out. And the more I hung out with Matt, the more guilty I felt at my secret longings for misfortune to befall him so that Maura would be freed up to fall in love with me, the guy who the gods of love surely knew was her perfect mate. The frustration of it all, coupled with my confusion at the fact that Maura would oftentimes hug me repeatedly before or after a performance or rest her arm around my shoulder when she was catching her breath after a dance number, made me completely unsure if Maura had any supressed romantic feelings toward me or not.

But I was about to find out.

And Now for the Chorus: Love Hurls

8/22/82

What I'm going to write in here tonight is something that shouldn't be written, and chances are that I'll tear it out before anyone else can see it. The reason I'm writing it is because I can't tell anybody what happened. I could lose a lot of good friends.

Last night, after "Guys and Dolls," I decided to skip Sampson's anniversary party and hang around with the cast. Julie, Maura, Libby, Sarah, and I stood around for a while, waiting for Sarah's boyfriend to pick her up. After he arrived and left, Maura, Julie, Russ, and myself went over to the Firehouse for pizza with the cast. I sat next to Maura and she was extra friendly to me, hugging me and such. Julie was depressed about Steve (what a soap opera!), so Maura and I decided to drive back to the Macomb, drop off Julie, and then go back to the Firehouse. We dropped Julie, and Russ decided to go home, too. So, Maura and I drove back to the Firehouse. Maura went in to see if anyone was still there but everyone had left. I must admit that I was glad, because I felt like talking to, and just being with, Maura. (You see, I've had a "crush" on her since Freshman English at Wayne). Neither Maura nor myself felt like calling it a night, so Maura said I could come over to her house to play video games (Her parents are out of town). Well, we drove over and started talking. When we were in the house, I made sure to sit on the opposite side of the coffee table (she's Matt's girlfriend and Matt is a good friend of mine). Well, after a while, we played video games and watched some TV. Then, we turned off the TV and decided just to talk with the stereo on. It was around 4:00AM (?). We talked for a while, then something happened. Something hit the window of the room we were in, and we both became very worried. That's when everything started. She held onto me because she was afraid. I, of course, held her. This went on for about an hour and a half. We just held each other and joked around like before. I wanted to kiss her bad but all I could think about was the fact that she's Matt's girlfriend. So, we went on talking and joking, but the joking grew less and less, and we started to hold each other more caringly. Then, Maura said, "I'm so glad that you're here with me. I was really scared." Then, she said in the usual friendly theater-tone, "Give me a kiss." Well, I did and it was all over. We went on kissing for hours, quite lovingly. I felt guilty, but I just couldn't stop. I've liked Maura for so long and to finally have her. We both admitted that we had been attracted to each other for a few weeks now. It was my dream come true. Around eight, I decided I'd better get going. We both agreed that this night would be our secret, and I was very sure that I could let the whole thing end right there. Ha! All day, *that's all I've been able to think about. I'm not hungry, I feel depressed because I'm leaving, I feel very worried that Matt and his sisters will find out (they are all good friends). One thing eases my worry a bit (not much). Maura said that about a month ago, Matt and her decided that they should both go out with other people. Hmm. I don't know. All I do know is that I'm falling more for Maura every minute. A whole bunch of us are going to Cedar Pointe Wednesday, and I hope everything can go normal. Maura is going to read my one-act tomorrow, I'm going to send her flowers, but I'll sign them so that only she will know who they're from. I don't know what I'm going to do. The emotions that I thought were dormant are now tearing me up inside. Remember, no one can see this.*

It was, in fact, a miracle.

The idea that Maura thought of me as anything other than a goofy friend was the greatest thing to happen to me since I was thirteen and I overheard my father telling my mother he thought I might be a genius (I had always assumed he thought I was a moron). Even though our encounter was G-rated—the Disney version of a steamy one-night stand— to me it was epic. It was pure romance, pure attraction gone wild, and a pure "we know this is wrong but we simply can't help ourselves" soap opera, in which I was one of the two lead actors.

Yes, I had made out with Matt's girlfriend. And I couldn't have been happier about it.

Well, except for all the guilt.

I went over the details of the evening. It really seemed like Maura had angled to get me back to her house and had led me toward our make-out session by keeping me there later and later into the early-morning hours. Unfortunately, because of my usual fears and my allegiance to Matt, I probably trimmed a few extra hours of physical contact off the event by not being more aggressive sooner. But it didn't matter, since I can safely say there was no way the evening's passion would have ever elevated beyond the make-out stage. I was simply too over-come. The entire time it was happening my only thought was "I can't *believe* this is happening," as if I were making out with the queen of England or Farrah Fawcett-Majors. To have the girl I had been pining for for so long suddenly be mine, body and soul, was nothing short of life changing. It was as if the gods had told me, "Yes, friend, you *can* have any girl you want, as long as you really think she's right." I knew she was right, and now I had the proof of an "in her house on her couch from four to eight in the morning while her parents were out of town lying on top of her even though we were fully clothed hand on her breast even though it too was fully clothed" make-out session to support my case.

The only question was whether it was something that affected her as much as it affected me.

And, more important, was there any chance of it hap-pening again?

I decided to add up the evidence.

The first thing I recalled that made me nervous was that, mere minutes after our make-out session had ended, the phone had rung and it was Matt. The shock of guilt that belted my body the minute I heard Maura chirpily say, "Oh, hi, Matt," was enough to send me fleeing to a monastery if not for the fact that my legs had become immobile in fear. Would Maura spill the beans to Matt? Was their new "let's go out with other people" pact so flexible and their attitudes so cosmopolitan that Matt might actually get me on the phone and ask me how I enjoyed lying on top of his girlfriend? Or was Maura suddenly going to be overcome with guilt and confess everything, saying tearfully that I had lured her back and forced her to make out with me, which would then result in Matt showing up and asking me to "step outside"? Fortunately, she chose option C, which consisted of her talking to him for several minutes in what sounded like the exact same conversation they might have had if she and I hadn't just spent the night together. She was so cool and casual that I even started to feel insulted. A little bit of shifting eyes and sweat on her brow would have at least made me feel like I'd had some effect on her. But Maura was a whole new breed of girl for me. She was almost a year older than I was, she had been in a real relationship for a long time, she was a dancer who was in tune with her body, and she was someone who actually had the maturity to have a "let's go out with other people" talk with her significant other, something I couldn't envision myself ever doing. Maura was the real thing. For her to have a night of passion with a fellow performer and then jauntily get on the phone minutes afterward and discuss her dinner plans with her boyfriend may simply be how the adult world works, I told myself. There's no way she couldn't have felt what I felt. The earth moved between those hours of 4 and 8 A.M., and we both had been changed forever.

Or at least I hoped *she* had.

I did indeed give her flowers as planned, but instead of delivering them myself, I had the florist drive them over, figuring it had to be the pinnacle of romance to receive roses this way—via a delivery man who I was sure would arrive at her door wearing a white suit, black tie, and a crisp white hat, looking like the milkmen in old black-and-white TV shows, holding out an armful of red roses to her and saying, "From a special someone, ma'am." It was only later that I discovered flower deliveries in our town were generally made by surly teens wearing dirty cutoffs and Blue Öyster Cult T-shirts with paint stains on the front. But Maura did call and thank me profusely for the flowers, sounding like they had actually pleased her and apparently didn't make her think I was a desperate stalker.

The part of my plan I was having trouble with was my brilliant idea to give her the one-act play I had written for my creative writing class. I saw it as the perfect way to increase her love for me, since women on TV and in movies always seemed to be impressed by guys who wrote artistic things like stories, poems, and songs. And so to hand her a complete one-act play forged by my very own pen would make me a veritable Shakespeare in her mind. The play, titled *A Peanut Butter Evening,* was my first attempt at writing something dramatic, and the touching story of a teenage boy who goes to a prostitute to lose his virginity, only to find that she is in fact his long-lost mother, seemed like the kind of mature work that would have her certain she would one day be escorting me to Stockholm to watch me collect my Nobel Prize for literature. But I just couldn't seem to find an opening in her busy schedule to deliver it to her. Admitting to myself that she was simply busier than I was, I told myself I would be seeing her on Wednesday for a day trip with the show's cast members to Cedar Point amusement park in Sandusky, Ohio, and so could hand my masterpiece to her in person. It was the perfect plan, despite the fact that Matt would also be in attendance. But I forced myself not to think about this.

In those first few days after Maura's and my evening together, I went through the most intense love pangs that I had ever experienced up to that point in my life. There's that feeling you get when you fall deeply, deeply in love with someone, and it's both the greatest and the worst feeling in the world. You can't eat, but it's not a pleasant feeling of appetite forgotten to airy thoughts of your beloved—it's more of a feeling of having a whole pineapple sitting sideways inside your stomach, thorny top and all. You feel alternately like you want to sing from the hilltops, and throw up. Love ties knots in your stomach like a Boy Scout going for his Emergency Preparedness merit badge; it pulls the ends of the rope too tightly when it gets nervous, and it has a hard time untying them when it does it wrong. My stomach in those days leading up to the Cedar Point trip felt like it was one of Pippi Longstocking's braids. There were times when my desire to see Maura, to kiss her and to have her reassure me that she still wanted me as much as that night we spent on her couch, was so intense that I felt like I couldn't breathe. I tried to keep my mind on other things but everything reminded me of her. It was the old observation about how whenever you're in love all you ever seem to hear on the radio are love songs, but for me it was multiplied by ten thousand. I became as emotionally hallucinatory as a schizophrenic on LSD. Maura's face was everywhere. Every woman on every billboard looked like her. Every actress on every TV show and commercial had one or more of her features: her eyes showing up in an episode of *M*A*S*H*, her lips making an appearance in an ad for Arid Extra Dry, her hair doing a one-scene walk-on during *Dallas,* her neck modeling a diamond necklace available only at the Meyers Thrifty Acres End of Summer Blow-out Jewelry Sale. There was no escaping Maura's face, her voice, her arms, her clothes, her perfume, her hold over me. She had entered my brain, and she was proving to be a very noisy tenant.

By the time the day of our trip to Cedar Point arrived, I was beside myself with anticipation.

However . . .

As soon as I pulled up in front of Matt's house to join the

car pool, I knew the day was going to be different than the one I had been hoping for. Because the personnel for this fun-filled outing to one of the Midwest's biggest amusement parks consisted only of the following people:

1. Maura
2. Matt
3. And me.

I don't quite know how it ended up to be this way, since the trip had been planned for about ten people and it's almost unthinkable that any Michigander in his or her late teens would turn down a trip to Cedar Point. But the gods apparently decided that there wasn't anything entertaining on their TVs that day and so made the decision to create their own private soap opera cast with the two people I was closest to that summer. I had originally envisioned this trip for Maura and me as being one of stolen kisses, of secret hand-holding on scary rides, of breaking away from the group with her under the guise of going off to buy souvenirs and then embracing romantically under the roller coaster as Matt and the others played carnival games and remained blissfully unaware of Maura's and my bliss.

But now it was clear that the day was going to go on one of two trajectories—that either Matt and I were going to end up confronting each other, or Maura and I were going to have to pretend that nothing had happened between us four nights ago.

Neither scenario worked for me.

However, the gods didn't seem to care much.

As we drove the two-hour trip to Sandusky, Maura and Matt sat in the front seat, and I sat in the rear. All my imaginings of Maura and Matt's strained and failing relationship evaporated as I watched them hang all over each other while Matt drove and Maura laughed at all his jokes and kissed the side of his face as if they were newlyweds. As I pretended to laugh along with Matt and act like I was having a great time, the pineapple in my stomach moved up into my chest and pushed its thorns into my rib cage. If an enemy army wanted information and decided to torture me, they couldn't have come up with a more effective method of breaking my spirit than putting me in the backseat of that car and making me watch Maura crawl all over Matt.

Unfortunately, there was little else to do on the two-hour trip than watch the heart-wrenching spectacle taking place in the front seat.

By the time we arrived at the amusement park parking lot, I felt like someone had drained all the air out of the car. I could only hope that being at an amusement park would divert my attention away from the fact that I was going to have to spend the next six to eight hours acting like I didn't care that Matt and Maura were still a couple who specialized in Public Displays of Affection. But the "amusement" part of Cedar Point quickly began to mock me, and the day saw me quickly descend into absolute misery.

To be honest, I really don't remember much at all about what we did. I know we went on rides and that occasionally I got Matt to sit with some stranger on a roller coaster so that I could sit next to Maura, but we were never out of his eyeshot, and so the charade was forced to continue for the entire duration of our fun-filled day. The only thing I do remember was the unrelenting gut-wrenching pain I was experiencing as Maura and Matt held hands and hugged incessantly and I tried to act like it wasn't tearing the heart out of me. Didn't Maura know how I was feeling? Didn't she care about me enough to at least not hang all over Matt? Or did she even still remember what happened between us that night in her living room, when we were holding each other and professing our attraction for one another and then spending several hours as close as we could be with all our clothes on?

Or . . .

. . . was that the problem? Had I once again so underwhelmed a woman with my backward ways that she had written me off even as our passionate co-mingling was taking place? Had she expected me, wanted me, to have sex with her that night? Was it even an option? Should I have done it? The more I thought about it, even though I was overwhelmed that night, had she tried to advance things beyond the make-out stage, I was convinced I would have given in, so intense was my attraction to her. But maybe that was the problem. As with Stacey, I had once again not initiated anything and so may have presented her with the ultimate turn-off, the proof that I was not boyfriend material, that I was an immature guy who made her laugh but who wasn't in league with a guy like Matt, who was clearly willing to do everything sensual and sexual with her. Or so I assumed.

There was no way to really know how sexually active Matt and Maura were without simply asking Maura point-blank. But by that time I didn't want to know. Maura had in the past few days gone from being another guy's girlfriend whom I pined over to being my saintly future wife and, like most guys in love, I didn't even want to think about her being touched by another man. However, I didn't have to think about it, because they were touching each other right in front of me every single minute of the day.

I finally had a few moments of respite when Matt ran off to grab a frozen lemonade. Maura laughed warmly as she watched after Matt, who was doing a funny Jerry Lewis run, and then she turned to look at me.

"How you doing?" she asked with a sudden tone of sympathy.

All the strength went out of me and I felt like I was going to burst into tears. "I'm dying," was all that I could muster.

"I know. I'm sorry," was all that she could muster back.

Her voice almost seemed to be saying, "I know this is hard but I have to do this to keep Matt from finding out." It had just enough empathy in it that it gave me the slightest hope that she still had feelings for me but was merely trying to protect my friendship with Matt. It didn't make watching them continue to hug and kiss the rest of the day any easier, but it did make me feel like there might be the slightest hint of a light at the end of the tunnel.

As we rode home that evening, Matt and Maura seemed more subdued, probably because we all were tired, having just spent the entire day in the humid midwestern sun. Matt was tapping his fingers on the wheel along to the radio, and Maura was staring out the passenger window, watching the Ohio countryside go by. As I sat and stared at the side of Maura's face, I saw her eyes glance at me without turning her head. A small, sweet smile played on her lips, and I saw her eyes shift down as if she was trying to point something out to me. I looked down and my heart skipped a beat.

Down between the passenger door and seat, her hand was reaching back, her fingers out to indicate that she wanted me to hold her hand. I glanced over at Matt. He was gazing hypnotically at the road, lost in thought. My heart pounding, I shifted forward in my seat, as if I had decided to lean on my knees, and took hold of Maura's hand. The wave of happiness and relief I felt at this was enough to almost erase the day of extreme pain I had just gone through. I glanced secretly at Maura's face again, and she gave me another small smile. And with that, Matt's Maverick levitated off the road and flew effortlessly through the dusky Ohio sky and over the Michigan state line, turning the two-hour trip into a nanosecond.

I was alive again. Because hope was alive.

When we arrived at Matt's house, I volunteered to drive Maura home and Matt agreed. I fully expected to be the recipient of another prolonged make-out session as soon as she and I were out of range of Matt's house, but Maura's body language and spoken language quickly made me realize this wasn't going to happen.

"So, when are you leaving for USC?" she asked.

"On Monday," I replied, putting emphasis on *Monday* to hopefully drive home the point that our time together was waning quickly.

"You know what?" she said, turning toward me and putting one leg under her to sit on. "It's probably a good thing that you're going. Because, if you were staying, we'd go out a few more times and then I'd have to tell Matt about us. I don't know how he'd handle it."

I was both pleased and confused by this last comment. My pleasure came from the fact she was saying she did indeed want to keep going out with me, but the confusion came from wondering just what she thought Matt might do if he found out. The ominous tone of her "I don't know how he'd handle it" seemed to say "because he might kick the shit out of you."

"I know. You're probably right," I said, half believing it. I would rather have had her admit that it would be impossible to live without me, and that she could no longer keep up the charade of her and Matt's relationship. But I also felt relief that I wouldn't have to deal with Matt and his perhaps unknown jealous rage before heading off to college. "But I'd like to see you a lot more before I leave."

"I'm around tomorrow night," she said with a smile that

fell somewhere on the border between encouragement and the pathetic act of throwing me a bone. I chose to interpret it as the former.

"Great. I'll come get you around seven."

We pulled up in front of her house and I prayed that at least a mini-make-out session would occur. However, she immediately put her hand on the door and opened it as soon as the car rolled to a halt. To stop her, I pulled my one-act play out from under the driver's seat.

It was time to put *Operation: Sensitive Artist* into effect.

"Hey, Maura," I said with just the right amount of shyness so that she wouldn't think I was anxious to show off my work to her. "I wrote this for one of my courses and was wondering if you'd read it." I didn't want to let her know that I was trying to get her to fall deeper in love with me after being dazzled by my talent, and so decided I needed a more benign and self-deprecating reason to engage her reading skills. "I'm not sure if it's working and so was wondering if you wouldn't mind giving me some notes."

"Oh, Paul, I'd love to," she said, sounding touched. I was certain that this would be followed by her leaping forward and throwing her arms around my neck to kiss me passionately, but she simply reached out and grabbed the play with one hand as her other hand threw the door open. "I'll read it tonight," she said, leaning into the car and then giving me an air kiss. And with that, she slammed the door and ran up and into her house.

Not exactly the exchange I was hoping for, but at least I now had a date set with her. And after a day like the one I'd just had, I was more than happy to take what I could get.

I drove over to Maura's house the next night with a stomach full of butterflies. I had decided to dress nicely and was decked out in my best pants and sweater vest. I wanted to look attractive but not so uncool as to go overboard by wearing a suit jacket. I wasn't sure if Maura was expecting us to go out to dinner or not, but I wanted to be ready. By the time I pulled up in front of her house, my heart was thumping loudly and my libido was at full throttle.

And into the batter's box I stepped. I was looking for a home run.

I knocked on Maura's front door and she opened it.

Maura was wearing wrinkled sweatpants and a sweatshirt, her hair up in a sloppy bun. She looked tired and out of sorts. And the sight of me standing in her doorway, dressed like I was on my way to a church social, apparently didn't make her feel any better.

"Oh, you're all dressed up," she said, as if I had just dumped a wheelbarrow of cat turds on her welcome mat. "We didn't say we were going out, did we?"

Strike one!

"Oh, uh, no, not really," I stammered, immediately feeling like the world's biggest nerd. "I just felt like putting this on because . . . all my jeans are in the wash. But I didn't have anything planned."

"Oh, good," she said, sounding relieved and rubbing her forehead the way one does when one has a headache. "Well, c'mon in."

She motioned me in as if I were there to fix the oven. As I entered her dimly lit living room, I could hear the sound of the TV coming out of the family room, the place that was formerly our lair of passion. As she signaled for me to sit, I looked through the doorway and saw the backs of her parents' heads as they sat watching TV on the couch that Maura and I had formerly made out upon. They neither acknowledged my presence nor looked like they were going to be vacating our love nest anytime soon.

Maura plopped down into the easy chair across from me and sighed loudly, rubbing her forehead again. "I'm sorry, I'm just having such a bad period day," she exhaled, alerting me to a fact that was about the last thing on earth I wanted to know.

Strike two!

As I tried to banish the sudden flood of stomach-churning mental images of what might be occurring inside Maura due to this "bad period day," she rubbed her temples again and then looked at me.

"So," she said with a sigh that said it was a big effort to be conversational, "how are you?" It was the tone you use when you really don't want to know how somebody is but you feel it's your duty as a human being to ask.

"Oh, I'm fine," I said, my disappointment at her condition barely hidden, knowing any hope of making out flew out the window the second the words "bad period day" left her lips. But before I could regroup, she reached down to the floor next to the easy chair and picked up my one-act script.

"So . . . I read your play," she said, sounding like a school principal who was about to expel me, "and, I don't know. I think it has a lot of problems."

STRIKE THREE! *YERRRRRRR OUT!!!*

We spent the next two hours sitting in her dungeon of a living room as she went page by page through my play and deconstructed every moment of my writing, using phrases like "I really didn't buy this" and "I have *no* idea what you were going for here," all while her parents laughed loudly at TV sitcoms in the next room. Maura kept her brow furrowed during the entire critique as she leafed back and forth through the pages of my play the way you would through a magazine that contained pictures of dead puppies. Her disdain for my writing in general and for this play specifically was so severe that she didn't even attempt to extend me the courtesy of trying to find a few positives with which to balance out the overwhelming negatives. It was the most scathing indictment of anything I had ever created, and it was coming from the woman I loved.

By the time Maura had finished tearing apart my play, I was exhausted. I thought about saying, "So, I guess we won't be making out anytime soon," but was too demoralized to be able to muster up even the smallest moment of sarcasm. Maura asked me if I was okay with her being so hard on my play and I fell all over myself convincing her that "this is what I wanted" and "hey, I told you I needed your notes." But inside I was torn between the desire to storm out of her house and wanting to break down in her arms. There's nothing quite as demoralizing as a bad review, but in Maura's case, her abuse of my one-act had given me a case of Stockholm syndrome. I wanted her to hold me, to tell me that it didn't matter whether or not I was untalented—that she loved me no matter what I did. But the only reaction I got from her after she had torn the guts out of my beloved one-act play was, "I'm really tired. Do you mind if we call it an early night so I can go to bed?"

I drove home with love songs playing on the radio and a sharp metal object wedged painfully inside my chest. I had no idea what to think now.

As I packed for my semester at USC on a sunny Friday afternoon, I was actually starting to get excited about going away to college, thanks to my less than stellar summer.

It was then that I received a phone call from Maura.

"Hey, whatcha doin'?" she asked breezily, a different person from the one I had seen the other night.

"Oh, just packing for college."

"When do you leave?"

"Monday."

"God, that soon, huh?" I was afraid to let myself think this way but it sounded very much from her tone like she was actually upset I was leaving.

"Yeah, I want to get out there a little early so that I can get settled in. Don't want to be dealing with apartment stuff after classes start." I made sure to use the word *apartment* so that she wouldn't think I was just a lowly freshman going off to live in some crummy dorm.

"That's smart. Hey, I just wanted to tell you that after *Guys and Dolls* tomorrow night, a bunch of us want to throw you a little going-away party. Will you have time to come out after the show?"

I was touched. But I didn't quite know how to read this. I analyzed her words. "A bunch of us want to" wasn't the same as saying "*I* wanted to," which would have meant that it had been *her* idea. But the fact that *she* was calling me and not Matt or anyone else from the cast made me wonder if she was merely giving credit to the others when in fact it *was* her idea to throw me a party. Was this a sign that her bad mood the other night actually *was* because of her bad period day and that she still had fond feelings for me? Did my inept dramaturgy not completely turn her off? Or was it just that my friends in the cast wanted to have a nice get-together in my honor and Maura had been chosen to call me? Whatever it was, there was no way I would ever have turned it down, and so I said to Maura, "That'd be great. I can't wait."

As we did our last performance of *Guys and Dolls* the next night, Maura was very touchy-feely with me. She would hug me or kiss my cheek or put her arm around me whenever we were within close proximity of each other. It was in that way that I had always been jealous of most of my life, when you would see a girl you liked hanging all over her older brother or a male friend whom she had known for a long time. Whether it was because desperation wafted off me perpetually like Hai Karate or whether my female friends have just never felt that close to me, I've never been the kind of guy that girls voluntarily hung on. I would sometimes become envious of students who endured some sort of tragedy at their schools simply because the TV news would be filled with pictures of emotional girls hugging and hanging all over the guys in their classes, even draping themselves over the guys' shoulders like human shawls at whatever memorial services or postmortem ceremonies they were attending, as if grief and sorrow were the ultimate aphrodisiac. And now that Maura was hanging all over me, I was both thrilled and nervous. My nervousness came from the fact that Maura was doing a lot of this right in front of Matt. But he always watched us with a smile, as if he was sure it was all just because we were great friends and that Maura would miss me the same way she would miss any of her other platonic friends from the show if they were moving across the country. And maybe that *was* what she was feeling. But, whatever the motivation, I was simply in heaven to have her so near.

After the play, we all gathered at Matt's house. His family had a cake for me that read "Good Luck, Paul!" with little fedora hats drawn around the edges in honor of our period costumes from *Guys and Dolls*. Pretty much the entire cast attended and, even though I knew the odds were low that any actor would ever pass up a party with free food and drinks, I was quite moved by the fact that so many people had shown up to say good-bye to me.

It became our usual evening of musical theater reverie, consisting of singing show tunes to either Matt's piano playing or, in the case of more athletic songs like "It's All for the Best" from *Godspell* and "I Am the Very Model of a Modern Major General" from *HMS Pinafore,* trying to keep up with the original cast recordings on the stereo. It was all great fun, with Maura constantly at my side, and made me realize what a fun summer I'd had after all. Maybe it *was* a good idea to have spent these months back at home in Michigan, I thought to myself. Because I had gotten to perform and I had made a lot of very good friends. The only thing I wasn't sure of was whether or not I now had a potential girlfriend, even if she was bound to be a top-secret, long-distance one.

As the party started to wind down, Maura dragged me into the backyard as Matt and his sisters were busy cleaning up. She took me outside in such a clandestine way, taking my arm and pulling me as she scanned around to make sure no one was watching where we were going, that I immediately became excited that something great was about to happen. As soon as we got outside, Maura pulled me into the shadows of the walkway next to Matt's house, threw her arms around my neck, and gave me a massive, extended, passionate kiss. It was more passionate than anything we had shared during our previous night together, partly because that evening was all about the kind of long, tender kisses that allow you to go on for hours. This kiss was of the *The War's Over!* variety, the kind of lip-lock that ends up on the front of newsmagazines and romance novels. The kiss was so deep and desperate that I fully expected Maura to beg me to take her to California; to tell me that she had realized in the last few days she simply couldn't live without me. However, when the kiss finally ended, she pulled away from me, stared into my eyes, and very pointedly said:

"I'll be here when you get back."

I practically floated home that night.

The next day, my parents drove me to the airport and I flew off to Los Angeles. I wasn't sad when I left. I was filled only with anticipation of my impending film school experience and my love for Maura. It was as if she were now in my heart, sitting warm and soothing in my chest. Whenever any worries or fears about starting at a new school on the opposite side of the world from where I had grown up loomed, they were easily quelled by remembering my kiss from Maura. The words "I'll be here when you get back" played through my head like a reassuring mantra, a guarantee that no matter what happened to me in the next few months, I had love and affection waiting for me when I returned to the Midwest. My soul continued to soar along with the airplane as we made our way across the United States to my future alma mater. Things were going to be all right.

My first semester at USC seemed to go by quickly. Between the five super-8 short films I had to make in my first production class, to my other required classes in both filmmaking techniques and the humanities, I was in a constant panic of trying to hit deadlines on all my assignments. I had roommates whom I really liked, and the gang that lived on my Faculty in Residence floor was eclectic and intellectual. I became best friends with the girl who lived across the hall from me and I was taken in by her parents, brothers, and sisters as an unofficial member of their family on holidays and weekends. I called my parents regularly and fell very much in love with the academic side of college life, even though I considered USC to be way too conservative for my tastes and fraternity row to be the home of all the guys who used to beat me up. So, all in all, one could say my first semester of real college life was a rousing success.

But I still missed Maura.

I thought about her constantly. I wrote scripts and short stories about her. I named characters in my movie pitches after her. I portrayed our love for each other in all kinds of plots and tales. I drew pictures of her in the margins of my notebooks. Whenever the stress of school would become too much, I would take myself back to our times together, reliving our night on her couch and our kiss in Matt's backyard in the shadows of the moonlight. I would hear her voice saying softly, "I'll be here when you get back" as I lay in bed and tried to quiet my brain so that I could fall asleep. I called her occasionally to say hello and to fill her in on my film projects. We always seemed to be limited in how romantically we could talk because her parents or my roommates were usually in the room. But she would always say, "I can't *wait* to see you at Christmas," before she hung up and my heart would pound. I watched various films in my head of our reunion, seeing myself running out of the airport gate, where Maura would see me, become emotional, and sprint through the crowd. We would then rush together and embrace, my bags dropping onto the ground as we hugged each other so tightly that we would almost squeeze the life out of one another. I imagined the future, with myself as a famous film director, squiring Maura on my arm to the Oscars, and how everyone I knew would see us and say things like "That is one beautiful wife you have there" and "Man, does she love you!" It was Maura who got me through my first semester of film school, and I counted down the days for three and a half months until I would get to see her again.

By the time Christmas vacation rolled around, I was almost out of my mind with anticipation for Maura's and my reunion. I could barely concentrate enough to study for my finals but used Maura's long-distance strength to empower myself. I called her to see if she'd be able to come and meet me when I arrived at the airport but, alas, I was landing in the afternoon and she still had an exam to take at Wayne State. I was disappointed but understood, and so we made plans to see each other the night after I returned home. The only thing I was unsure of was how I'd be able to make it through my first night back without seeing her. But I told myself that all good things come to those who wait and, since she was the best good-thing in my life, I was willing to be patient and spend my first night back with the parents who were paying to put me through college.

On the next day, as I counted down the final hours until I would see Maura, the phone rang. It was her.

"Hey, you want to meet up at The Hoagie Station?" she asked in a chipper voice. "A bunch of people from the troupe are getting together and they'd love to see you."

As much as I had missed my theater pals, I wasn't really looking for a reunion with them on this night. My plan was to spend an evening alone with Maura, being close with her and rediscovering our temporarily separated love. But part of me wondered if maybe this was going to be Maura's way to introduce us to the world as a couple. The image of her hanging all over me in front of them the way she used to hang all over Matt seemed like it might actually be the perfect way for us to launch our new lives together.

I arrived at The Hoagie Station, which was a local T.G.I. Friday's–type restaurant and bar that specialized in beer and hoagie sandwiches. My heart was pounding harder and harder as I walked toward the door, knowing that Maura was inside. I could imagine her scream when I entered the restaurant, picture her jumping out of her seat to rush through the tables and then throwing her arms around me and planting a deep and joyful soul kiss on my mouth. Granted, it was a modified version of my airport fantasy, but since that scenario hadn't materialized, it was something that I now wanted to experience here. My hand practically trembling in anticipation, I reached out, pulled open the door to The Hoagie Station, and stepped inside.

And, as usual, my heart sank.

For there, sitting at the head of a table filled with ten of my friends from the theater, were Maura and Matt. Maura was sitting in Matt's lap with her arms around his neck, and she was laughing and kissing the side of his face. They not only looked like the same happy couple I had left months ago—they actually looked *happier*. There was something about them that almost screamed, "We just had the best sex of our lives!" When Maura looked over and saw me standing there, she gave me the kind of smile you would give a person whom you hadn't seen for a couple of hours, and a wave that could have easily said, "Oh, hi, Grandpa. I didn't know you were coming over." Before I could deal with my grief and heartbreak at this, the rest of my friends jumped up and gave me a hero's welcome, hugging me and shaking my hand and patting me on the back and peppering me with all kinds of questions about my semester, giving me the kind of attention that just minutes earlier I would have considered to be too low-key if it had come from Maura. She, however, just continued to sit on Matt's lap and smile at my reunion with my fellow cast members, as if she were my mother and I was her son. When I finally worked my way through my friends to where Maura and Matt were sitting, Maura stood up and opened her arms out to me the way a priest might do if he was welcoming a new parishioner into the fold. She gave me a hug whose only passion was the extra squeeze she gave my back before letting me go so that Matt could also hug me hello. I felt like I was congratulating them at their wedding.

As I sat at the table and spun stories about my first semester of film school—getting laughs with recollections like the time I had my roommate play a corpse that suddenly comes back to life and in tensing his body to do so he accidentally blasted an enormous fart—I was absolutely dead inside. For some reason, each of my humorous stories acted as more and more of an aphrodisiac for Matt and Maura, who would laugh uproariously at each punch line and then kiss and snuggle further into each other in anticipation of what I would say next. I felt like I should tell a sad, dramatic story just in case it might have the opposite effect and turn them against each other, but the only sad, dramatic story I had to tell was the one that was taking place at that very moment. I was the life of the party and I was in hell—a nerdy, delusional Pagliacci. The only solace I took was in the enormous hoagie sandwich I was devouring, which smelled a little odd and tasted a bit strange but which seemed to be doing a good job filling the void in my body left by Maura, who had burst out of my chest more violently than the thing that came out of John Hurt's chest in *Alien*. By the time the party started to wind down, I was desperate to get out of there and never see Maura again.

I drove home feeling awful. My stomach was aching, and the back of my throat had the hot feeling that comes with swallowing one's bile all evening. The ordeal had zapped so much energy out of me that I felt like I had the flu. As I got closer to my house, I couldn't even cheer myself up with any of my favorite radio stations, which all happened to be playing songs I loved. My stomach hurt more and more and soon I felt like I couldn't even breathe. By the time I pulled into our driveway, I could barely stand to walk into the house.

I came into the living room where my parents were sitting and watching TV. I was surprised to find them both up, but then realized that I had mentioned I was going to be seeing Maura and they were clearly curious about how it went. The pain and nausea in my stomach were almost doubling me over as I sat on the couch.

"Hey, hey," my dad said jovially, "there's the big movie director."

"So?" said my mother in her most girly voice. "How was Maura?"

"I . . . she . . ."

And with that, I stood up and projectile-vomited all over the living room carpeting. My mother screamed and my father jumped out of his recliner. Feeling a second wave immediately heading up my esophagus, I tried to run down the hall toward our bathroom but only succeeded in painting the hallway walls and carpeting with another huge blast of the contents of my stomach. "Oh, God" was all I heard out of my mother regarding the mess I had just made of the most heavily used sections of our house as I dropped down in front of the toilet I had gone to the bathroom in my entire life and proceeded to vomit into it everything that had entered my body in the past twenty-four hours. It was the kind of vomiting that is so gut-twisting you wouldn't be at all surprised to see your actual stomach come out of your mouth and hang there. The entire bathroom reeked of tainted hoagie as I continued to puke for the next hour and a half, crying like a five-year-old and saying things like "Oh, no, please, not agai—" as my stomach constricted over and over and futilely tried to force out even the memory of the ptomaine-filled chopped beef submarine I had wolfed down just hours earlier.

I couldn't eat for the next two days, but this time it wasn't because of love pangs for Maura—it was because my stomach had been so wrenched and contracted by vomiting that I literally couldn't put anything into it. My whole body was sore and it was everything I could do simply to stand up. And when Maura called a few days later to wish me a happy holiday and I told her what had happened, she simply said, "Oh, that's terrible. I'm sorry," and then proceeded to tell me what she was buying Matt for Christmas.

I tried to feel mad at her for the rest of the trip, but I just didn't have the energy. And I realized I didn't have a good case against her. After all, she hadn't lied to me when she told me at the end of the summer that she'd be there when I got back. She indeed *was* there when I returned, and thanks to her presence, I ended up eating a food-poisoned hoagie from a place I would never have gone to if she hadn't invited me to go there in the first place. But it was my fault for never asking her point-blank at any time during the past four months if she had any real feelings for me and, more important, if she had any intentions of ever breaking up with Matt. I chose, as always, to avoid hearing anything potentially negative, hoping that everything would work itself out with no effort on my behalf whatsoever. And, of course, it didn't. When does it ever? If you want something in life, you have to at least expend a *little* energy and inquiry on it, right?

Three days after the Hoagie Incident, my mother took me to the Coney Island restaurant at our local mall. It was one of the places she and I always went throughout my life whenever we were trying to cheer ourselves up. My stomach was still sore and I was nervous I wouldn't be able to eat. But once the hot dogs arrived and my mom started asking me questions about my failed reunion with Maura, my appetite came back. And as the two of us ate and made a lot of noise while I ranted about Matt and Maura and my mother got into one of her laughing jags, the ones she usually fell victim to whenever I would tell her some tale of woe that had befallen me, I realized how much I missed her while I had been away at USC.

Mauras may come and Mauras may go, but at the end of the day, I only had one mother. And at that moment I was suddenly very happy that she had been there when I got back.

The Final Reprise

Right around my fortieth birthday, I was in Los Angeles International Airport waiting to catch a plane when I heard someone say, "Paul Feig?" I looked up and saw Maura, looking exactly the same as she always did, as beautiful as ever. We hugged and chatted, and the entire time I was desperate to know if she was still with Matt, even after all these years.

"Hey, I'd like you to meet my daughter and my husband," she said brightly.

Expecting to see Matt jump out from behind a post and yell "Surprise!," I looked over as Maura signaled across the gate area to her husband. As he made his way over to us, I took the greatest pleasure in seeing that he was not Matt, and was in fact a very normal, pleasant-looking guy who didn't seem like he had done a day of musical theater in his life. And as I shook his hand and then met their young daughter, I was smiling ear to ear.

Hey, Matt beat me out of every role I ever wanted in my life. The least I could do was get to enjoy the fact that there was one role neither one of us ended up getting—the role of Maura's husband.

Hey, just because I'm older now, I never said I was any more mature.

BOOK FIVE

Close Encounters of the Nerd Kind

Please Do Not Read This Chapter

Seriously. Don't.

I am not trying to be cute or provocative by telling you this. I do not ask you to avoid this chapter because I'm trying to be clever. I am not trying to be Lemony Snicket.

I really don't want you to read this.

Then why am I writing it?

Honestly, I don't know. Maybe it's because I feel the need to confess, in the hope that other guys will tell me that they too have done what I am about to tell you I attempted at one point in my life, and thus assuage my embarrassment. Maybe it's because I want any women reading this to see the extent to which guys will go in order to try to make up for the fact that we're not all confident enough and good looking enough to automatically get girlfriends and wives who can keep us from doing desperate acts like the one I am shortly to tell you. Or maybe it's just to try to get a laugh out of something fairly horrifying that I did. Sort of like the whole point of this book, I guess.

Whatever the case, when all is said and done, I'd be happier if you simply didn't read this. Especially if you're a woman.

Because you'll probably be very put off by it.

And by me.

I know my wife sure was when she read it.

But, with that said, here goes . . .

* * *

Okay, wait. Never mind those three snowflake thingies I just typed. First I have to make a small disclaimer. You have to realize what had happened to me between my episode with Maura and the one I'm about to tell you so that I can put this embarrassing tale into context and try to save a little face.

First of all, I had already graduated from USC film school at the time this occurred. It took me two and a half years because of required classes I had to take that didn't transfer over from Wayne State, but I made it through and received my degree (cum laude, no less). And during my time at USC, even though I had crushes galore on a myriad of pretty girls on campus and in my apartment building, I didn't do any dating whatsoever and thus became one of the few people in the world to have exited my college career with my virginity firmly intact. I guess I had grown so gun-shy about girls because of my Michigan experiences that I was desperate to avoid tainting a new state by littering it with women whom either I was fleeing or who, more likely, were fleeing me. Simply put, I had lost my nerve for dating and sex and relationships, and so I buried myself in the platonic safety of my schoolwork and friends and walked onstage to get my diploma on graduation day as chaste as a newborn baby.

But inside, the suppressed ocean of my libido was roiling like the perfect storm.

I moved into an apartment with a friend from film school and immediately threw myself into my first real job in the film industry, working as a script reader for a Hollywood producer. This kept me busy enough to continue unthinkingly on my course of nondating, since I always had piles of screenplays that I had to read and write synopses for. In the moments when I would be gripped by extreme loneliness and desperation, it was beginning to seem like I had spent so much energy the last few years convincing myself I wasn't going to date that I couldn't mentally switch out of that mode and do anything proactive about it. But the urges to engage in some arena of human sexuality were knocking on my door like the LAPD with a battering ram. Suddenly every woman I saw was attractive and completely unattainable. It didn't help that I felt quite unappealing living in southern California and working in the entertainment industry, a goofy-looking twenty-two-year-old virgin in a city that contains a higher ratio of beautiful people to ordinary people than a nighttime drama on Fox. I didn't know how to meet women, I didn't know where to meet women, and I didn't have the nerve to talk to them even if an opportunity arose. I was terrified of being rejected, and I was certain that my growing sexual desperation was so outwardly apparent that just saying hello to a woman would result in her screaming for the police.

In short, to use the vernacular of a colorful backwoods character, I was hornier than a sailor after ten years at sea. And my lonely method of carpal-tunnel release was no longer getting the job done. I needed a human touch, or I needed a different kind of touch, and I had no idea how to get it.

And now, if you're kind, you'll simply pity me, stop reading here, and go on to the next chapter, which is still pretty embarrassing, but nowhere near as bad as what I'm about to tell you.

It's your last chance. I'll even give you a page break and a formal direction to help make it less difficult:

Please proceed to page 273.
Thank you for your cooperation!

Still here, huh? Well, then, read on at your own risk.

You've been warned . . .

There were lots of rumors flying around when I was growing up about guys who could please themselves orally. There were at first stories in junior high about contortionists and yoga guys in India who were so limber that they could simply bend their bodies in half in such a way that their mouths would end up right in front of their genitals. When I first heard about this, I didn't even know what oral sex was and so assumed that this skill meant they had the ability to look at themselves more closely, in case a detailed visual inspection of their privates was required when a physician was not available. But as the years went by and I learned more about human sexuality and sexual practices, I started to realize the titanic possibilities this skill presented.

It was at this same time that my cousin Philip told me a story he had heard about a guy who was so committed to acquiring this talent that he enlisted his wife to begin sitting on his back as he leaned forward and tried to bend down far enough to have quality face time with his manhood. Apparently the very open-minded husband-and-wife team did this over the course of several months until they had trained the man's back muscles and spine to behave in such a way that he no longer required the assistance of his spouse's body weight. Why any self-respecting wife would participate in helping her husband achieve this skill was never fully explained to me, other than that perhaps the woman simply didn't want to perform the act herself and so figured that if she helped her husband learn how to do it on his own, she'd be freed up to spend the time she'd have lost fellating her husband pursuing other more worthy endeavors. Whatever the explanation, the story at that time just seemed weird and deviant to me, something that two scary people who had forsaken all else for sex had taken part in. And this, coupled with my longstanding fear of God getting mad at me for the simple act of masturbating, made the thought of actually trying anything like this myself nonentertainable.

By the time I had gotten through high school, these stories had taken on a life of their own. There was the tale of the man who was so desperate to self-please that he had two vertebrae removed from the middle part of his back to make himself more pliable (what he told the doctor in order to get this surgery I couldn't imagine). There was the man who slept in a chair with a barbell on the back of his neck each night until he achieved success. There was even the guy who had his best friend break his back in the center so that even though he could no longer walk, he could spend all day at home folded in half like an omelette, engaging in a nonstop act of self-love.

All these stories horrified me, and all made a lasting impression.

But it wasn't until those desperate days when I was the world's loneliest script reader that they all came flooding back.

Here's the deal. I had begun shopping in a lot of second-hand clothing stores in the most eclectic parts of Los Angeles. And in all of these stores were women, both customers and employees, who were different from any females I had ever encountered before. These were the cool rock 'n' roll and punk girls with green and pink hair wearing Doc Martens and red plaid pants held together with safety pins; the ones clad in schoolgirl skirts and leather jackets with chains and paintings of skulls on the back; women with tattoos and piercings and thick black mascara and lipstick and eye shadow who liked bands like the Dead Kennedys and

Black Flag. And, for some reason, they were more and more becoming the stuff of my masturbatory fantasies. This was probably due in part to the fact that you could tell many of them were extremely attractive under all their rebellious accoutrements. But their biggest draw, I'm embarrassed to say, was that because of the way they presented themselves, you got the feeling they were probably more willing than other more "normal" girls to indulge in carefree acts of sexual expression.

In other words, using the crudest of terms, they looked like girls who might give you a blow job.

However, I was not the type of guy who would ever go out specifically seeking anything this overtly sexual, nor did I have the nerve even to approach them to request a date, since I knew that, on the off chance they'd say yes, we'd end up in a bar or club in which the odds were extremely good that I would be beaten to death. And so I simply kept my mouth shut and stared longingly at them when I knew they were looking in the other direction.

It wasn't until one day when I was shopping at a used-clothing store in North Hollywood called Second Hand Rose that I got up the nerve to talk to one of them. Feeling particularly bold on a sunny Saturday afternoon, I struck up a conversation with the very attractive salesgirl behind the counter. She had dark hair that was cut into a Dorothy Parker bob with bright red streaks and was styled to look like she had just crawled out of bed. She was also wearing an old prom dress with spaghetti straps, torn fishnet stockings, and big black combat boots. The effect was stunning because it seemed to cry out to me that her motto in life was "I'll do anything with anybody in bed." However, I have no idea if this was true or not. She very possibly could have been a born-again Christian for all I knew, but in my mind (and what's more powerful than the mind of a desperate virgin in his early twenties?) she was possibly the woman who could usher me into true maturity, curing all that ailed me like that stuttering guy who could suddenly talk after he has sex with the nurse in *One Flew Over the Cuckoo's Nest*. On top of this, she was actually being nice to me as I was buying a green suit from the 1950s that somebody's grandfather had probably passed away in. At times, I was almost certain she was flirting with me as she laughed at all the lame jokes I was nervously trying to impress her with. Every bone in my body wanted to ask her out but, as usual, I simply couldn't muster up the courage. I paid for my suit, gave her a brotherly "Thanks, good-bye," and then hightailed it out of there to run back to the safety of my apartment.

At home in my sad little bedroom, I tried to envision the punky prom dress–wearing sales clerk entering my bedroom and seductively removing all her clothes, telling me that she had hoped I would ask her over the minute she set eyes on me. I tried to imagine her coming over to me and pushing me back on my bed, then kneeling to perform the act that most men fantasize the women they find attractive will do. But it was the vividness of this fantasy and the inability of my powers of self-manipulation to re-create anything that might indeed feel like the "real thing" that caused me to realize that my current means of release were simply not going to do the trick. I needed an actual woman or I needed to give up.

And it was then I remembered the stories I'd heard since junior high.

It was not a proud moment by any means, and I sat and debated for a good long time over whether I should actually stoop low enough even to consider trying to perform this act upon myself. First of all, I knew from past urban legends that it generally took surgical alteration of the spine or the love and hard work of a very liberal wife to get one even close to being able to accomplish this sexual circus trick. But I also knew that I had excelled in gym class whenever we did tumbling or stretching, and so because of my inherent limberness I possibly had a better shot at being able to fold myself in half than most other men. It seemed like the choice was mine to make. The only question was would I ever be able to look at myself in the mirror again if I did it. It seemed to me like once you had blown yourself, you were pretty much on a path that took you out of the running for having a normal, respectable life. It'd be sort of difficult to sit around with family and friends knowing that in the privacy of your own room you were doing something to yourself that, according to the most prudish amongst us, the jury still seems to be out on the morality of, even as an act between two consenting adults. Lord only knew what the karmic ramifications of doing it to yourself were. However, I also knew chances were good that I wouldn't be able to do it anyway. And so, overwhelmed with the bad decision-making that seems to occur when one's libido takes charge, I decided I should lock the door, close the blinds, and see if I could do the impossible.

I stripped off my clothes and sat on the edge of my bed. Feeling as self-conscious as if I were in front of a studio audience, I tried to bend my head down toward my midsection. Very quickly, I realized how ill designed the human body was to accomplish this move and was fully able to comprehend why so much work had to be put into it by the people who had cracked the code. However, I was absolutely convinced at that moment that I could make my body give in if I only put a little sweat and ingenuity into it. I laced my fingers together behind my head and pulled down as hard as I could. However, the closest I could bring myself into range of my goal was slightly less than a foot. Using the same techniques I'd been taught in gym class stretching exercises, I alternated between pulling my head down for a five count, then resting for another five count, in the hope that my neck and back muscles would slowly give way. However, after about ten minutes of this, all I had accomplished was a sweaty back of the neck and a lower rib cage crushing all my internal organs. Figuring that the laws of physics were working against me, I looked around for something that might help provide me more torque.

I grabbed an old Mickey Mouse towel I'd had since I was a kid and slung it around the back of my neck. Then, pulling down on both sides of the towel with my hands, I tried to force my head down further. Alas, this too only resulted in more rib cage pain and the sad realization that I'd never be able to look at my favorite old beach towel ever again without dredging up terrible memories of this low point in my life.

Now feeling a strange mix of disgust, frustration, and determination, I sat back and tried to figure out a new way to do this. Everything I had heard in all these self-oral-copulation success stories had revolved around the experimenter forcing himself to overcome his body's structural security system while in an upright, seated position. But perhaps this was far too traditional thinking. Perhaps one of the problems, as I had just discovered, was physics. Maybe one could never get one's head and shoulders to bend far enough forward simply because it was not possible to make one's upper-body muscles contract strongly enough on their own to overcome the resistance of the spine. Some sort of fulcrum was needed. And other than the guy who cut out part of his back, all those who beat the odds used an artificial weight to force their bodies into submission. Since I had neither a set of barbells nor a fellow human being whom I would ever dare bring into this degenerate experiment of mine, I had to figure out something else to force my face into my crotch.

And then it hit me, the "Aha!"/"Eureka!" moment for which I'd been waiting.

I would use the weight of my own body.

Figuring that since the human head weighs only a fraction of what the rest of the body weighs, I realized I could use that lopsided ratio to produce enough pressure on my neck and back muscles to make them give. It seemed almost genius. Perhaps I was about to uncover a secret ability that men's bodies had been provided with by evolution but, because of the puritanical mores of our current society, had been suppressed over the generations. Perhaps I was about to become the Leonardo da Vinci of masturbation. I was so giddy with the spirit of discovery that I momentarily forgot how utterly misguided what I was about to try was.

I rolled onto my bed and did a handstand against the wall. Then, very slowly, I bent my head forward so that my shoulders were on the mattress and my chin was pressed against my chest. Then I lowered my legs down in front of me, trying to turn my body into something shaped like the letter G. The pressure on my neck was enormous, but the softness of my mattress seemed to be providing enough give to make it bearable. As I lowered my hips downward, I couldn't believe it. I was actually a few scant inches away from my goal. However, "a few scant inches" wasn't good enough for what I was trying to accomplish.

As the pressure on my face felt like my head was a children's party balloon being filled to the breaking point with helium, I reached over and grabbed my pillow. It seemed to me that with just the slightest extra bit of angle that putting the pillow beneath my head would give me, I was mere seconds away from being able to never have to find a girlfriend as long as I lived.

I jammed the pillow behind my head and was suddenly face-to-face with the appendage with whom I had been trying to meet. I was less than an inch away and, even though my back and neck were now screaming with pain, I knew that if I simply relaxed and let the weight of my upended body continue to do its work, I would be shouting "Mission Accomplished!" within seconds. The pressure being exerted upon my head and face was gargantuan, and my eyes felt like they were bulging out of their sockets worse than Arnold Schwarzenegger's were in the climatic scene on the surface of Mars in his 1990 science fiction hit *Total Recall*. Suddenly realizing that I might not survive the wait for my muscles to slowly give in, and due to the fact that I felt like I was going to pass out from all the blood rushing to my head, I figured that one good bounce via my shoulders would bring my goal to fruition.

And so I bounced.

And it was then that I heard the "pop."

At first, it didn't feel like anything more than a hot burst of air on the back of my neck. However, within a few moments, I suddenly realized that something had gone very, very wrong. I slowly tried to unfurl myself like a red carpet being unrolled in front of a movie premiere but found that every part of my body was against this. The childhood warning of "If you make a face like that, it'll stay that way" took on a whole new catastrophic meaning as I fell over sideways on the bed, my body feeling like it was locked in this doughnut shape into which I had willingly put myself. I lay on the bed for several minutes, trying to catch my breath and hoping that I wasn't about to die of a stroke or a brain aneurysm from all the pressure to which I had just subjected my cranium. The thought of being found dead in this less than dignified position was sure to guarantee the one thing I didn't want out of life: a funny death. Ever since as a kid I would hear my peers snicker and laugh derisively at the urban legend that "Mama" Cass Elliot had died choking on a ham sandwich—which was supposed to be comedic because of the irony that a fat person would die while eating—I have been afraid of dying funny. I have always thought that for one's legacy to be a humorous demise would be the worst of indignities, and now I was suddenly terrified of the vision of the police coming in and finding me curled up on my bed in a position that they would immediately decipher as the shape one gets into when one is trying to blow oneself. I could only imagine the phone call that would be made to my parents.

"Um . . . Mr. and Mrs. Feig, we have some tragic news for you. I hope you're sitting down."

"Oh, my God. What is it?"

"Your son is dead."

"Our . . . son . . . is . . . *(gasp)* . . . what happened . . . ?"

"He was trying to perform oral sex on himself and the pressure he caused within his brain killed him."

A long period of silence, followed by: "You must have the wrong number. We don't have a son. Good-bye."

I tried not to panic. It's simply that you've overstretched muscles that you've never used before, I told myself, and so they were now rebelling. If you just lie here and try to relax, they'll also relax and then you can put this whole terrible episode behind you.

I lay in wait for what felt like hours, but which I'm sure was only a few minutes. Carefully, I tried to move my legs. They responded fairly well, but very quickly my lower back spasmed. It felt like I had been punched by one of the Seven Dwarves, and I made such a sharp guttural yelp of pain that I then spent the next few minutes worrying if my neighbors had heard. I took a few deep breaths and tried again. I was able to painfully straighten my lower back, my spine feeling like it was filled with walnut shells. Then, as I attempted to uncurl my middle and upper back, a sharp pain shot through my rib cage and thought that I had somehow gotten my heart hooked onto one of my ribs and had just torn it open. I made yet another guttural cry that I was convinced my neighbors had heard and waited for the icy hand of death to grab me by the shoulder, laughing in my face at the ridiculous way I had caused my accidental summoning of him. Fortunately, the Grim Reaper apparently had better things to do on that day and, once I was able to catch my breath, I straightened my crushed rib cage and rubbed my sore chest. Figuring I was home free, I straightened my neck. And it was then that I quickly realized something.

I hadn't straightened my neck.

I *couldn't* straighten my neck.

My head was bent forward like that of an old woman in the final stages of osteoporosis. I tried again to lift my head but a sharp pain like a nail being pounded into my spinal cord hit me, and I immediately put my chin back down onto my chest.

"Oh no," was all I could think.

I'd heard enough "funny" stories over the years of people showing up in emergency rooms with any manner of paraphernalia lodged within their anal cavities and had always had as good a laugh over it as the next guy, although I always found the stories to have an inherent sadness to them. The idea that somebody would be so desperate for some simple, albeit misguided, solo sexual gratification that they would resort to sticking a lightbulb or a pool ball up their hinder always made me feel bad to be laughing at their misfortune. Granted, it was a pretty nontraditional activity, and one whose self-stimulatory allure I couldn't relate to, but who are any of us to judge what other people find enticing, as long as it's not hurting anybody else? Live and let live, I've always said. And now that I suddenly found myself faced with the prospect of having to go to the emergency room and seeing the cause of my neck trauma described on my hospital report as "dislocated upper vertebrae resulting from overarticulation due to an inexplicable attempt to perform self-fellatio," I found a new and profound sympathy for those emergency-room laughingstocks.

What if I broke my neck? I thought, in a panic. I'd always assumed that when you broke your neck, it was a highly dramatic event, the result of being thrown from a motorcycle like Evel Knievel while trying to jump over the fountain at Caesar's Palace or having your head twisted sideways by a ninja or a Green Beret as you guarded the general's tent in a war movie. But maybe I had broken it simply by putting the entire weight of my body on the main bone structure in charge of keeping my head and brain aloft and active. Maybe I had just ruined my life because I was desperate to know what oral sex felt like and because I was too awkward and afraid to try to find someone who could eventually do it *for* me.

Talk about curiosity killing the cat.

I sat on the edge of my bed with my head hanging down like a sleeping wino and tried to think pleasant thoughts. It's just a strain, I told myself. The muscles just need to relax and then things will be fine. It'll be a little stiff for a few hours but then after a good round of stretching and calisthenics I'll be back to my normal, not-trying-to-blow-myself self. Try to work out the knot, I told myself, like a helpful physical therapist.

I slowly started to lift my head again but, alas, the pain stabbed me just as hard.

I dropped my head back down.

I let out a helpless little whimper.

I was in big trouble.

I really had no idea what to do. Should I call an ambulance? Could I drive myself to the emergency room with my chin glued to my solar plexus? And what would I tell the doctors when I got there? I broke my neck because I was doing a handstand and my arms gave out? I was playing on a Slip 'N Slide and slid headfirst into a tree trunk? I was in a WWF wrestling match and was pile-driven by Hulk Hogan? There seemed to be no good explanation for how I had injured myself so badly except for some watered-down version of the embarrassing truth. Which would then enter me into the pantheon of stories that begin "This guy I know told me about a friend of his who worked in an emergency room . . ."

And so I realized that there was no way I could go to the hospital. To tell anybody what had happened was just too humiliating. The secret would have to die with me. I would simply have to suffer. If my injury turned out to be life ruining, then obviously I deserved it. Whether or not God was still after me over the whole masturbation thing, some kind of otherworldly revenge was being meted out and I would merely have to accept my fate and display my new handicap as I walked among the decent people in this world, like Hester Prynne bearing her town-appointed shame in *The Scarlet Letter*. However, where she could stand tall and defiant in the face of moral hypocrisy, I could merely spend the rest of my life trying to invent reasonable-sounding excuses to explain why my neck was now shaped like a boomerang.

The phone rang. I debated whether to answer it or not but figured that it might be my only chance at getting a lifeline to the outside world in my fragile condition. I reached over to grab the receiver, causing another sharp pain to stab in my neck. Stifling a moan, I picked up the phone and slowly brought it to my ear.

"Hello?"

"Hi, dear!" came my mother's perky voice. "Did I catch you at a bad time?"

"No, no," I said as casually as possible to the woman who had given birth to me, feeling immediately more weirded out to be talking to her at this moment than I had ever been in my life. "How are you?"

"I'm fine," she said. "What are you doing?"

". . . nothing."

"You sound out of breath. I didn't catch you napping, did I?" She said this with one of her girlish giggles that meant somehow the accusation that I'd be sleeping in the middle of the afternoon like an out-of-work drug addict was supposed to be funny.

"No, I was just exercising."

"Oh, well, make sure you stretch first. Don't want to pull anything."

Now you tell me. "What's up?" I asked. "Is everything okay?"

"I just wanted to say hi," she said. Then she paused oddly and sighed, as if she was embarrassed. "This is probably going to sound funny but, well, I don't know. I just had the strangest feeling that you might be hurt. You're okay, right?"

The chill that ran up my spine threatened to push the earth into a new ice age. I immediately went into the forced, defensive casualness that usually leads a jury to conclude a defendant is lying about something. "Of course I'm not hurt. God, why would you think that?"

"I don't know. Just a feeling."

As a kid, I'd grown up watching television shows that were always making jokes about and references to "women's intuition" but always figured it was some mystical force that only TV mothers were blessed with. My mother had never before displayed this power that I was aware of, and so I could only figure that it took an event of monstrous proportions to create such a disturbance in her Force. The only question was whether her superpower was advanced enough to let her know exactly *how* I had hurt myself.

"I'm *fine*," I didth protest too much.

"Well, I'm glad *you* are. Because I've got the worst sore neck."

And at that I snapped my head up, shocked. I felt another pop, and a screaming pain shot through my skull and spine. "OWWWW!!!" I yelled.

"I knew you were hurt!" she said, less out of concern and more out of being proven correct.

"I just stubbed my toe," I lied through gritted teeth, my head spinning in the aftermath of the sudden assault of pain. However, my head was now upright and my neck seemed to be pliable. Whatever I had just done had snapped my vertebrae back into their normal state, and I was immediately hit with the relief that it seemed my neck wasn't broken after all.

"Well, *see*," my mother said, giggling again and sounding vindicated. "I *knew* you were hurt. I just called a bit too early, I guess."

My neck was sore for at least a week after that, and every time I'd move it too quickly I would get a dull stab of pain that reminded me of the misguided act I had tried in my bedroom on that lonely afternoon. And the Freudian cloud of discomfort that surrounded me from this event that saw my mother fixing my neck in an otherworldly way guaranteed I never, never again attempt to get my body to do anything sexual that it was not structurally designed for.

And to this day, whenever it rains, I still get a dull pain in my neck. It's not exactly what you'd call a cool ailment like a football injury or an old war wound that one can use to predict the weather but, hey, at least I didn't hurt anybody else doing it. That's gotta count for something, right?

And so, what is the moral of this tale? I have no idea.

And why did I tell it? I have no idea.

And what do you think of me now that you've read it? I have no idea.

Look, I *told* you not to read this chapter. From now on maybe you'll listen to me.

And, by the way, it does sort of feel like it's going to rain today.

The Book of Miracles

Otherwise Called
How the Author Lost His Virginity

CHAPTER 1

1 I had been trying to get Jeri to sleep with me forever.

2 Actually, it was only nine months, but it really felt like forever.

3 It was 1986, I was now twenty-four years old, and I was still a virgin.

4 And, needless to say, after a lifetime of self-enforced celibacy, I was now officially desperate.

CHAPTER 2

1 I met Jeri in an improvisational comedy class I was taking and we had quickly become friends.

2 I fell in love with her the minute I saw her onstage.

3 She had long blond hair, was tall and thin, and had a very cute face.

4 She was also very funny.

5 It seemed like a match made in heaven.

6 The only problem was that she wasn't at all attracted to me.

CHAPTER 3

1 I tried everything to break her down.

2 I was her best friend.

3 I was her confidant.

4 I was her chauffeur.

5 I was her writer.

6 I spent all my free time with her.

7 I bought her presents.

8 I formed an improv group with her.

9 I befriended her parents.

10 I befriended her grandparents.

11 I bought her dinners.

12 I took her to movies.

13 I spent all my money on gas to drive the thirty miles to her house.

14 I did everything but succeed in convincing her that she should make me her boyfriend.

15 But I refused to give up.

CHAPTER 4

1 I don't want to make it sound like I had suddenly turned into a guy who was simply looking to get laid.

2 I was really in love with Jeri and so found myself more and more each day feeling like this was the woman I wanted to marry.

3 True, we had as much not in common as we did in common, and in retrospect, we had less in common than we did in common.

4 But if you just could have seen her the way I saw her back then.

5 Everything about her was what I had been looking for in a woman.

6 She was a real Teri Garr type, and Teri Garr was my dream girl, especially in her *Close Encounters of the Third Kind* days.

7 I was very physically attracted to Jeri, and I would often find myself fantasizing about sleeping with her, which in many ways was a real first for me.

8 In the past, I had always tried to avoid thinking of girls I was in love with in such an overtly sexual way, feeling that if I kept my desire for them on a purer level, then God would see how sincere my love for

these girls was and He'd let them fall in love with me.

9 Then I'd be able to marry one of them and finally get to have sex for the first time in my life.

10 But with Jeri, whether it was because I was so certain that she was destined to be my future wife or it was simply that at the age of twenty-four my hormones had become so out of control from years of suppression that they wiped out any and all fear I had of angering God by considering premarital sex,

11 I was willing to do anything to get her to sleep with me.

12 But nothing was working.

CHAPTER 5

1 For six months, she was impenetrable.

2 Literally.

3 Anything I did that seemed in the least bit like I was hitting on her or trying to act like we had a possible romantic future was met by an angry glare and a stern "Don't even think about it."

4 It didn't seem possible that she couldn't muster up some romantic feelings for me.

5 We had nothing but great times together whenever we hung out, and there was a definite attraction between us, whether she was willing to admit it or not.

6 I was positive about it.

7 Then I found out one day that she had been engaged about a year before I had met her, and that her fiancé had broken up with her right before their wedding.

8 And so I realized that I had been paying the price for the damage that some other guy had done so many months ago.

9 One bad apple *did* indeed spoil the whole bunch, girl.

10 "I just don't want to fall in love with anybody again," she said, "not this soon.

11 Besides, it might ruin our friendship."

12 And all I heard in those words was the following:

13 "Because if I didn't keep telling myself I didn't want a relationship, I would fall in love with you in a heartbeat."

14 And that was when I knew I had a chance.

CHAPTER 6

1 I spent the next month and a half working extra hard to break her down.

2 I hung out with her every night and every weekend.

3 I took her anywhere she wanted to go, no matter how much it cost.

4 I made mental notes of every album and book and piece of clothing she saw in the mall that she said she liked, and then I bought them for her as gifts.

5 I sent her flowers.

6 I took her dancing.

7 I did everything in my power to convince her that I wasn't a jerk like her ex-fiancé.

8 I wanted to prove to her that I was her soul mate.

9 And I think she started to believe it.

CHAPTER 7

1 It was then that something happened in my favor.

2 It wasn't a good thing for anybody else, but it did definitely help me out.

3 Jeri's mother almost died.

4 Her appendix burst and she was rushed to the hospital.

5 Fortunately, she was fine.

6 But who was right there with Jeri, helping her through this tough time?

7 You got it.

8 This seemed to be the event that was needed to knock things loose in the love-resistance department.

9 It was only a matter of days after this, while sitting in my car in the parking structure outside our improv class, that Jeri and I finally made out.

10 It wasn't anything more than a make-out session, but to me it was the end of the war.

11 It was magic on par with anything from David Copperfield's Vegas act.

12 It was an event of such surreal happiness that I kept expecting I was going to wake up and find myself French-kissing my pillow.

13 The old saying goes, "All good things come to those who wait."

14 Well, I had waited about eight months and the anticipation of this had made it not only a good thing, but the greatest thing that had ever happened to me up until that point in my life.

15 It was better than with Stacey, and better than with Nancy.

16 Yes, it was even better than with Maura.

17 It was true, pure love.

18 I was convinced of it.

CHAPTER 8

1 We made out in my car that night so long and so intensely that we literally fogged up all the windows.

2 When Jeri saw the fog, she got upset, as if she would be horribly embarrassed if anybody from our improv class had seen my steamy car and realized what was going on inside it between her and me.

3 It wasn't exactly what you'd call a rousing endorsement of our love but, hey, at least I had just gotten to make out with her for an hour.

4 Whether she wanted to believe it or not, she had given in to my geeky charms.

5 Well, that or she just figured it was time to toss me a bone.

6 Believe me, I wasn't too proud to accept a little charity back then, because charity or not,

7 I was in.

CHAPTER 9

1 Jeri and I continued to have make-out sessions, although it always seemed to take a lot of coaxing on my behalf.

2 There was definitely an element of "What have I done?" coming from her every time I'd try to engage in a re-creation of our car encounter.

3 The problem was that Jeri was a master at keeping me completely insecure.

4 You see, I came away from that first night of passion feeling quite cocky.

5 I figured that since she had given in to my advances, I was now in the driver's seat of our relationship.

6 The catbird seat, if you will.

7 I thought that it would finally be I who was pulling the strings and deciding exactly how and at what speed our relationship was going to progress.

8 But Jeri clearly didn't see it that way.

9 And one of the biggest sticking points for us was her relationship with my roommate Carl.

CHAPTER 10

1 I had also met Carl in my improv class, and he had quickly become my best friend, even moving in with me when my former roommate moved out.

2 He, Jeri, and I had become sort of a threesome, and we tended to hang out together quite a bit.

3 Jeri always seemed to be at her happiest when the three of us were out laughing and joking and having a good time.

4 And she started to worry that this fun dynamic was going to end now that she and I were moving toward being a full-fledged couple.

5 And so she started trying to push us back into our friends-only mode.

6 I, however, had tasted the forbidden fruit of her love and was now completely determined to keep our romance going.

7 And so the level of tension in our relationship climbed to new highs.

8 Even after what I considered to be successful and loving make-out sessions, she would only minutes later lament how much she wished that we were back to our old dynamic, the three of us roaming Los Angeles like a traveling comedy troupe, having carefree fun like an American version of *Jules et Jim*.

9 To me, her longing for Carl to become our third wheel in the immediate aftermath of our make-out sessions was like being told somebody would prefer going to McDonald's instead of continuing to eat a gourmet meal I had spent all day cooking.

10 Her sadness and frustration at the fact that our dating was cutting into her time with Carl immediately began to take its toll on me, and I soon found myself even more obsessed and insecure about our relationship.

11 Which seemed to be exactly what Jeri wanted me to feel.

CHAPTER 11

1 The next month became a colossal game of Who's in the Catbird Seat Now?

2 When I would become defeated and demoralized by her rejection of me, she would suddenly warm up and instigate a make-out session.

3 When I would become confident and jubilant over our love, she would suddenly become cold and distant.

4 One night, after an improv class, several of us went out to a bar for a drink.

5 While we were all talking and having a great time, Jeri asked Carl if he would come over to her house for Thanksgiving.

6 The problem with this for me was that *I* was going over to her house for Thanksgiving, and I had assumed that the reason she had asked me was that it was going to be our first official holiday together as boyfriend and girlfriend.

7 I had visions of sitting around with Jeri's parents as she and I held hands and put our arms around each other and showed her folks what a great son-in-law I was going to be.

8 But to have Carl also there was simply going to turn it into a "Hey, Mom, can my goofy friends from school come over to our house for dinner?" kind of event, in which Carl and I would be of equal importance.

9 Fortunately, Carl told her he had

other plans.

10 But I continued to stew for the rest of the evening.

11 And when we got into the car for me to drive her home, she turned my stew into a twelve-course meal by saying, "I'm so upset that Carl can't come over for Thanksgiving," sounding like she really truly was upset.

12 "I thought you just wanted *me* to be there," I said, sounding far whinier than I had planned.

13 My whine didn't go over well, and Jeri immediately launched into a tirade about how our new relationship was ruining her life.

14 "We're not a couple, you know," she said disdainfully, "so stop acting like we're married or something."

15 She then proceeded to tell me that she wasn't going to get into a serious relationship for a long time and maybe even ever.

16 She said that traditional relationships were outdated and something that progressive people like her didn't indulge in anymore.

17 And then she told me that she was too concerned about her freedom and her friends to have a possessive boyfriend.

18 "I'm a bird," she said.

CHAPTER 12

1 I went home that night completely out of my mind.

2 I kept hearing her voice saying the words "I'm a bird" over and over in my mind.

3 "I'm a bird" to me translated into "I'm so empowered by the fact that I know you're devoted to me that I can now claim not to care about relationships simply because I know you're not going anywhere and so I

will continue to push you away in order to keep you from ever leaving me."

4 And yet I didn't know for sure.

5 Maybe she *was* a bird.

6 Maybe she had been so burned by her ex-fiancé that she had purged any and all need for a boyfriend or husband out of her life.

7 Maybe I was destined to chase after her forever, never realizing that she truly didn't want to be in a relationship.

8 Maybe I was always to be her frustrated friend who occasionally gets to make out with her whenever she's feeling promiscuous and charitable but who never has the remotest chance of winning her over, heart and soul.

9 Maybe I'd even end up being stuck in a threesome of friendship with her and Carl for the rest of my life, constantly trying to one-up Carl in her eyes, always thinking I was on the verge of breaking through when in fact she was to remain as immune to my attentions as a militant lesbian would be to the advances of a cat-calling construction worker.

10 I now had no idea.

11 But I knew that I had to find out.

CHAPTER 13

1 I saw her the next day and had a mini-breakdown in front of her.

2 I didn't plan on being this uncool and desperate, but my frustration and virginity were driving me to emotional instability.

3 "Why are you so against being my girlfriend?" I asked, trying not to cry.

4 "Because I don't want to get tied down to anybody," she said with a smile that showed she was either

amused at my distraught state or else she had me right where she wanted me.

5 She took a breath and said,"I'm a—"

6 "Bird," I said, rolling my eyes. "I *know*."

7 And then, from out of nowhere, I said the following words:

8 "I just want to be close with you."

9 It didn't come out the way I thought it would, as if my intention was to say, "I want you and me to be in a close relationship."

10 It came out sounding exactly the way my subconscious and my libido wanted it to, even though the part of my brain that had grown up afraid of any and all sensuality and terrified of what God would say if I ever decided to have premarital sex would be horrified.

11 She got a strange smile, the kind you get when you think somebody's going to ask you for money but then they simply end up asking you if you know what time it is, and then she said the following words:

12 "If you're just talking about having sex, then that's fine."

13 I felt something snap inside my head.

14 I stared at her, unsure if she meant what I just thought she meant.

15 "What do you mean?" I asked dumbly.

16 "Do you mean you'd have sex with me, Jeri?"

17 She shrugged her shoulders in what I felt was a slightly forced display of nonchalance and said, "Sure."

CHAPTER 14

1 Now, if this was a normal story about a normal guy, the next thing I would be writing about was how we then immediately had sex.

2 But, alas, as you are painfully aware if you've made it this far through my book, I wasn't a normal guy when it came to things like sex, and so all her statement did was send me into a fevered journey of self-reflection.

3 In other words, my brain went haywire.

4 I simply thanked her as if she had just informed me that she would help me organize my closets, and then we had dinner and I drove her home.

5 And the whole time we were together that evening, I kept looking at her and asking myself if, now that I realized the choice was mine to make, this was the woman to whom I was actually going to allow myself to lose my virginity.

CHAPTER 15

1 The thing is, on top of the fact that I had so many anxieties growing up about masturbation and how God would react if I were to have premarital sex, I had also made a pact with myself many years prior that I was going to wait until my wedding night to lose my virginity.

2 As much as it was a fear of going against everything that I was taught in Sunday school, it was also a desire to be romantic.

3 To me, there just seemed to be something so pure and wonderful about having your wedding night be the first time you experienced the ultimate act of physical love.

4 I had lectured various people on this in the past, mostly as a reaction against the promiscuous society I had grown up surrounded by:

5 First the hippies and free love of

the 1960s, and then the sexual nihilism of one-night stands and faceless disco sex of the 1970s;

6 And now that I was in the middle of the 1980s in Los Angeles, which were looking to be every bit as nonromantic and fast-living as the previous two decades, I wanted more and more to harken back to what I then believed to be more innocent times.

7 This desire was then reinforced when, surprisingly, many people I discussed it with agreed with me.

8 A lot of people had told me stories about how bad their first time was, about how they wished they had waited, about how they also longed for a more innocent time.

9 One person had even told me about a couple he knew who, once they got engaged, had decided not to have sex again until their wedding night months later, so that it would feel like their first time.

10 All this positive feedback for my wholesome plan made me hang on to my desire to hold off my desire more and more.

11 The only thing I didn't consider was that everybody who was telling me how admirable my goal was was actually having sex on a regular basis.

12 So, of *course* what I was saying sounded admirable; *they* didn't have to do it.

13 I had worked hard—really, really hard—to do what I had been taught in Sunday school and in the Bible and by what I assumed was the voice of God and by the various clergymen and preachers and evangelists I had heard over the years about resisting temptation and about looking away from the body and about how it was a sin to have sex before a person was

married and yet the one thing that none of them had bothered to tell me was HOW I WAS SUPPOSED TO NOT GO INSANE DURING THE PROCESS OF DENYING MYSELF AN ACTIVITY THAT ALL HUMANS ARE GENETICALLY PROGRAMMED TO DO!

14 Even the "cool guy" preachers and religious lecturers I'd hear on TV who were telling me that they'd lived a life of debauchery and casual sex before they realized it was the wrong way to go and then found God had at least gotten to *have* sex so that they could discover it was "wrong."

15 But I was expected to just take their word for it and not think about the fact that they were probably able to be so cool about sex exactly because they'd *had* enough of it to keep them from losing their minds by the time they hit twenty-four.

16 But, because I was so programmed by my upbringing and my religion to do what was "right," I felt like I had to make a monumental decision regarding Jeri and so realized I had three options:

17 I could stay on God's good side and turn down Jeri's offer of sex and simply continue trying to break her down enough to get her to marry me in order to make it to our wedding night;

18 I could decide to give up on her and keep masturbating incessantly while I continued looking for the perfect woman who would fall in love with me and marry me and then, on our wedding night, treat me to the God-ordained, sent-from-the-heavens, a-okay-with-every-religion-and-religious-leader-on-earth evening of beautiful, morally acceptable lovemaking;

19 Or . . .

20 I could say "Oh, what the hell" and finally have sex for the first time in my life with a woman I was sure I loved.

21 I had no idea what I was going to do.

22 And that was when Jeri and I went to Beatlefest.

CHAPTER 16

1 Jeri wanted to go and I took her, and the minute we got there, I knew the day was going to be terrible.

2 First of all, the main exhibition hall was filled with hundreds of tables with vendors hawking anything and everything that had the word *Beatles* written, engraved, stamped, embroidered, or scrawled on it in Magic Marker.

3 The whole thing was just a blatant grab for people's money by guys who probably made up the exact same merchandise bearing the name of any and all music groups from the Jimi Hendrix Experience to Perry Como simply to make a buck.

4 Then, there was the theater where they were showing Beatles movies and videos.

5 When we entered, *A Hard Day's Night* was being projected, and as each of the Beatles appeared on the screen, many of the women sitting in the audience began to scream.

6 Now, in case you find me too humorless about this, it wasn't the "Hey, check out how funny it will be if I scream just like the girls in the movie" kind of audience participation fun, like when one person always yells "TURN IT UP!" after the really loud THX trailer rattles the speakers before a movie begins (which made me laugh the first time somebody did

it, but after hearing someone yell this every single time I've been to the movies in the past fifteen years, it seems to have lost every last iota of its comedic power).

7 No, this was the screaming of a bunch of people who were firmly planted in the past and who were desperately trying to get back whatever spark they had in their lives when they first actually had a reason to scream at the Beatles,

8 And it just came off to me as kinda pathetic.

9 To make matters worse, John Lennon's tragic end had occurred barely five years earlier and the sight of middle-aged women screaming for a dead man was right up there on the depressing meter between New Year's Eve at Grandma's house and shopping for coffins.

10 By the time Jeri and I had spent the entire afternoon looking at shoddy merchandise and watching every interview the Beatles ever did and she yelled at me for not having a better attitude, I was extremely angry that my day had been wasted on such a depressing event.

11 We finally left.

CHAPTER 17

1 Jeri was in a really bad mood as we headed back to my house to make dinner.

2 She was complaining about everything: my driving, my attitude during the convention, the traffic, the songs on the radio.

3 I was at the end of my rope.

4 When we got inside my house, she continued her nonstop grousing, this time about how cold it was.

5 Suddenly, I felt all the patience

drain out of my body and I turned to her and yelled, "ENOUGH with the complaining!"

6 I then steeled myself for a fight.

7 But to my surprise, Jeri started laughing.

8 Taking this as a license to continue, I started ranting about everything she had put me through that day.

9 The more I ranted, the more she laughed, as if telling me that she was well aware of how unbearable she and the day had been.

10 And suddenly she and I were having a great time.

11 And before I knew it, we were making out.

12 As we rolled around on the couch, my eye kept wandering over to my bedroom door.

13 Jeri was being so responsive to me that I was suddenly consumed with the thought that this might well be the moment of truth.

14 We were in my house, we were getting along great, we were feeling passionate toward each other, and I was horny as hell.

15 And so, before my brain could even comprehend what my body was doing, I scooped Jeri up as if I was Tarzan and carried her into my bedroom.

CHAPTER 18

1 And the Lord spake unto me:

2 God: "What are you doing?!"

3 Me: "I think I'm going to have sex with Jeri."

4 God: "But you're not married."

5 Me: "I know, but I'm thinking about marrying her . . . eventually. You know . . . if she'll let me."

6 God: "Well, thinking about getting married and being married are two different things. You can't do this."

7 Me: "Oh, c'mon, I've waited *twenty-four years*. I've done pretty much everything You've ever told me to do."

8 God: "Ha! That's a laugh."

9 Me: "All right, I mean, I know that I've never been good about the whole masturbation thing, but even You have to admit it's amazing that I've stayed a virgin for all this time. I could have blown it years ago with Nicole and Nancy."

10 God: "Yeah, right. You didn't do anything because you were too afraid of getting naked in front of them. It had nothing to do with doing what *I* wanted you to do."

11 Me: "That's *so* not fair! I've done everything in my life because I was trying not to make You mad. I've bent over backward in order to follow the rules You set for all of us to live by. And even You have to admit that there's hardly anybody else out there who sticks to them the way I do, especially *these* days."

12 God: "Hey, if everybody else jumped off a cliff, would you do it too?"

13 Me: "Oh, please. That's the lamest argument I've ever heard. Besides, I've been standing around for years watching everybody else jump off the cliff and the problem is that they all seem to be having a great time on the way down while I'm having a lousy time up on top. Why do I have to be the only one stuck up here? Why can't I be like those rock 'n' roll preacher guys who get to have tons of sex and take drugs and drink themselves into a coma and then *still* get to be all holy and stuff?"

14 God: "Because those guys didn't know what they were doing when they were disobeying Me. *You* do!"

15 Me: *"And this is the thanks I get?* Having to be all frustrated and guilty and trying to deny how I'm really feeling all the time? *That's* how a person who's doing everything You think is right is supposed to feel?"

16 God: "Well . . . yeah. You'll get your reward in heaven."

17 Me: "I CAN'T WAIT THAT LONG!!!"

CHAPTER 19

1 I set Jeri down on my bed.

2 I looked at her.

3 I can't do this, I told myself.

4 She looked at me, waiting for me to make the next move.

5 She really looked good.

6 I glanced over at my closet and saw my old Mouse Trap game from when I was a kid up on the top shelf with all my other old games I had brought from Michigan years earlier.

7 "You wanna play Mouse Trap?" I asked, hoping that she would laugh and then say something sexy like "Get over here, Mr. Feig" and then start to undress me.

8 However, she gave me a look that said I wasn't going to get anything unless I initiated it myself and said, "Sure, I'd love to play Mouse Trap."

9 And so we played Mouse Trap.

10 On my bed.

11 Two full games.

12 Not just the way we all used to play it when we were kids, where we simply built the mouse trap and then set it off a bunch of times.

13 No, we sat there for an hour rolling the dice and moving our mice and putting down a piece whenever the board told us to.

14 I don't remember who won each game but I was starting to feel like the loser.

15 As Jeri started to crank the wheel that would hit the boot that would then send the metal ball rolling down the rickety stairs which set the mousetrap in motion, I looked at her and realized how much I wanted to do what I had spent my life wondering if I would ever be able to have the courage to do.

16 The time had come.

17 I was going to have sex.

CHAPTER 20

1 And the Lord spake unto me.

2 Again.

3 God: "Holy shit, you're gonna do it, aren't you?"

4 Me: "I think so."

5 God: "You're just going to throw twenty-four years of self-restraint right out the window?"

6 Me: "I think so."

7 God: "You're going to give up that feeling of superiority you've always felt over all the jocks and the cool guys and cheesy disco guys you've been so judgmental about and just become one of them? You're going to be as bad as the frat guys at USC you always used to overhear talking about their sexual exploits? You're going to never be able to say to yourself that you're a virgin ever again?"

8 Me: "It's sort of starting to look that way."

9 And God sighed.

10 God: "And you're cool with that?"

11 Me: "I don't know, to be honest. I feel like the only reason I wouldn't do

it now, other than the fact that I'm really nervous and completely freaked out at the thought of having to get naked in front of Jeri, would be to prevent myself from feeling like I was losing something I thought was important. But I think I want to experience what real love and real sex feels like more than I want to be able to wake up tomorrow morning and know that I had still never slept with a woman."

12 God: "So, you're saying . . ."

13 Me: " I want to lose my virginity. And I want to lose it right now."

14 And the Lord tried to say something, stopped Himself, sighed, shook His head, and left the room.

CHAPTER 21

1 I picked up the Mouse Trap game from the bed and gently set it down on top of my dresser.

2 I turned and looked at Jeri, who stared back at me, waiting for me to state my intentions.

3 And then I jumped on top of her.

CHAPTER 22

1 We rolled around on the bed for a while, making out and laughing.

2 My brain continued to spin as I grappled with the fact that I was really going to have sex.

3 There was one small problem.

4 Actually, it was a very big problem.

5 I had to go to the bathroom.

6 Bad.

7 Like the way you have to go to the bathroom after you've had five large iced teas and then stood around out in the cold shivering.

8 But I was convinced that if I got up and left the room and took the two to four minutes it would take to do such a major round of urination, Jeri would have enough time to think about things and decide that she didn't want to have sex with me.

9 And I wasn't willing to take that risk.

10 So I tried not to think about it.

11 Which was impossible.

CHAPTER 23

1 I began to undress her.

2 Or I began to *try* to undress her.

3 She was wearing a sweater that seemed to have ten thousand buttons and, having never undressed a woman before, I wasn't aware of the fact that women's buttons were reversed from men's.

4 I fumbled and tugged and grappled with those buttons as if I were on an episode of *Happy Days*, and I was trying hard to keep kissing her on the mouth so that she couldn't say "What the *hell* are you doing?"

5 I had often told myself that when I actually ended up undressing a woman for the first time, I would make sure I was good at it, so that I wouldn't come off like every guy in a teen sex comedy.

6 But, alas, that's exactly how I was coming off.

7 Jeri finally moved my hand away and undid the buttons herself.

8 She gave me a look like she was going to laugh or make a joke about my total inexperience with female clothing, but I think the look on my face made her realize that I was in far too fragile a state to endure any ribbing, good-natured or otherwise.

9 Although maybe that look on my face was simply from the enormous amount of urine I was holding in my bladder.

10 Hard to tell.

11 We started to kiss again and I was able to deal more competently with the buttons on her shirt.

12 With every button I undid that brought me closer to her bra, I waited for her to say "Stop!" or "You know what? This isn't right."

13 But, fortunately, she didn't.

CHAPTER 24

1 I got her shirt off and then decided that I should hold off on the bra and instead get her shoes and pants off first.

2 In my mind, I had an order that I had played out over the years in my masturbatory fantasies.

3 It was always that I would first get a woman down to only her underwear, both top and bottom.

4 Then the bra would be removed.

5 And then and only then would the panties be removed, thus resulting in a completely nude woman.

6 Her total nudity was the one thing I had always promised myself, ever since I was a kid and saw a copy of *Oui* magazine behind the counter of our local convenience store (we used to pronounce the name of that magazine "Oy," by the way, as if it was filled with pictures of old naked Jewish women).

7 On the cover of the magazine I was able to glimpse for only the briefest of seconds was a photo of a woman sitting in a completely white room without a stitch of clothing on.

8 It had so blown my mind and piqued my interest back then that I had vowed the first time I was with a woman, she too would be completely nude.

9 The thing I wasn't sure about was whether I would be too.

10 However, undaunted, I started to take off Jeri's boots.

CHAPTER 25

1 I couldn't.

2 They too, like her sweater, were possessed of some otherworldly security system that saw them being held in place by the world's most obtuse zipper.

3 I tugged and pulled and tried to get a better grip on the zipper tab, which was the size of a miniature pine needle.

4 Once again, I was trying to do this while kissing her so that I could stop her from uttering any possible protestations, and so the angle at which I was having to reach down to her boot while engaging her head meant that I had neither the leverage nor the visual take on the situation to guide me.

5 And, once again, Jeri came to my rescue.

6 She sighed and pulled out of our kiss, then bent over and unzipped both of her boots.

7 Trying to salvage my masculinity, I stopped her from removing her boots and proceeded to do it myself, which was yet another ordeal, since they seemed to be as hard to remove as a cowboy's after he's been out in the heat of the desert all day.

8 I tugged so hard that I started getting visions of me breaking her ankle and ending our evening of passion in the emergency room.

9 Fortunately, they finally popped off.

10 I was having a lot of angst about whether or not I should be looking at her during all this.

11 I knew from movies that generally there's either a playfulness to the

undressing of one another during the lead-up to sex, or else there's an exchange of long, intense stares of passion between the two involved parties.

12 But suddenly I was afraid of what I might see if I looked at her.

13 Part of me was worried that I'd see her staring with that "I just smelled something really bad" look that women get when they've decided they're disgusted with you.

14 The other part of me was afraid I'd look up and see her trying not to laugh.

15 Either option was a no-go for me, since both would lead to the destruction of my already fragile ego.

16 The only look that would make me feel better would be an "Oh, you're doing everything I love/This is perfect and you are an amazing lover" look from her.

17 Which I was certain wasn't the look on her face.

18 And so, like a kid working in a coloring book with his tongue sticking out the side of his mouth in concentration, I simply stared at the task at hand and kept my eyes on the road.

CHAPTER 26

1 I started to take off her socks.

2 "Man, you're really going all the way, aren't you?" she said in what could have been interpreted either as a supportive chuckle or a total slam.

3 I chose to simply ignore it and pulled off her socks, surprised that she would even consider having sex with them on.

4 Socks off, Jeri was now officially in her underwear.

5 Phase One accomplished.

6 Time to begin Phase Two.

CHAPTER 27

1 I started to go for her bra clasp but she quickly reached back and unhooked it before I was even within reach.

2 Clearly she wanted to avoid the inevitable.

3 And before I could even process it, she pulled off her bra and was completely topless.

4 I felt like somebody hit me in the face with a blast of water.

5 I had stared at naked breasts in magazines for my enitre life, but this was the first time I had seen a pair up close and personal.

6 Trying to remain cool, I simply returned to my itinerary and moved on to her underwear.

7 But, once again, she seemed to see trouble a-brewin' and so quickly lifted her midsection off the bed, pulled down her panties, then lifted her legs and pulled them off, tossing them onto the floor.

8 And there she was.

9 Completely naked.

10 On my bed.

11 All for me.

12 Man, did I have to go to the bathroom.

CHAPTER 28

1 I quickly realized that, even though she was naked, I still had all *my* clothes on.

2 Even my shoes.

3 It suddenly made the whole scene feel cheap, as if I had abducted her and was about to do something illegal.

4 I knew the moment had come for me to undress in front of a woman for the first time in my life.

5 And I immediately realized that

I had completely screwed everything up.

6 I had always assumed that in the lead-up to sex, the undressing happened mutually, in that as I undressed the woman, she would at the same time be undressing me, so that, without even realizing it, we would both magically be naked and, more important, be naked under the covers.

7 However, in my race to get her undressed so that she couldn't back out of having sex with me, I had placed myself in the absolute worst possible situation . . .

8 I was going to have to strip, right in front of her, while she had nothing else to do but watch.

9 Stripping down in gym class was bad enough, because you knew you were surrounded by guys who wanted to beat you up, and so the shedding of one's clothing was tantamount to taking off one's body armor.

10 But now that I was faced with having to strip in front of a woman whom I was trying to impress, undressing in gym class seemed almost like a pleasurable event.

11 Because not only was I about to deal with my fear of exposing myself to another human being, this human being was also someone whom I was asking to then interact with my body in the most personal way imaginable, short of surgery.

12 I had to deal with my embarrassment, my neuroses, and my discomfort while at the same time dealing with the very real concern that Jeri might not find my naked body to be attractive.

13 I thought about turning out the light but then realized that the overhead light wasn't on anyway.

14 The only light in the room was coming from the small reading lamp next to my bed, but that was right next to Jeri and for me to go over and turn it off seemed like I was telling her that I had some sort of deformity or hideous birthmark that would turn her stomach if she saw it.

15 No, I realized that, ready or not, passion-inducing or not, I was now going to have to get naked.

16 And so the only plan I was able to come up with to feel like I had the slightest bit of control over the situation was my decision that I should get undressed very quickly.

17 Which, of course, proved to be impossible.

CHAPTER 29

1 I quickly took off my shoes, undid my belt, unzipped my fly, and pulled down my pants.

2 But then I didn't know what to do with them.

3 At this time in my life, I wasn't wearing jeans.

4 I instead spent a lot of what little money I had on clothes that I felt represented my personality, and at this point in time, I felt my personality was best represented by wearing retro pleated pants with bowling shirts and Converse high-top sneakers.

5 I was also very neat with them and was loath ever to simply toss my clothes onto the floor.

6 But I knew that were I to head over to my closet and start neatly pulling out hangers to make sure my clothes weren't going to get wrinkled, it might be taken as being a tad bit on the unpassionate side.

7 I had seen plenty of movies in which a couple would send their gar-

ments flying all over the room as they prepared to make love, or else the camera would follow the trail of strewn and twisted clothing up to a bed that contained a pair of postcoital lovers, but both of those scenarios had occurred from the mutual undressing process that I had already missed.

8 And so I wasn't sure exactly what rules applied to someone in my situation.

9 Finding a halfway point that would allow me to look like I was passionate enough not to care too much about my clothes but that would also help me avoid making a trip to the dry cleaner's the next morning, I took my pants and placed them over the back of my desk chair, making sure to secretly fold them on the crease.

10 That out of the way, I now was struck with the image of myself standing in front of Jeri wearing my shirt, socks, and underwear, much the same way my father used to walk around the house after taking his evening dump.

11 Either the shirt would have to come off next, which would result in me standing in my socks and underpants like a nerd at a massage parlor, or the underwear or socks would have to be attended to first.

12 I opted for the socks, which took about two seconds to remove.

13 So much for stalling.

14 It was now a question of underwear or shirt, and I quickly did the math.

15 To take off the shirt first would be to make the removal of my underwear a major event, since it would turn my groin into the focal point of the room at that moment.

16 However, to take off the underwear first meant that I could use the length of my bowling shirt to obscure my most private of parts, which was an extremely comforting thought right then.

17 And so it was decided.

18 It was time to take off my underwear.

19 In front of a woman.

20 Driven by the fact that I knew I couldn't look like I was stalling in front of Jeri, I took a deep, internal breath, placed my thumbs inside the elastic waistband of my briefs, and, feeling the way it must feel when you go skydiving for the first time and decide that it's time to jump out the open door into the abyss and possible death, I pulled down my underwear and felt the cool breeze of nakedness hit my reproductive organs.

21 I had done it.

22 I was, by all accounts, naked.

CHAPTER 30

1 Using the camouflage of my bowling shirt as cover, I quickly dashed toward the bed, bending my knees in such a way as to keep the bottom of the shirt covering my manliness.

2 Even though I was obscuring my most prized possession from her view, just knowing that I was naked in that area was mind-bending to me.

3 It felt strange, as if I were running around in a hospital gown; that feeling of being naked when everyone else around you is dressed, like in one of those dreams where you're walking the halls of your old high school in the nude hoping nobody will notice.

4 Except now there was a reason for my nakedness, and that reason was also naked and looking at me as I was climbing into bed with her.

5 I unbuttoned my shirt, trying to

make it look like it was perfectly natural to finish undressing once one was already under the covers, and then tossed it over to the chair where my pants were hanging.

6 The shirt missed the chair and landed in a heap on the floor, and I had to override my instinct to get back out of bed and pick it up.

7 This decision was made easier because of the fact that I was now completely, utterly, totally, in-the-raw, wearing-my-birthday-suit, starkers nude.

8 Now what? I thought to myself.

CHAPTER 31

1 Everyone seems to want to tell you about the birds and the bees when you're a kid, but nobody ever tells you what you're supposed to do *before* you get to the birds and bees part of sex.

2 The only training I had ever received in the fine art of foreplay was from Woody Allen movies and episodes of *Love, American Style*.

3 I knew from enough love stories and comedies in which women would complain about what selfish lovers their boyfriends and husbands were that a lot of stuff was supposed to happen before one got down to the actual intercourse part of sex.

4 But what was a guy supposed to do to fill up that presex time to make his lover scream with desire?

5 Or at least keep her from yawning with boredom?

6 I knew that kissing was a big part of it and so Jeri and I set about doing that, but as we were, even though I was enjoying the new sensation of feeling my unclothed body against the unclothed body of a woman, I was more preoccupied with trying to figure out what I was supposed to do next.

7 I knew from overhearing enough locker room talk and the reading of various sex scenes in novelizations of movies like *The Towering Inferno* that at some point, oral sex was to take place.

8 Clearly I knew what oral sex was when it came to a woman giving it to a man (oh, my neck), but Jeri wasn't making any moves that indicated she was thinking about heading in a southward direction, and there was no way in the world that I would have had the courage to ask her to do it.

9 Plus, I now had to go to the bathroom even worse than before, due to all the excitement of the moment.

10 Heck, I always have to go to the bathroom ten minutes into an action film if I drink even a sip of water before it starts, so you can imagine the levels of overproduction my bladder was working at during my first time in bed with a woman.

11 And so the thought of her going down there and possibly prolonging the amount of time between our lovemaking and a trip to the bathroom was beyond comprehension.

12 But maybe it was my duty as a man to perform oral sex on *her*, I thought.

13 It definitely seemed like something a passionate and caring lover would do for his lady, but there was one problem:

14 I had no idea what oral sex on a woman entailed.

15 I'd never even seen a woman's most intimate of parts up close, let alone had to deal with the mechanics of it.

16 I suppose this is where magazines like *Playboy* do a bit of a disservice to the inexperienced.

17 Because their pictures always strove to be more artistic and less graphic, the female anatomy down there as shown in their magazine always appeared to me the way a riptide appears to an inexperienced swimmer:

18 There's something on top that you can see, but whatever lies beneath is a complete mystery that you know must have a lot more going on inside it than you could ever imagine.

19 Besides, making such a bold move as working my face all the way down to her midsection seemed like I would be guaranteeing her an experience she would not soon forget.

20 I just didn't want it to be something she wouldn't forget because it was the worst thing she'd ever experienced.

21 And so I decided to stay up top.

22 And since I couldn't think of anything else to do, I knew it was probably time to get directly to the main event.

23 And it was then that I realized the next problem.

CHAPTER 32

1 For whatever reason, whether it was nerves or embarrassment or the pressure or simply because I had to go to the bathroom worse than a guy who just won a drinking contest at an Oktoberfest, I wasn't fully . . . um . . . you know . . .

2 . . . at attention.

3 I knew that if I could just excuse myself and run into the bathroom to urinate that I'd probably be fine, but the thought of leaving her right then

was even more unthinkable than it had been before.

4 To give her that big of an out at this crucial moment now seemed almost irresponsible.

5 Full bladder or no full bladder, I would have to press on.

6 It was at this moment that I congratulated myself on having asked a question during sixth-grade health class that at the time had made me the object of much ridicule.

7 When we were being told in sex education how the man's penis was used during intercourse, I raised my hand and made what I thought was a perfectly legitimate inquiry:

8 "Is there any chance that during sex you could accidentally go to the bathroom inside the woman?"

9 Everybody laughed uproariously and looked at me like I was insane.

10 But I really wanted to know, because I really was concerned.

11 The teacher, who was a young woman, gave me an understanding smile and said, "No, Paul, there's things inside you that prevent that from happening."

12 Little did I know what an M. Night Shyamalan moment this was for me, since that info was only this minute having major relevance in my life.

13 But now that my accidental urination fears had been allayed, the more disturbing question of why I wasn't in the solid state in which a man is supposed to be in order to perform the ultimate act of love was still unanswered.

14 Since my first instinct is always to jump to the worst possible conclusion about anything to do with a defect regarding my body, I immedi-

ately started to wonder if I was in the process of finding out that I was in fact impotent.

15 It had never been a problem for me when I was by myself, and in fact whenever Jeri looked at me in any sort of romantic way since I'd known her I'd had the same problem that plagued me years before in front of the photography section at the local bookstore.

16 But maybe it was a different case altogether when one was with a woman, I thought.

17 Maybe it was possible to be impotent with a woman even though you weren't impotent on your own.

18 Or did that even make sense?

19 And was this indeed my problem?

20 Or was it simply a complication from all the things that were going on in my head and bladder at that moment?

21 I had no idea but I knew that, in order to keep Jeri from getting up and leaving, I was going to have to forge ahead.

22 Somehow.

CHAPTER 33

1 I figured that in the process of getting myself into Jeri's anatomical place where all the magic was supposed to happen, my attention problem would take care of itself.

2 But, alas, this brought up the *next* problem:

3 How did one get *in* there?

4 Figuring that Jeri, who had already had sex in her life, would give me some assistance if I got myself into a position that indicated I was ready for action, I placed myself on top of her and waited for her loving guidance.

5 I'd still be there today if I had

waited any longer.

6 Jeri's hand sort of hovered around down there for a bit, but clearly she had no intention of actually taking control of the situation.

7 The only good thing to come out of it was that the presence of her hand so close to that which had only ever been touched by me seemed to cure my former problem, albeit not as fully as I had expected.

8 But it did seem like enough to get the ball rolling, if you will.

9 I just had to figure out exactly into where the ball was supposed to roll.

10 I once again have to lay some of the blame on the doorstep of the Playboy Mansion for what happened next, as well as nature itself for designing something that was so confusing at first glance.

11 You see, the female midsectional anatomy that I had seen for so many years in the pages of *Playboy* seemed to make perfect sense.

12 There was a triangle of hair, and so it went to figure that within the center of that triangle would be where one would find an entrance, since putting an entrance in the center of objects seemed to be a pretty standard design in all things, be they man-made or nature-made.

13 And so, seeing that I was going to receive no help from Jeri, I decided to take the initiative and do things myself.

14 And like a guy who figures he can fix cars just because he's looked at pictures of them in magazines all his life, I set forth to begin hitting a home run with Jeri.

CHAPTER 34

1 If you've ever accidentally tried

to get in a door and, instead of realizing on the first try that it's not going to open, you then begin to pound and push and pull on the door until somebody walks up and says, "What are you doing? They welded that door shut years ago," then you'd have some idea of what I spent the next few moments doing in bed with Jeri.

2 I was certain that the place where a man's anatomy fit inside a woman's anatomy had to be in the center of that triangle, on the front of her pelvis.

3 When I was having no luck finding it, I started poking around within this Bermuda Triangle, probing the real estate within it like an oil company looking for an opportune place to drill.

4 But there was nowhere to go.

5 What was wrong with Jeri? I wondered.

6 Was she a virgin too?

7 Did it take a first time to open up what needed to be opened up down there?

8 Was there some sort of operation needed that hadn't been performed?

9 Or was I doing this wrong?

10 It was at that moment that Jeri *finally* came to my rescue.

11 She reached down and grabbed me, then looked me in the eyes, gave me a small sympathetic smile, and said, "You really don't know what you're doing, do you?"

12 If I wasn't so frustrated at how completely inept I was at sex, I would have been embarrassed.

13 But like a bank robber who has accidentally locked himself in the safe and is rescued by the police just before he runs out of air, I was too relieved to be getting assistance to

care about any other consequences, and so I said, "Hey, I *told* you I've never done this before."

14 And with that, Jeri laughed and put me exactly where I was supposed to go.

CHAPTER 35

1 Now, I wish I could say that the story ended there, that the screen then cut away to waves crashing on a beach and fireworks going off and a train going into a tunnel.

2 But it didn't.

3 Simply put, I was completely confused.

4 I had imagined what sex might be like, but beyond that, I really didn't know what to do.

5 Granted, I had actually seen a couple of soft-core pornographic movies in college and witnessed people seeming to have sex in them.

6 But, oddly enough, I had never really connected up what the actors in those films did to what is required for actual nonpornographic sex.

7 I guess I had assumed that all the thrusting and pounding and grunting was something that was being done simply for the benefit of the camera, and that in real life, one simply had to get inside the other person and sex would then magically happen;

8 that whatever motion I had supplied whenever I was performing the rope feeling upon myself was automatically taken care of by something inside this mysterious organ of the woman.

9 Yes, friends, I really was that clueless.

10 And not only was I confused about why I wasn't feeling anything,

but I was also confused as to why I didn't even feel like I was *in* anything.

11 Once again, my ignorance was on display.

12 I always assumed that the opening on a woman was small and so going inside it was much like forcing your finger into a pop bottle.

13 It was a struggle to get it in, but once you were in, you really knew it.

14 I had the sensation that I was in something, and yet I wasn't sure if it was her or simply the sheets on my bed.

15 What was up? I wondered.

16 Is Jeri just abnormally big?

17 Or am I just abnormally small?

18 I didn't like the possible affirmative answer to either one of those questions.

19 As I lay there and tried to figure all this out, I could feel Jeri staring at me, wondering what I was doing.

20 I looked at her, wondering the same thing.

21 "Well," I thought to myself, trying to send a telepathic message her way, "make it do something."

22 She was clearly thinking the same thing about me because after a few moments, she shifted as if she was growing impatient.

23 In retrospect, she must have thought I had either frozen in fear or that I was performing some Satanic ritual on her, in which I lay very still while I drew the life force out of her.

24 But when she shifted, I felt something.

25 And, yea, it was very good.

26 I moved again, and once again it felt good.

27 And then I began to replay in my head a scene from the porno movie we had watched in my college apartment that had made me queasy at the time, and lo and behold, it turned out that the actors in the film weren't just showing off for the camera.

28 They were doing what everyone needed to do to have sex, from my parents on down to the most primitive natives in the deepest reaches of Africa.

29 And it was kinda working.

30 But I still *really* had to go to the bathroom.

CHAPTER 36

1 I continued to do what was required and soon felt that the rope feeling was fast approaching.

2 Even though I was now officially having sex, I knew that until I actually completed the act, it wouldn't truly be official.

3 Or at least it wouldn't be to me, who had waited twenty-four years to do this.

4 But then, just as everything was about to reach its peak . . .

5 The rope feeling went away.

6 I was immediately hit with a wave of panic.

7 What happened? I asked myself.

8 Where did it go?

9 And then, to make matters worse, the rope feeling wasn't the only thing that went away.

10 As they say in the army:

11 "At ease."

12 My body was acting as if I had finished whereas my mind and my libido knew for certain that I hadn't.

13 I didn't know what to do but realized that this probably wasn't going to play well with Jeri.

14 Maybe it was a sign that I had to now run to the toilet, no matter

what the consequences, and actually go to the bathroom.

15 But my brain was doggedly determined.

16 I had to do this, and I had to finish this, and I had to finish this *now*.

17 I hadn't waited all these years and thrown out a lifetime of self-control just to have my first time be incomplete and unsatisfying.

18 My mission was now crystal clear:

19 I was going to get this job done.

CHAPTER 37

1 I told my bladder to sit down and shut up.

2 I told my midsection to wake up.

3 I told my libido to liven up.

4 And I ran for the finish line.

CHAPTER 38

1 I wish I could say that this tale had a happy ending.

2 It kinda does.

3 And it kinda doesn't.

4 As I worked away, my bladder literally throbbing in pain, I felt the rope feeling once more approaching.

5 I steeled myself for the high point of my first sexual experience.

6 And with all the fanfare of a returning army, it arrived.

7 Kinda.

8 I have to be honest: To this day, I don't know if anything happened or not.

9 It was some kind of peak, but it didn't feel remotely like the rope feeling I was used to.

10 But I pretended it did.

11 And thus I believe I became one of the few men in the world to ever fake an orgasm.

12 By that point, I don't think Jeri cared much anyway, and part of me was simply thrilled that I was finally going to get to go to the bathroom, a long-awaited event that turned out to feel even better than the sex had.

13 Jeri and I got dressed and tried not to feel weird around each other.

14 I walked her out to her car and we kissed good night.

15 And then I went back inside, relived the event in my mind, and performed the rope feeling, a sexual act that I was actually good at.

16 It was the sexual equivalent of eating at someone's house whose food doesn't fill you up, and so you stop to get a hamburger on the way home.

17 Proud moment or not, at least it felt the way I knew it should.

CHAPTER 39

1 So, my first attempt at sex had taught me a lot, and I had finally shed the virginity that had made it all the way out to California and through college and into my career with me.

2 However, all I could think of at that moment was a song my father used to play over and over again on our stereo, a tune that was on a Peggy Lee album, the only album my father owned.

3 "Is That All There Is?"

4 Peggy Lee sang in my head as I sat on my couch and watched a Marx Brothers movie that was playing on the late show.

5 "Is that all there is?"

6 "Tonight," I thought as I watched my comic hero Groucho running amok with his two brothers through an old-fashioned college set, "I hope that's all there is.

7 Because if there's any more, I don't think I can take it."

Happy Trails from the G-Rated Gigolo!

I am now married.

I am now happy.

I have a wonderful wife.

I didn't marry Jeri.

In fact, we broke up a couple months after she helped me lose my virginity.

Our second time trying it, things went a lot better.

We had a couple of good months to help me become competent.

I think I did okay.

However, with the tension of sex gone, we quickly realized we weren't at all right for each other.

Which is why I now believe that people should have sex before they get married.

I don't mean to step on anyone's toes or morals by making that judgment, and you don't have to take my advice if you don't want to.

I just know that I personally wasn't able to think objectively or rationally about a potential spouse before I was able to sleep with her.

But, lest you think I ended up going too far the other way after losing my virginity, I'm not ashamed to admit that I've only ever slept with three women in my life.

One was Jeri.

One shall remain nameless.

And one was, and is, and always will be, my wife.

So maybe it was okay I waited so long.

And that I didn't sleep around.

And that I didn't listen to God.

Or whoever He, or he, was.

Look, at the end of the day, like it or not, we are all sexual beings.

It's how we keep the human race going.

It's what our genes are programmed to do.

And so if we get too down on ourselves and try to suppress all our bodies' urges, then we'll only succeed in making ourselves crazy.

Trust me.

It doesn't mean you should go nuts and sleep with everything in sight.

First, make sure you feel love for the other person.

Second, make sure the other person feels it too.

Third, make sure you're both old enough.

Then, if it seems right, give it a shot.

You know . . . make sure you protect yourself and do everything that the world of science and medicine tells you you're supposed to do in order not to get yourself into an "unwanted" or "unexpected" or life-threatening situation.

But then, if you really feel strongly about it, and if you both agree on it, and if you both have respect for each other, and if you're not going to hurt anybody else by doing it . . .

Do it.

'Cause at the end of the day, no matter where we live, no matter what we believe, no matter how we dress, what we eat, what we look like, what we watch, what we like, what we hate, or what we think we know about the world, at the end of the day, there's only one thing that none of us can logically disagree with.

We're all just human.

Even geeks.

Also by Paul feig

Kick Me
0–609–80943–1
$12.95 paper

Written in side-splitting and often cringe-inducing detail, Paul Feig's <u>Kick Me</u> takes you in a time machine to a world of bombardment by dodgeballs, ill-fated prom dates, hellish high school bus rides, and other aspects of public school life that will keep you laughing in recognition and occasionally sighing in relief that you aren't him. <u>Kick Me</u> is a nostalgic trip for the inner geek in all of us.

"It's shocking that one person could have so many humiliating experiences and even more shocking that he chose to remember them."
—Ira Glass, host of <u>This American Life</u>

THREE RIVERS PRESS • NEW YORK

Wherever books are sold
CrownPublishing.com